DUMBARTON OAKS STUDIES

ᴈᴄ VII ᴚᴑ

BYZANTINE SILVER STAMPS

BYZANTINE SILVER STAMPS

ERICA CRUIKSHANK DODD

With an Excursus on the

Comes Sacrarum Largitionum

by

J. P. C. KENT

The Dumbarton Oaks Research Library and Collection
Trustees for Harvard University
Washington, District of Columbia
1961

Distributed by
J. J. Augustin, Publisher
Locust Valley, New York

Library of Congress Catalog Card Number 61–16953
Printed in Germany *at* J. J. Augustin, Glückstadt

In Memoriam

Leonid Antonovich Matsulevich

1886–1959

Preface

During the last hundred years there have come to light numerous silver vessels belonging for the most part to ancient church treasures or barbarian hoards and stamped with Byzantine "hallmarks." Some were chance discoveries along the shores of the Mediterranean, in Russia, in the Balkans, and in Western Europe; others were found in archaeological excavations, while a few had been preserved above ground. Many of these vessels are decorated with reliefs which are closely dependent, iconographically and stylistically, upon classical traditions—so closely dependent, in fact, that the vessels were at first thought to be Hellenistic, while the stamps, which are purely Byzantine in character, were assumed to have been applied at a later period. Subsequent investigations, however, have proved this view to be untenable.

At the turn of the century the first serious study of the stamps, and their interpretation, was undertaken by O. M. Dalton in England and Iacov I. Smirnov in Russia.[1] In 1928 M. Rosenberg of Germany published a revised edition of his catalogue of goldsmiths' marks of medieval and later periods in which he included the stamps on about sixty Byzantine silver objects,[2] and in 1929 the Russian scholar Leonid Matsulevich elaborated upon the work of Smirnov and produced a study (in German) which not only contributed to the interpretation of the stamps but also provided the first stylistic grouping of the relevant objects in the Hermitage Museum.[3] Both Smirnov and, later, Matsulevich cited a number of instances where the stamps had been damaged when the relief was worked, or where they bore other indications of having been applied before, rather than after, the vessel was finished. It thus became clear that the stamps provide a *terminus post quem* for the relief, and may indicate, moreover, a provenance or workshop for the object. They furnish, therefore, documentary evidence upon which may be based the stylistic and iconographic study of silver, with or without control marks.

The work of Smirnov and Dalton was confined to the interpretation of a limited group of stamps; that of Matsulevich, though larger in scope, dealt almost exclusively with objects in the Hermitage. Since Rosenberg published his catalogue, more than forty additional silver vessels with Byzantine control marks have been discovered.[4] These additional examples throw new light on

[1] For these authors, see *infra*, References Cited in Abbreviation.

[2] See *ibid.*

[3] Matsulevich, *Byz.Ant.*

[4] Nos. 4, 5, 6, 10, 18, 23, 24, 25, 26, 27, 29, 32, 37, 38, 39, 40, 41, 42, 43, 44, 45, 46, 48, 49, 50, 53, 72, 74, 76, 78, 80, 82, 84, 85, 86, 87, 90, 95, 98, 99, 101, 102, 103. The list is not exact, as Rosenberg published some objects without publishing their stamps, and photographs of these have now been procured. Other objects are included in the present catalogue on the strength of the fact that they are known to bear stamps though no photographs or descriptions are available. No. 103 is not stamped but engraved (p. 22).

vii

the interpretation of the stamps, and before progress can be made in solving stylistic and iconographic problems pertaining to Byzantine silver, all the available information regarding the stamps must be marshalled systematically. It is to this task that the present study is devoted. Concerned solely with the stamps, it is intended to provide a basis for future research in broader fields.

The book is divided into three parts: Part I presents a classification and analysis of the stamps and explains the method of dating. Part II explores the type of organization that applied them, and takes up the question of provenance. Part III is a catalogue in which all the stamped objects now known are included; wherever possible the stamps themselves are illustrated and described, and in the descriptions emphasis has been placed on those points that throw light on the date of the stamps and help to place them in a chronological sequence. For each object the principal bibliographical references are given. In the text the vessels are referred to by the number under which they appear in the catalogue.

August 1960   Erica Cruikshank Dodd

Acknowledgments

In the course of preparing a work such as this, which undertakes to present a complete survey of a class of objects distributed among museums and collections in many countries, one must call upon the cooperation and generosity of numerous persons in several fields, and it is with pleasure and gratitude that I present here the names of those to whom I am accordingly indebted.

The following officials made it possible for me to study, at first hand, silver objects and the relevant documents in their charge, to discuss these objects with them personally, and to obtain photographs and casts of the objects: Msgr. Anselmo Albareda, O.S.B., Biblioteca Apostolica Vaticana; M. J. Babelon, Cabinet des Médailles; M. E. Coche de la Ferté, Louvre; Dr. A. Dikigoropoulos, Department of Antiquities, Nicosia; Mr. William Forsyth, Metropolitan Museum of Art; Mr. Peter Lasko, British Museum; Mrs. Vera Ostoia, Metropolitan Museum of Art; Dr. G. Ristow, Staatliche Museen, Berlin; Dr. Hermine Speier, Musei e Gallerie Pontificie; and Mr. Philippe Verdier, Walters Art Gallery, Baltimore.

From many other sources I have received information about stamped objects, as well as photographs and casts, for which my thanks are due in particular to the following officials: in West Berlin, Dr. Peter Metz, Dr. G. Daltrop, and Dr. Claus Zoege von Manteuffel of the Ehem. Staatliche Museen; in Bologna, Dr. G. A. Mansuelli, Soprintendenza alle Antichità; in Budapest, Dr. M. Párducz of the Hungarian National Museum; in Istanbul, Dr. Rüstem Duyuran of the Archaeological Museum; in Kharkov, Prof. Voevodin of the Historical Museum; in Kiev, Dr. R. I. V'ezzhev of the Institute of Archaeology; in Moscow, Prof. A. P. Smirnov of the State Historical Museum; in Riga, Mr. M. Ashmanis of the Museum of the History of the Latvian SSR; in Turin, Dr. Carlo Carducci of the Museo Archeologico and Dr. Noemi Gabrielli of the Galleria Sabauda; and in Vienna, Dr. S. M. Auer and Dr. Rudolf Noll of the Kunsthistorische Museum.

Because of the large number of stamped objects in the Hermitage, my task could not have been accomplished without the untiring help of Miss Alisa Banck, Curator of Byzantine Antiquities, who provided me with documents, information, and photographs of all relevant objects in her charge—also, in many instances, with plaster casts—and made it possible for me to study closely and to photograph the objects from Russia shown at the Byzantine Exhibition in Edinburgh in 1958. Most memorable are the letters received from Prof. Leonid Matsulevich. Eager to help even during the period of his last illness, he sent me material and documents from his own files, and gave generous advice from his profound knowledge of the subject; my warm thanks are due also to Prof. Jeannette Matsulevich for continuing this help after her husband's death in 1959.

I am indebted, too, to other scholars who procured for me the documentation of objects not accessible to me personally: Prof. Paul Underwood and Mr. Lawrence Majewski of the Byzantine Institute were instrumental in securing photographs and casts from the Archaeological Museum, Istanbul; M. Henri Seyrig, then Director of the Institut Français d'Archéologie in Beirut, provided me with detailed information about, and casts of, the stamps on the chalice in Jerusalem (no. 18); Miss Alison Frantz's excellent photographs of the Mytilene (Lesbos) objects are an important contribution; and Mr. Marvin C. Ross kindly brought to my attention the dish in Moscow (no. 74), as well as a number of other objects, and secured photographs for me.

I am grateful to Mme Marguerite Mallon for permission to publish the plate in her collection (no. 25); to Father Bruneel for allowing me to publish the chalice in Jerusalem; to Mr. V. Loevinson-Lessing for permission to reproduce the photographs from the Hermitage; and to the Antiquities Department of the Royal Greek Government, which, through the kind offices of Mr. A. N. Pilavachi, Counselor of the Royal Greek Embassy in Washington, granted me permission to reproduce the stamps on the silver vessels from Mytilene.

The material presented here was originally part of a doctoral thesis submitted to London University in the summer of 1958 under the title "Studies in Early Byzantine Silver." The first two years of work on this thesis were made possible through a Junior Fellowship at Dumbarton Oaks. Later I received grants from the Humanities Research Council of Canada and the Canada Council, as well as the Horton-Hallowell award from Wellesley College. In preparing the study for publication I was greatly helped by two generous grants from McMaster University, Hamilton, Ontario, and by a second grant from the Canada Council. The publication itself was furthered by a contribution from the Humanities Research Council using funds provided by the Canada Council. To all of these organizations I wish to express my deep gratitude.

Among those who contributed toward the actual production of the publication, I am indebted to Mr. John Blair for the preliminary drawings and tables and to Mr. Frank Haentschke, of the Freer Gallery of Art, Washington, for later revisions of these; to Mr. Anthony Kitzinger for plotting and making a preliminary drawing of the map as well as for assistance in checking details; and to Miss Brenda Sens and Miss Carol Cross, of the Center for Middle Eastern Studies, Harvard University, for secretarial help.

Of inestimable assistance were the counsel and criticism of Mr. Philip Grierson, who read the entire manuscript, recommended changes and additions, and revised the section dealing with coins; of Professors Henri Seyrig and George Ostrogorsky, who made valuable suggestions concerning a number of specific points; and of Mr. John Beckwith, Victoria and Albert Museum, who took personal and patient interest in this work over a long period.

ACKNOWLEDGMENTS

I am deeply indebted to my colleagues at Dumbarton Oaks who gave generously not only of their time but also of their knowledge in their respective fields. Mr. John S. Thacher, Director, most kindly made available to me every facility at Dumbarton Oaks and lent his personal interest. The assistance of Mrs. Elizabeth Bland was invaluable in the study of pertinent objects in the Dumbarton Oaks Collection. To Mr. George Soulis I extend my thanks for his help with the translation and transliteration of Russian, and to Mrs. Fanny Bonajuto for locating and securing essential photographs and for checking references. For thorough editorial assistance I am most grateful to Miss Julia Warner.

Much credit goes to my family and to the many friends and colleagues at Wellesley College, the Warburg and Courtauld Institutes, and McMaster University, who have had a close association with me during the writing of this book.

Above all, I wish to thank both of my supervisors, Dr. Hugo Buchthal under whose wise guidance the original thesis was drafted, and Professor Ernst Kitzinger who, from the beginning of my work and throughout its development, has given uncounted hours of encouragement, counsel, and active interest. This volume could not, in fact, have been attempted or produced without his assistance.

E. C. D.

Table of Contents

List of Stamped Objects and Illustrations

xv

LIST OF STAMPED OBJECTS

xvi

LIST OF STAMPED OBJECTS

xix

PART I

CLASSIFICATION AND ANALYSIS OF THE STAMPS

THE stamps to which this study is devoted are found on more than one hundred silver objects of the early Byzantine period. Before examining the stamps themselves, some remarks on the method of working the silver are in order, though this is a subject which will not be treated in detail.[5]

While knowledge of the methods and tools used for this work is incomplete, it is clear from the marks left on the silver that a rotating device like the lathe was employed. A small hole, generally termed the centering point, appears exactly in the center of many pieces. Frequently there is evidence that the back was hammered with tools of different shapes, and H. Maryon has shown[6] how the relief on some objects was chased on a thick sheet of silver entirely from the front. L. A. Matsulevich observed that certain objects having deep relief, like the mythological plates in the Hermitage, are nevertheless smooth on the reverse, with no indication of how the relief was achieved, and he suggested that in such instances the object was made of two separate thin sheets of silver joined together after the front one had been worked by the artist. Examination of other silver objects supports this view and one of the Cyprus plates in New York (no. 61) may be cited as an example. In this plate, the reverse of the relief shows clearly on the back of the plate within the circle of the footring, but outside the footring the surface is quite smooth. The plate is bordered by a rolled rim, achieved by carrying the edge of the bottom sheet of silver over the top sheet. This method sometimes permitted another design to be incised on the back of the plate outside the footring (e.g. no. 9). Many objects, however, are obviously made of only one sheet of silver, for example, the Riha paten (no. 20) on which the relief was beaten from the back so that the design of the entire obverse surface can be seen on the reverse. Chalices, candlesticks, and vessels of complicated form were fashioned of a single, thin sheet of silver.

As was pointed out in the Preface, examination of the vessels in the Hermitage by Smirnov and Matsulevich yielded the fact that the stamps were applied before the decoration was completed, and this conclusion is supported by the

---

[5] A good bibliography for ancient silver metallurgy will be found in R. J. Forbes, *Metallurgy in Antiquity* (Leiden, 1950). The following are among the pertinent references: J. Percy, *Metallurgy: The Art of Extracting Metals from Their Ores. Silver and Gold* (London, 1880); H. Blümner, *Technologie und Terminologie der Gewerbe und Künste bei Griechen und Römern*, IV (Leipzig, 1887); Walters, pp. x–xiii; F. von Bissing, "Zur Geschichte des Silbers und des Electrons," *Acta Orientalia*, IV (1925), pp. 138–141; H. Carpenter and J. M. Robertson, *Metals* (London, 1939); *A History of Technology* (ed. Charles Singer and others, Oxford, 1954–1956), vols. I, II.

[6] H. Maryon, "The Mildenhall Treasure, Some Technical Problems," *Man. A Monthly Record of Anthropological Science*, XLVIII (1948), pp. 25–27, 38–41; *idem*, "Metal Working in the Ancient World," *AJA*, LIII (1949), pp. 120–124; also *The Mildenhall Treasure* (British Museum Handbook, London, 1955), pp. 15–19.

investigation of additional silver objects in the present study. The stamps on the Riha flabellum (no. 21), for instance, must have been applied before the feather decoration of the back surface was traced, for the decoration cuts into the corner of the cross stamp and the working of it has erased part of the cross. On no. 35 rings incised on the base have clearly cut off parts of the stamps. In the case of the chalices—the Tyler Chalice (no. 8) is a good example—the stamping instrument seems to have been applied after the silver had been cut but before the base was finally fashioned, since it would have been virtually impossible for the stamping to have been placed so deep in the base, after it had been finished, without danger of both disfiguring the stamp and denting the base. On many objects, the area around the centering point is worn and parts of the stamps are erased (no. 38) or the centering point itself has broken a stamp (no. 44). Moreover, on the plates with an incised niello design (e.g. no. 42) the wreath in the center may break through the stamps on the reverse.

Among forty-seven stamped vessels which the writer was able to examine personally, thirty-seven give every indication that the stamps were applied before the vessel was finished;[7] three seem to have been stamped after the decoration was complete;[8] and in seven instances[9] there is no clear indication one way or the other. If the vessels studied by Matsulevich are added to these, the total number is increased by at least twenty-seven.[10] Matsulevich considered most of his examples to have been stamped before the object was completed, although he does not specify in each case how this conclusion was reached. In many other instances either the reproduction is sufficiently clear to indicate when the stamps were applied, or an adequate description of the stamps is available.[11] The preponderance of objects stamped before being decorated is such as to warrant the conclusion that it was customary to stamp the vessel before it was completed, and the stamps may thus be considered as a *terminus post quem* for the finished vessel. In those few examples where this rule was not observed, special circumstances prevailed.

At this point it should be added that the vessel was roughly shaped before it was stamped. The significance of this fact will be considered below in connection with the purpose of the stamps and the administrative system of controls. For the time being it is enough to note that the stamps were applied in such a way as to fit the shape of the base of a particular vessel (e.g. the oblong base of no. 75) and not necessarily bunched in groups as was the custom for circular plates (e.g. nos. 6 or 57); in the case of chalices, they were applied before the base had been finally fashioned, though certainly after the sheet of silver had been cut, for they are disposed around the inside lip of the base (see *supra*).

---

[7] Nos. 8, 10, 13, 14, 19, 20, 21, 24, 25, 33, 34, 35, 37, 38, 39, 44, 45, 46, 52, 53, 54, 58, 59, 60, 61, 62, 63, 64, 65, 66, 70, 80, 85, 87, 90, 91, 92.

[8] Nos. 89, 99, 103.

[9] Nos. 2, 4, 28, 47, 78, 88, 98.

[10] Nos. 1, 6, 7, 9, 15, 16, 23, 26, 30, 31, 36, 51, 55, 56, 57, 67, 68, 72, 73, 75, 76, 77, 79, 84, 94, 95, 100.

[11] Stamps applied before the object was decorated: nos. 12, 17, 18, 22, 27, 32, 40, 41, 42, 43, 49, 74, 83, 96, 97. Stamps applied after the object was decorated: no. 101. Examples where the reproduction is not sufficiently clear to indicate when the stamps were applied: 3, 5, 11, 29, 48, 50, 69, 71 81, 82, 86, 93, 102.

Stamps were thus applied to silver vessels at some point during the process of manufacture, after the ultimate use of the refined silver had been determined and the vessel shaped but before the decoration was finally completed.

We turn now to the stamps themselves and consider their development from their first appearance to the time when they fell into disuse.

A. SILVER BULLION, GOLD BARS, AND GRAFFITI. THE SQUARE STAMP

The practice, still in use today, of stamping vessels made of precious metal with an official sign indicating their fineness, and thereby setting them apart from objects made of more ordinary materials, represents a comparatively late development in the history of the use of gold and silver. Indeed, the stamps or marks to be described here are the earliest essays in this practice. In very ancient times there was apparently no control over the quality of metal used by the gold- or silversmith, nor any mark to identify the maker. In the classical Greek era the names of craftsmen were scratched on red- or black-figured vases, and as early as the fifth century B.C. individual artists' names may have been inscribed on silver and gold vessels as well.[12] The custom of thus inscribing an object with the name of the artist may have had both practical and social or psychological significance; it may have reflected the status achieved by the craftsman in Greek society, but in the case of precious metals it must also have served to guarantee the quality of the metal. Early in the classical period, moreover, indications of weight are found scratched on the bottoms of such vessels.[13] This practice served as a more positive evidence of quality, and graffiti of this type continue to be found on vessels long after the classical period. The custom is undoubtedly connected with that of using gold and silver vessels (either whole or broken into fragments for bullion) as currency for such purposes as the payment of debt or tribute.[14] From the second century B.C. actual stamps inscribed with the maker and workshop were used on terracotta and bronze objects.[15] No doubt this development occurred in the cheaper media because the objects were manufactured in great quantity in large workshops, and it would have been too laborious to sign them individually; but no stamps have been found on gold or silver objects of a date earlier than the fourth and fifth centuries A.D., and the earliest of these stamps are on gold and silver ingots, rather than on shaped vessels.

[12] G. M. A. Richter, in *AJA*, XLV (1941), p. 388; cf. Daremberg and Saglio, *Dictionnaire des antiquités grecques et romaines*, I (Paris, 1887), p. 805, note 263.

[13] Signs of weight are found so frequently on silver objects that it is hardly necessary to refer to specific examples. A discussion of the significance of this practice is found in Grünhagen, pp. 65–67.

[14] *Ibid.*, pp. 65–66; Pacatus, *Panegyricus Theodosio Augusto dictus* (*Panegyrici latini*, Teubner ed. [1874], p. 294), XII:26; *Cod. Theod.*, VII:xxiv:1; XII:vi:13; XIII:ii:1.

[15] J. Déchelette, *Les vases céramiques ornés de la Gaule Romaine*, I, II (Paris, 1904); F. Oswald and T. Davies Pryce, *An Introduction to the Study of Terra Sigillata, Treated from a Chronological Standpoint* (London, 1920), with full bibliography and appendix of potters' names, pp. 273–276; for more recent bibliography, see M.-T. Lenger, "Timbres amphoriques trouvés à Argos," *BCH*, LXXIX (1955), pp. 484–508; for bronze objects, Th. Schreiber, *Die alexandrinische Toreutik* (Leipzig, 1894), p. 395; H. Willers, *Die römischen Bronzeeimer von Hemmoor* (Hannover-Leipzig, 1901), *passim*; A. Radnóti, *Die römischen Bronzegefässe von Pannonien* (Budapest, 1938), pl. XVII.

In contrast to the marks previously considered, the stamps on bullion are not only inscribed with an individual name and perhaps the place of origin or the workshop, but also bear an indication of their official character. The busts of three emperors occur in a stamp on a silver ingot found near Hanover. They have been identified as Valentinian III (who came to the throne in A.D. 425), Galla Placidia, and Theodosius II (d. A.D. 450) and thus date the stamp between 425 and 450.[16] The same ingot also bears a stamp containing a seated Tyche holding a scepter and a sphere, and an inscription identifying the figure as the city of Rome. On gold bars from Transylvania are stamps containing the busts of Theodosius the Great (A.D. 379–395), Honorius, and Arcadius.[17] Among the stamps on these bars is one with the seated figure of a Tyche identified by inscription as the city of Sirmium. Silver ingots found in England and Ireland bear the inscription EX OFFI(CINA), or a variant thereof, followed by a proper name.[18] These inscriptions, busts, and city goddesses suggest that the stamps were not applied by a private individual but by some bureau of control established to regulate traffic in the precious metals, and that they represent, therefore, a form of government authority. The individual names inscribed in the stamps on these bars are not likely to be the names of craftsmen, but rather of officials whose duty it was to guarantee the quality and weight of the metal. It is known that metal in bulk was evaluated by weight for purposes of tax payment,[19] and the stamps on the bars thus represent an official guarantee of unadulterated metal. It was probably inevitable that as the power of the central government became stronger, its control in financial matters should extend to all forms of traffic in the precious metals.

The stamps on vessels from the fourth and fifth centuries represent the next step in this development. Only five such stamps are known, one on each of an equal number of vessels (nos. 81–85). They are all of a similar type, square or slightly rectangular, and contain a seated Tyche[20] similar to those on the gold and silver bars. This Tyche again lends the stamp an official character, for it is unlikely that the silversmith would have been allowed to depict the local divinity on a stamp bearing his personal signature and serving his own private purposes. Moreover, the stamp on no. 81 is inscribed in Greek with the words

[16] Willers, op. cit. pp. 232–233, pl. XI: 1a; Sir Arthur Evans, "Notes on the Coinage and Silver Currency in Roman Britain from Valentinian I to Constantine III," Numismatic Chronicle, 4th Ser., XV (1915), pp. 488–519, esp. p. 496; M. Rosenberg, Der Goldschmiede Merkzeichen, I (Frankfurt a. M., 1922), p. XXX, fig. 7; Grünhagen, p. 66. Sir Arthur Evans assigns the imperial busts to Theodosius I and his two sons, Arcadius and Honorius, and dates the bars accordingly at the end of the fourth century. More recent opinion favors a fifth-century date.

[17] Willers, op. cit., p. 229, pl. XIII: 1f. Rosenberg, op. cit., p. XXIX, fig. 6; Sir Arthur Evans, op. cit., p. 490. These busts have also been associated with Valentinian I (Emperor of the West from A. D. 364 to 375), his brother Valens (Emperor of the East in 364–378), and his son Gratian (named Co-Emperor in 367) (F. Kenner, "Römische Goldbarren mit Stempeln," Archaeologisch-Epigraphische Mittheilungen aus Oesterreich-Ungarn, XII [1888], pp. 1–24; see also, ibid., pp. 66–73).

[18] Sir Arthur Evans, op. cit., pp. 508–519; Walters, pp. 31, no. 118, 52, no. 196; Journal of Roman Studies, XXXV (1945), p. 91.

[19] See note 14, and Amm. Marc., XX:iv:18; Cod. Just., X:lxxii:5; X:lxxviii; see also Le livre du Préfet, II:8 (ed. Jules Nicole, Geneva, 1893), p. 24.

[20] Only no. 85 is too damaged to show the figure distinctly.

ΑΒΑΛΑΤΟΣ ΣΦΡΑΓΙΣΕΝ. The Tyche on this stamp closely resembles the figure on a coin struck by Valentinian II (A.D. 383–392) and may be dated in the late fourth century.[21] The inscription leaves no doubt in the mind of the reader that the concern was not with the person who made the vessel but with the one who stamped it; in other words, with the quality of the metal as guaranteed by the stamp of Abalatos, and not with the artistic merits of the vase. The inscription is in Greek, moreover, which suggests an Eastern rather than a Western origin for the vase, and, as Zahn pointed out, the name Abalatos is in itself Eastern. The stamp on no. 82 is also inscribed in Greek and is in most respects like that on no. 81. The Tyche in the stamp on no. 83 is different only in that she is represented in profile; she holds an unidentifiable object and a scepter and her left foot rests on a prow. A similar goddess in profile with globus crucifer and a scepter is found on coins from Constantinople in the reign of Theodosius II (A.D. 408–450).[22] As the bowl was found with coins of Theodosius II and Valentinian III (d. 455), it may reasonably be dated in the first half of the fifth century, a little later than the stamps on nos. 81 and 82. Laffranchi has shown that the representation of Constantinopolis on coins from this period can be distinguished from that of Roma by the fact that she has her left foot resting on a prow.[23] Since this feature appears in the representation on the stamp and since, moreover, the stamp is inscribed with the letters CONS, there can be no doubt that it was applied in the capital. The stamp on no. 84 may be related to the one on no. 83 and dated accordingly; the stamp on no. 85, although in very bad condition, seems to resemble that on no. 81.

Of these five surviving stamps, three bear marks of Eastern origin and may be reasonably closely dated; the remaining two are scarcely legible. So far no stamps at all have been found on gold vessels, but this is probably due to the fact that few such vessels have survived; some may well have been stamped in this period.[23a] Nor were all silver vessels stamped. Numerous objects have come down to us from the fourth and fifth centuries without any such marks. These five are the only extant examples of such an early date documented in this way; at the same time their stamps survive as the first indication of a form of official control of the traffic in precious metals other than for coinage purposes. This was a kind of public assurance that became a permanent fixture only in the later middle ages.

B. IMPERIAL STAMPS

To the reign of Anastasius I (A.D. 491–518) belong the first stamps in the series called "Imperial." This term is used because the reigning emperor's

---

[21] R. Zahn, "Spätantike Silbergefässe," *Amtl.Ber.*, XXXVIII, no. 10 (1917), cols. 263–304, see esp. cols. 271–277 and 292–296.

[22] Ratto, pl. IV, nos. 153–155, 169–179, and *passim*.

[23] L. Laffranchi, "Un nuovo medaglione aureo di Teodosio I e la figura di Constantinopolis," *Studi di numismatica*, I (1940), pp. 69–82; *idem*, "Appunti di critica numismatica. I. La data finale della personificazione di Costantinopoli ed i medaglioni aurei del tempo Teodosiano," *Numismatica*, VII (1941), pp. 33–39.

[23a] Cf. J. Heurgon, *Le trésor de Ténès* (Paris, 1958), pp. 22, 28 (stamp on gold fibula).

portrait and/or his name, written either in full or in monogram form, appear on one or more of the stamps on each of the vessels concerned. The series extends from the reign of Anastasius to that of Constans II (A.D. 641–668). Like the busts on stamps of gold and silver bars, these devices lend the stamps an official character that in itself suggests governmental authority.

The stamps of the reign of Anastasius I occur on five silver vessels (nos. 1–5) and are of five different shapes: round, hexagonal, triangular, square, and oblong with an arched top. This last shape, which also occurs throughout the rest of the Imperial series, will be designated hereafter simply by the adjective "long." Four stamps are found on each vessel under Anastasius and among these at least one of the standard shapes is repeated twice. Vessels nos. 1, 2, and 3 each have two round stamps, one hexagon, and one triangle. The round stamps on no. 1 appear to be identical, containing a bust of the Emperor circumscribed in Latin DN ANASTASIVS PP AVG, a form used commonly on his coins.[24] The hexagon and the triangle contain monograms of the "box type." This kind of monogram is formed by grouping subsidiary letters around one central letter form, and it is so termed to distinguish it from the "cross type" that was developed later in the sixth century. Rosenberg has attempted to read the worn monogram in the triangle, while the one in the hexagon is barely distinguishable; in any case, it is clear that neither can be read as the name of Anastasius. Both monograms are circumscribed by different and unrelated individual names in Greek characters. The stamps on the plate of Paternus, no. 2, are similar in form to those on no. 1, except for two significant changes: although both round stamps contain the bust of the Emperor and one of them is inscribed with his name in Latin, the second is inscribed with an individual name in Greek characters, MHNNA, much like the hexagon and the triangle of no. 1; moreover, in the hexagon is a monogram which can be read to give the name of the Emperor in a form used on his coinage:[25] $\aleph$. This box-type monogram also served for Justinian (*infra*, p. 13), for the letters may be so arranged as to read either name, but in this case, as in nos. 4 and 5, the association with the inscribed name of the Emperor in the accompanying stamp assures the identification. On the same plate, no. 2, the triangle contains a box-type monogram different both from that of the Emperor and from the one in the triangle of no. 1; it may be read to give the name IWANNOV. The hexagon and the triangle are inscribed with the names of individuals in Greek characters, bearing no relation to the names in the stamps of no. 1. The stamps on no. 3 are like those on nos. 1 and 2 in type, except that both the round ones are inscribed with individual Greek names; the name of the Emperor is not to be found, and the box type monogram IWANNOV, corresponding to the monogram in the triangle of no. 2, occurs along with the busts in the round stamps, as well as in the triangle. These stamps are assigned to Anastasius I on the basis of their relationship to the stamps on nos. 1 and 2. On object no. 4, a new shape

---

[24] Wroth, I, p. 1 ff.

[25] Wroth, I, p. 7, no. 59, pl. II: 2; cf. E. Kitzinger, "The Sutton Hoo Ship-Burial. V: The Silver," *Antiquity*, XIV (1940), p. 42.

is introduced, the long stamp. It is repeated twice, along with two identical hexagons, and contains the bust of the Emperor and his name previously found in the round stamp; it contains also a monogram different from those previously observed, and not yet deciphered. In the hexagon is the monogram of the Emperor, similar to the one in the hexagon of no. 2, and the name ΘωΜΑ. Finally, no. 5 shows two long stamps, one hexagon and a square, the latter being the only instance of a square among the stamps of Anastasius. The long stamp resembles those on no. 4, containing the bust and name of the Emperor in Latin, and again a different box-type monogram. Although in form the hexagon is similar to the hexagons already described, in this instance it contains a monogram which is not that of Anastasius. His monogram is found instead in the square stamp, where it is circumscribed by a name in Greek.

The portrait of the Emperor thus occurs in one or another of the stamps on each vessel. In all but one of the stamps the bust is shown full face and wearing a diadem with a trefoil ornament. This portrait is similar to that used later for Justinian I (Table I: Type 1, see *infra*), and will be referred to again. In the round stamp on no. 2, which is inscribed with the Emperor's name, the bust is wearing a plumed helmet rather than a diadem with a trefoil ornament. This portrait type corresponds to contemporary coin portraits of the Emperor Anastasius, a fact which suggests that this stamp may be earlier than the stamps with the "Justinianic" portrait. The stamps on at least three objects show, in addition to the monogram of the Emperor, another and different monogram which will be termed the "secondary monogram." Circumscribing the portraits and the monograms are proper names, and there is a tendency to replace the name of the Emperor, which is in Latin, with that of an individual in Greek. These names and monograms are inscribed in the same way on stamps throughout the Imperial series; that is, the forms remain the same, although the persons to whom they refer constantly change, and a discussion of their meaning is reserved for the end of this section so as to include the entire series. Apart from the recurring patterns described, no very consistent development can be traced among the stamps on these first five objects. There are four on each object, but they occur in different combinations. Coming as they do after the isolated square stamps of the fourth and fifth centuries, they imply the establishment of a new system of control of silver under the direct authority of the Emperor Anastasius; but their lack of uniformity suggests that this system had not yet assumed a fixed character.

The stamps of Anastasius were the forerunners of a new system of control marks introduced in the reign of Justinian I (A.D. 527–565), a system which was established so securely that it survived, with very few changes, for one hundred and fifty years. During this period, five different standard shapes were generally applied to each silver vessel; four of these, the round, the long, the square, and the hexagon are similar to their counterparts under Anastasius; in addition, a new shape, a stamp in the form of a cross was introduced. All are inscribed in Greek characters. Occasionally one shape may be repeated on the same vessel and another omitted, but the total number remains the same. In some instances, only four stamps are visible,[26] and it is possible that where this is the case the fifth stamp was worn away or destroyed while the decoration of the vessel was being finished.[27] This may also have happened to three objects — nos. 71, 74, 79 — where only one stamp can be seen. On the other hand, some of these objects belong to a period when the Imperial system of stamping was breaking down,[28] and the irregularity may be a further sign of the disorganization of controls. On five objects, nos. 44, 54, 55, 64, 65, more than five stamps are visible. In each case one or more of the extra stamps are very much worn and it can be shown that no. 54, at least, and probably no. 55, were stamped on two different occasions,[29] which suggests a similar explanation for nos. 44, 64, 65. The overwhelming majority of the objects concerned, however, have five stamps each. Altogether there are *seventy-five* objects with Imperial stamps (nos. 6–80), exclusive of the stamps from the reign of Anastasius. Two of these are inadequately published (nos. 79, 80). The following description concerns the stamps on the remaining seventy-three objects.[30] Two sets of stamps are found on nos. 17, 54, and 55, which increases the number of stamp *groups* to seventy-six.[31] Each of the five shapes of stamps will be considered as it developed throughout the entire series.

The round stamp contains the bust of the ruling emperor circumscribed by the name or title of an individual in Greek characters.[32] These "portraits" are similar to the busts on the stamps of Anastasius. Their resemblance to contemporary coin types, first observed by Matsulevich, was used by him in *Byzantinische Antike* to date the principal objects with which he deals. Matsulevich described five main types of busts; today we can distinguish eight different types, each of which can be compared with a representative coin type. They cover the reigns from Anastasius I to Constans II, and are described and illustrated in Table I.

The busts of Type I are similar to the busts on coins struck by Justinian I (A.D. 527–565) in 538/39 and after. This bust is also frequently found on the coins of Justin II (A.D. 565–578).[32a] It is true that the coin type is of a military character, showing the emperor full face and wearing helmet and armor,

[26] Nos. 17, 18(?), 34(?), 61, 69, 75. For documentary references to the five stamps, see p. 26f. The suggestion has been made that four stamps may have been used on silver of inferior quality. That this is *not* the case is proved by Rutherford J. Gettens and Claude L. Waring, "The Composition of Some Ancient Persian and Other Near Eastern Silver Objects," *Ars Orientalis*, II (1957), p. 89, nos. 17–24, where it is shown that silver with four stamps is of as good a quality as silver with five.

[27] See nos. 20, 21, 22, 49.

[28] See *infra*, pp. 12, 31, 33.

[29] See the entries for nos. 54 and 55 in the Catalogue.

[30] Rosenberg published about forty-five of the seventy-three objects. The additional numbers are given in note 4.

[31] Although the distinctions between the two sets on nos. 54 and 55 are open to question on minor points because several of the stamps are badly worn, these uncertainties do not affect the following argument and for the sake of convenience the two objects are considered as bearing two independent sets of stamps, as does no. 17. The additional stamps on nos. 44, 64, and 65 are too worn to be considered independently.

[32] On no. 78 there is a round stamp of the normal kind and, in addition — a single exception to the rule — a round stamp containing a monogram; see pp. 12, 21.

[32a] Cf. Wroth, I, pls. IV: 11, 12 (Justinian); XI: 1 (Justin II).

whereas the stamp type is of a civilian character, showing the emperor in a cloak and wearing a diadem; but there are close analogies between the two types: the helmet on the coins is surrounded by a diadem having a frontal ornament with three small projections; this trefoil-like arrangement is found also in the silver stamps and in both cases the circular ornament which supports the trefoil may be omitted and the projections depicted widely separated, losing all relation to the original design.[32b] The bust in the stamps is nimbed and while the nimbus does not occur on the obverse of normal solidi, the emperor may occasionally be nimbed on coins even in the sixth century.[33] A variant of Type 1 occurs in a stamp from the reign of Anastasius on the plate of Paternus, no. 2. This stamp shows the Emperor helmeted and in three-quarter view. Such a bust is found on Byzantine coins beginning with the early fourth century and is used consistently until the time of Justinian I.[34] It is found regularly on the coins of Anastasius; but most stamps of Anastasius show the full-face type and anticipate by several years the adoption of that type for the coinage of Justinian in 538/39.[35]

Type 2 is similar to Type 1, except that the diadem with trefoil ornament is replaced by a crown with a small, circular, raised ornament in front. The bust corresponds to a coin type adopted by Tiberius II Constantine (A.D. 578–582). On these coins the same crown appears either with a helmet or supporting a cross, and so it continued under Mauricius Tiberius (A.D. 582–602).[35a] Moreover, on some coins Tiberius II is shown wearing, instead of his armor, a paludamentum like that worn by the bust in the stamps.[36] The stamps concerned may thus be dated in the reigns of Tiberius II or Mauricius. There is also, however, one bust of this kind in a stamp belonging to the reign of Justin II (no. 27), that is, to a period when it had not yet appeared on the coins. This is another instance where the stamp type anticipates the development in coinage. Type 3 is similar to Type 2, but is even closer to the coin types of Tiberius in that the Emperor is without nimbus and the crown has a circular ornament supporting a cross. Types 1, 2, and 3 cover the sixth century, the only significant change being in the headgear of the emperor. This small distinction was, indeed, noticed by Matsulevich,[37] but he had no evidence to show how the different types overlapped the several reigns. Moreover, in the stamps of this period, except for Type 3 (of which there is only a single example), the busts are nimbed

---

[32b] This omission is normal on coins of the sixth century, but the complete design appears regularly on coins of the late fifth century.

[33] Cf. a coin from the joint reign of Justin I and Justinian, showing the two Emperors seated and *en face*: Wroth, I, pl. IV: 5, 6. A nimbed figure of the emperor is also found on rare silver coins from Constantinople: Sabatier, I, p. 178, nos. 7, 8, pl. XII: 6, 7; Wroth, I, p. 29, nos. 26, 27; pl. V: 1, 2.

[34] J. Maurice, *Numismatique constantinienne*, I (Paris, 1908), p. 151, no. 5, pl. XIV; Sabatier, I, pls. III ff.; Ratto, no. 40 ff.

[35] Wroth, I, p. xci. Wroth regards this full-face type as an innovation made by Justinian and considers it to be a portrait of this Emperor. Its earlier use in the stamps by Anastasius suggests that it was not an individual likeness of either Emperor but, rather, a formal type-portrait adopted by Anastasius and used by his successors.

[35a] Cf. Wroth, I, pls. XIII: 17 (Tiberius II, ornament with cross); XVII: 3 (Mauricius, ornament with helmet).

[36] Wroth, I, p. 110, nos. 38, 39; pl. XIV: 7, 8.

[37] *Byz. Ant.*, p. 82.

and for this reason Matsulevich classed *all* nimbed portraits in the sixth century. Type 3 shows that the nimbus may be dropped before the end of the sixth century, while, on the other hand, it appears again on stamps from the seventh century.

Type 4a introduces two innovations: the bust is nimbed, but the crown worn by the emperor does not have pendants and the portrait is bearded. The beard of Phocas (A.D. 602–610), as it was portrayed on normal coin issues in the East,[37a] was distinctively long and pointed. It is as recognizable on the stamps as on the coins of this Emperor. The only distinction between Type 4a and Type 4b is that the nimbus is omitted in the latter; so the relationship between the coin and the stamp types becomes even closer.

Types 5–7 all belong to the Emperor Heraclius (A.D. 610–641). Type 5 continues in the tradition of the Phocas portrait except that Heraclius' beard is short, if indeed there is a beard at all.[38] The crown has pendants of the sixth-century type and is surmounted by a circular ornament. This type corresponds to the effigy of the Emperor on his coins 610–613, except that in the usual coin type he wears a helmet, or, if he does wear a crown, its ornament is surmounted by a cross.[39] The portrait is nimbed. Type 6 occurs most frequently on the stamps of Heraclius and corresponds to coin types from the years 613–629/30.[40] On the stamps this type occurs with minor variations. In all of them the Emperor is dressed in a cloak; he wears a bushy beard, cropped hair and a crown. In Type 6a he is nimbed and on the front of the crown there is a circular ornament recalling earlier types in the series. Type 6b is similar to Type 6a, except that the nimbus is omitted. In Type 6c the ornament on the crown is embellished with a cross, as it normally is on contemporary coins. Type 6d, which shows the ornament on the crown surmounted by a trefoil decoration,[40a] occurs only twice in the Imperial series, and both times in the long stamp. It is nimbate. Type 7 portrays Heraclius as he appears on his coins between 629/30 and 641.[41] In the stamps, as on the coins, the Emperor wears a crown with a cross; he has a long beard with rather formidable mustaches and no nimbus.

Type 8 belongs to Constans II (A.D. 641–668). It differs from the bust of Heraclius in the distinctive shape of the face and in the fact that the Emperor carries a globus crucifer. This bust corresponds to the coin portrait of

---

[37a] Cf. Wroth, I, pl. XX: 4, 5.

[38] In the year of his accession, A.D. 610, Heraclius shaved his beard which had previously been long and bushy: Georgius Cedrenus, *Historiarum compendium*, I (Bonn, 1838), p. 714. The information agrees with the portrayal of the Emperor on coins from the first two or three years of his reign (see *infra*) and it helps support our chronological grouping of the silver stamps of the reign of Heraclius, since those with an effigy of this type appear at the head of the sequence on other grounds also.

[39] Wroth, I, p. 211, no. 205, pl. XXV: 1; Grierson, *Num. Chron.* X, p. 69, 38a, pl. IV. For the dating of these coin types and excellent illustrations, see Grierson, "Solidi of Phocas and Heraclius: the Chronological Framework," *Numismatic Chronicle*, 6th Ser., XIX (1959), pp. 131–154. Unfortunately, this article appeared too late to be referred to throughout this text.

[40] Wroth, I, p. xxiv; pl. XXIII: 4, 8.

[40a] Cf. Wroth, I, pl. XXIII: 11, where the crown has a similar ornament.

[41] *Ibid.*, pl. XXIII: 9, 10–12.

Constans II between 641 and 651/2, in which the Emperor also carries a globus crucifer.[42]

The busts in the round stamps can thus be associated with coin types from the reign of Anastasius I to Constans II, and on this evidence alone the entire series can be attributed to the sixth and first half of the seventh century. In the case of stamps from the seventh century the emperors portrayed can be identified fairly readily, but in the sixth century only three slightly different portrait types were used for the stamps throughout five reigns and the dating of an object on grounds of the portrait alone is correspondingly vague. Frequently the bust in the round stamp is too badly worn to be distinguished, or the round stamp may be entirely missing. Although a similar portrait is found in the long stamp (to be discussed presently), in cases where neither bust is clear the most positive criterion for dating lies in the imperial monogram in the square and hexagonal stamps.

The square and hexagonal stamps are similar in kind and may be considered together. Each contains a monogram in the center and a name or title in Greek letters around the periphery. The hexagon generally has, in addition, a mark of religious character, either a cross (e.g., no. 37) or a nimbed bust (e.g., no. 56). On two objects (nos. 45, 46) the nimbus is crossed and thus indicates that the bust portrays Christ. In two other stamps (nos. 72, 73) the bust appears to be winged. In one instance only is this general arrangement varied: the hexagon of no. 77, contains a large bust of a saint and a circumscribed name, but no monogram.[43] In no instance is the name inscribed in the square the same as that in the hexagon and there seems to be little relationship between them; but it is of great importance that the monogram in the square very frequently spells the same name as the monogram in the hexagon. Table II illustrates how frequently this occurs. From the beginning of the reign of Justinian I, to the end of the reign of Constans II there are thirty-one stamp groups in which the monograms in both the square and the hexagon are at least partially legible.[44] Among these thirty-one groups (or sixty-two stamps), only six instances (or twelve stamps) occur in which the monogram in one stamp is not the same as in the other (nos. 28, 29, 36, 41, 76, 78). It follows that there is generally a relationship between the monograms in question, and wherever one is not legible it is most likely to have been the same as the other.

Furthermore, again in the great majority of cases, this monogram spells the name of an emperor, and specifically the emperor (or one of the emperors) with

[42] Wroth, I, p. 255, note 1; pl. xxx: 12–15. In the round stamp of no. 75 the Emperor has a fairly short, full beard, which, according to Wroth, was worn by Constans II from *ca.* 646–651/2. It is difficult to judge whether or not the busts in the round stamps of nos. 76 and 77 are bearded, but it is possible that they are without beard and thus belong to the years 641–*ca.* 646. The round stamp on no. 78 is hardly distinguishable.

[43] The religious character of these stamps is discussed in A. Alföldi and E. Cruikshank, "A Sassanian Silver Phalera at Dumbarton Oaks," *Dumbarton Oaks Papers*, 11 (1957), p. 244.

[44] Neither monogram is legible on nos. 18, 24, 53, 71, 74. Only one monogram, either in the square or the hexagon, is legible on nos. 6, 10, 14, 16, 17A, 17B, 19, 20, 21, 22, 23, 26, 35, 40, 42, 43, 47, 48, 49, 50, 51, 52, 54A, 54B, 55B, 58, 59, 60, 61, 62, 63, 64, 65, 66, 67, 68, 69, 70, 75. No. 77 is also excluded since the hexagon does not contain a monogram.

whom the bust in the round stamp is associated. Among the seventy-six stamp groups, there are seventy-one in which at least *one* of the two stamps, either the square or the hexagon, is legible, and sixty-seven times out of seventy-one, at least *one* of these monograms reads the name of an emperor. This is a substantial proportion of the total number. It points to the conclusion that the monograms in the square and the hexagon are, as a rule, not only identical, but both also spell the name of the emperor portrayed in the round stamp.

In all, there are only eight exceptions to this rule and they are marked on Table II in dark ink.[45] On only one object (no. 77) does neither stamp contain a monogram with the name of an emperor. These stamps belong to the reign of Constans II, when the system of controls was deteriorating.[46] The same circumstance explains the irregularities on nos. 75, 76, and 78. No explanation for the irregularities among the stamps on nos. 28, 29, 36, and 41 is entirely satisfactory. Nos. 28 and 29 belong to the reign of Tiberius II. It is suggested that, since his reign lasted only four years, the stamping system may not have become fully organized during so brief a period. In one of the stamps on no. 29 the monogram of Justin II seems to have been re-used. Also, among the stamps of Tiberius the monogram of Constantine occurs, and the same monogram appears again in the hexagonal stamps of nos. 36 and 41, where the accompanying square stamps bear the monograms of Phocas and Heraclius respectively.[47] Whatever the reason for these minor variations, the fact remains that, taking the entire group of square and hexagonal stamps, there is an evident relationship between their monograms and the portrait of the emperor in the round stamp, a relationship which has not been sufficiently recognized in the past. The monogram has occasionally been connected with the emperor when the portrait in the round stamp was clear, but it has not usually been used as a guide to the date of an object. Yet, since the monogram in the square and hexagonal stamps generally agrees with the portrait in the round stamp, it follows that in cases where the portrait is not recognizable, the object may frequently be dated by the monogram alone.

Monograms like those of Phocas and Heraclius can hardly be read to yield any other name, but other monograms are not so easily interpreted. Once it is established that the squares and hexagons contain as a rule an imperial monogram, we are justified in choosing among several possible readings one which corresponds to the name of an emperor. For example, the monogram ⬥ could

---

[45] Nos. 28, 29, 36, 41, 75, 76, 77, 78. Nos. 1 and 5, also marked in dark ink, are excluded since they belong to the reign of Anastasius; on nos. 11, 12, 13, 25, 37, 38, 39, there are slight variations in the monograms in question, but they do not affect the present discussion. In every case they involve only a variation in the form of monogram or in the spelling of the emperor's name (see also note 54).

[46] See *infra*, pp. 31, 33.

[47] In the case of no. 28, the monogram in the hexagon reads Constantine and it is possible that the monogram in the square spells the Emperor's first name. It is known that Tiberius assumed the name Constantine on his accession (Wroth, I, p. xx, note 3). Some of the coins of Tiberius are inscribed with his first name on one side and his second on the other (Wroth, I, pp. 106–107). A similar explanation applies to no. 41 from the reign of Heraclius, for this Emperor named his son, Heraclius Constantine, co-Emperor in 613 (see no. 94; Grierson, "Solidi of Phocas and Heraclius; The Chronological Framework," *Numismatic Chronicle*, 6th Ser., XIX [1959], p. 142). There seems to be no equally valid reason for the use of this monogram by Phocas for the hexagonal stamp on no. 36.

read either MAPKOV or MAVPIKIOV, but the latter reading is undoubtedly the correct one. In this manner, it is possible to decipher monograms that have not previously been read. Along with the portrait in the round stamp, Table I gives the monogram (or monograms) of each emperor as it appears on his stamps.

The monogram �, or , was assigned by Matsulevich and Rosenberg to either Anastasius or Justinian, since it contains all the letters of both names: NACTIOV. Indeed, it was certainly shared by both Emperors, for it can be seen not only on the coins and stamps of Anastasius, but also on capitals of St. Sophia,[48] St. John at Ephesus,[49] and, possibly, S. Vitale in Ravenna,[50] where it refers to the Emperor Justinian. There is another form of this monogram that could refer to either name and which, as it is found in the stamps, has been assigned to both Anastasius and Justinian. The only difference between it and the first monogram lies in the fact that an additional line is used to form the letter A: . This type is widely represented in the churches of Justinian and occurs on the brass collars and capitals of St. Sophia far more frequently than does the first.[51] It is found again on the capitals of the church of Sts. Sergius and Bacchus[52] and of St. Irene.[53] The church of St. Sophia was built in the years from 532 to 537, and presumably the capitals on the columns of the nave, on which both monograms occur, were put in place toward the beginning or middle of this period. The second monogram must have been in use well before the church was finished, or at least by *ca.* 536. Other variations of the first monogram were used by Justinian in his churches, but the second type was the form most commonly employed. On silver, it occurs only in stamps which can be attributed on other grounds also to the reign of Justinian rather than to that of Anastasius. For these reasons the monogram can probably be considered a variation instituted by Justinian alone and not shared by his predecessor.

The monogram of Justin II (IOVCTINOV) is identified here for the first time. It is similar to that of Anastasius and Justinian but lacks the A and thus cannot represent the name of either of these Emperors. Once, on no. 25, a variation occurs with an epsilon, which yields the reading

[48] Lethaby and Swainson, p. 293: F. 2.

[49] *Forschungen in Ephesos* (Österreichisches archäologisches Institut), IV, 3 (Vienna, 1951), p. 122, fig. 22, pls. XXVIII: 1; XXX: 1, 2; XXXI: 1, 2; R. Kautzsch, *Kapitellstudien* (Berlin-Leipzig, 1936), pl. 36, no. 567 a, b.

[50] Diehl, *Ravenne* (Paris, 1928), p. 133; see also *Archaeologia*, XLV (1880), p. 425. This monogram exists in a slightly different form among the Justinianic capitals of Caričin Grad: Dj. Mano-Zisi, "Les fouilles de Caričin Grad en 1949–1952," *Starinar*, III–IV (1952–1953), p. 143, fig. 28.

[51] See e.g. E. M. Antoniades, *Ekphrasis tes Hagias Sophias*, II (Athens, 1908), figs. 250, 302, 307, 313; Lethaby and Swainson, p. 293: C. 1, D. 1, D. 2, G. 1, H. 2, J. 1, K. 2, L. 1, M. 2, N. 1, O. 2. P. 2; E. H. Swift, *Hagia Sophia* (New York, 1940), p. 52, figs. 3, 4, p. 65, fig. 8.

[52] J. A. Ebersolt and A. Thiers, *Les églises de Constantinople* (Paris, 1913), p. 47, fig. 24.

[53] W. S. George, *The Church of Saint Eirene at Constantinople* (Oxford, 1912), p. 21, fig. 7, pls. 16, 23. It is found also on a bronze weight of Justinian in the Louvre: Daremberg and Saglio, "Exagium," *Dictionnaire des antiquités grecques et romaines*, II (Paris, 1892), p. 876, fig. 2850; H. Leclercq, in Cabrol and Leclercq, *Dictionnaire d'archéologie chrétienne et de liturgie*, IX² (Paris, 1930), col. 1778, fig. 7145.

IOVCTEINOV.[54] This monogram is found in the squares and/or hexagons on seven silver objects (nos. 20–23, 25–27). The objects concerned, which include the well-known patens from Riha and Stuma and the plate with the bust of "Euthenia," may be dated, therefore, within the thirteen years of the reign of Justin II (A.D. 565–578). It might be said that this monogram could also refer to Justin I (A.D. 518–527), but the secondary monogram is of the cross type, a type which, as will be shown, did not develop until after *ca.* 536. This circumstance, together with other factors to be considered later, places these stamps in the reign of the second Justin (see *infra*, p. 16 and note 67).

The monogram in the square stamp of no. 28, an object attributed on other grounds to Tiberius II Constantine,[55] is unfortunately not very legible. The monogram in the hexagon reads KШNCTANTINOV. It is known that Tiberius assumed this name on his accession.[56]

The monogram of Mauricius 𝕏 occurs on two silver objects (nos. 30 and 31) that have in the round stamp a bust of Type 2 (Table I). These two sets of stamps are exceptional in the Imperial series in that the imperial monogram is found in the long stamp, as well as in the square and hexagonal stamps.[57] Although the stamps are badly defaced, by combining all six examples a monogram that reads MAVPIKIOV can be pieced together.

The monograms of Phocas and Heraclius have been identified before and it is necessary only to observe that in stamps dating from the early part of Heraclius' reign his monogram differs slightly from the one that appears in the later stamps. On objects which on other grounds can be placed early in the sequence, the P in the monogram is combined with the H: ⊩ ("type b"). On stamps later in the sequence, the P is attached to the stem of the ȣ, and the resulting design is more balanced: ⊩ ("type a"). In two instances (the square stamps of nos. 69 and 70) the P seems to be entirely missing ("type c").

Among the stamps of Constans II we have already observed irregularities; it would appear that this Emperor used a similar monogram to that of his predecessor in two hexagonal stamps (nos. 76, 78). His given name was, indeed, Heraclius.[57a]

---

[54] For a similar spelling of the name of Justin, see *Corpus Inscriptionum Graecarum*, III, no. add. 4366.i³. A monogram very like the monogram of Justin II is found on certain "Vandalic" coins in the British Museum, which have been assigned to Anastasius I: W. Wroth, *Catalogue of the Coins of the Vandals, Ostrogoths and Lombards ... in the British Museum* (London, 1911), p. 33. In this case it is probable that the monogram refers to Justin I.

[55] See Catalogue entry for no. 28.

[56] See note 47.

[57] See p. 15 *infra*. This monogram differs from the cross-type monogram used on Mauricius' coins (Sabatier, I, pl. XXVI: 20). For variations in the form of this monogram, see Tables I, II, and III.

[57a] A monogram that reads "Constantine" and thus might refer to Constans II occurs in the long and cross stamps of no. 75 and in the cross stamps of nos. 76 and 77. The monograms in long and cross stamps are discussed *infra*. They do not generally refer to an emperor, and since Constantine is a common name, it would be rash to conclude that these stamps are an exception to the rule. If, on the other hand, these monograms do refer to the Emperor, they contribute to the unusual features that distinguish the stamps of Constans II (pp. 8, 12), and may be explained on the same grounds: namely, that the system of controls was deteriorating (pp. 31, 33).

The long stamp always contains a small bust, a monogram beneath it, and a name or title inscribed on the sides. The bust is generally identical with the one in the round stamp, and so may likewise be considered a means of establishing the date. Two objects, nos. 55 and 56, provide exceptions to this rule, since in these groups Type 6c occurs in the round stamp and Type 6a in the long. The long stamps on these objects and on no. 54 have another peculiarity: they have inscribed just below the bust the two letters X and Θ. Matsulevich suggests that these may be officina marks similar to those found on coins,[58] but since these irregularities are found on only three objects the question remains open. The monogram and the inscribed name in the long stamp will be discussed together with those on the cross.

The cross stamp contains only a name and a monogram. The name is inscribed at the ends of the arms of the cross and the arrangement of the letters is not uniform throughout. The earliest cross stamps, from the beginning of the reign of Justinian (nos. 6–14), are of a rather crude shape with square, blunt arms of equal length, though on nos. 10, 12, and 13 the arms have a slight flare. All the letters of the name are upright and must be read first from top to bottom and then from left to right.[59] In somewhat later examples from the reign of Justinian and in some of those from the reign of Justin II, the name is still read in the same way but the arms of the cross are decidedly flared.[60] This type of cross stamp also occurs under Mauricius (nos. 30, 31) and even in the reign of Phocas (no. 34). As early as the reigns of Justin II and Tiberius II (nos. 27, 28), however, the form more frequently adopted is one in which all the letters are placed upright, if read from the center of the cross clockwise around the arms. All but one of the cross stamps from the reign of Phocas, and all those from the reign of Heraclius, are of this type. The shape of the cross and the arrangement of the letters may thus be used within broad limits as a means of dating an object.

The monograms in the long and cross stamps (Table III) are, in all but four examples, identical with each other. The four exceptions to this rule, which involve two pairs of identical stamps, are marked on the table in dark ink. As has been noted above, the long stamp of nos. 30 and 31, repeats, for unexplained reasons, the monogram of the emperor in the accompanying square and hexagonal stamps. On nos. 70 and 71, it is the cross stamp that has a monogram resembling that of the emperor.[61] On all the other stamps in question the monogram differs from that of the emperor, and in order to distinguish it from the latter it will be termed the "secondary" monogram.

The secondary monogram also provides valuable means of dating an object.

[58] "Arg. byz.," p. 300. Matsulevich also found the letter Є below the bust in the round stamp of no. 77 (this would appear rather to be the clasp of the emperor's paludamentum, but the reproduction is not very clear). There may be a connection here with the Θ and the X and also the Є which by the end of the eighth century replace the mint mark on coins (Wroth, II, p. 402 and *passim*).

[59] See nos. 6, 7, 8, 9, 12, 13, 14, in which the inscriptions are clear.

[60] Nos. 15, 16, 17, 19, 20, 21, 22, 23, 25, 26?.

[61] In other instances the monograms in the long and cross stamps differ only in minor respects, i.e. in the placing of the letters or in the spelling of the name (e.g. nos 25 and 33). Compare the variations in the imperial monograms noted *supra* (notes 45 and 57).

In the first place, its form changes. Weigand observed[62] that there were two types of monograms in use during the reign of Justinian, both of which are represented in St. Sophia. The first is the box type found in the stamps of Anastasius and used for the name of the Empress Theodora on at least one of the capitals of St. Sophia (532–537).[63] Shortly thereafter, a new form seems to have been adopted for Theodora, probably for the sake of convenience; in this type all the letters of the name are placed on the arms of a cross, with the Θ in the center.[64] This type, called the "cross" or "cruciform" type, is used consistently for Theodora on the capitals of St. John at Ephesus[65] and, in a slightly different (perhaps earlier) form, in St. Irene.[66] This appears to be the first occurrence of the cruciform monogram and, like the second of Justinian's box-type monograms, it may be dated shortly before St. Sophia was finished, that is, around A.D. 536. A similar change of type occurs in the secondary monograms in the long and cross stamps; on objects which on other grounds can be assigned to the reign of Justinian these monograms may be either of the box or cruciform type. After the reign of Justinian, on the other hand, this monogram is invariably cruciform. Since for the monogram of Theodora the transition occurred around A.D. 536, it is likely that the monogram in the long and cross stamps changed at about the same time. Thus the monogram that reads IOVCTINOV can be assigned to Justin II (A.D. 565–578) rather than to Justin I (A.D. 518–527), for on all objects where it occurs (nos. 20–27) the monogram in the long and cross stamps is of the cross type and is accordingly later than *ca.* 536.[67] Only the imperial monogram preserved the older form for a time; Justinian and the three succeeding emperors used the box type in the square and hexagon. Phocas, however, adopted the cruciform monogram, as did Heraclius.

Even more important for the dating of the stamps is the repetition of the secondary monogram in corresponding stamps on different objects. The full meaning of this monogram will be discussed below in connection with textual evidence for the control system underlying the stamps. At this point it should be observed merely that the recurrence of identical monograms makes it possible to form groups among objects within the reign of a single emperor (e.g. nos. 41–50). It may be suggested that in such cases the monogram refers to a single official and that therefore the stamps were applied at approximately the same time. Table III illustrates how frequently this repetition occurs, and in the Catalogue the objects are so arranged that the secondary monograms fall together in blocks (indicated by heavier dividing lines).

---

[62] "Ein bisher verkanntes Diptychon Symmachorum," *JDAI*, LII (1937), p. 130; see also Dalton, *Arch.* 57, p. 167.

[63] Lethaby and Swainson, p. 293: E. 1, E. 2.

[64] *Ibid.*, p. 293: F. 1 (B. 2 shows another variant of the cross type).

[65] *Forschungen in Ephesos*, IV, 3, pls. XXVIII: 3, 4; XXIX: 2; Kautzsch, *Kapitellstudien*, pl. 36, no. 567 c and e.

[66] George, *The Church of Saint Eirene at Constantinople*, p. 21, fig. 7; pls. 12, 16, 23.

[67] The assignment of these stamps to Justin II is further supported by other criteria: the imperial bust type, the relationships with stamps from the reigns of Justinian I and Tiberius II Constantine, the identification of the *comes sacrarum largitionum* (p. 29), and the shape of the cross stamp. The sum of these factors makes it impossible to ascribe the stamps to Justin I.

Since this method of dating is subordinate to that based on the imperial monograms, it is revealing that the consecutive groups thus formed never run counter to the sequence dictated by the latter; nor do these groups conflict with the order established on the basis of the imperial bust types or of the shape and form of the cross stamp. In only one instance is the secondary monogram repeated on objects from different reigns, and the objects involved (nos. 27 and 28) belong respectively to the reign of Justin II and to that of his successor, Tiberius II. If the same official is represented by the secondary monogram in both groups of stamps, it follows that he was in office during the reigns of both Emperors. The first object, then, belongs to the end of the reign of Justin II, and the second to the beginning of the reign of Tiberius II.

Finally, the individual names and titles inscribed in all five stamps suggest other means of dating and make it possible to place the stamped objects in a close chronological sequence within the imperial reigns and also within the groups formed by the secondary monograms. The inscriptions are generally common personal names. Although CXOΛACTIKIC, ΠΑΤΡΙΚΙC, and KOMITAC resemble titles of officials, they are also used as personal names.[68] The same cannot be said, however, for ΛΑΜΠΡΟΤΑΤΟC and CΕBACTOC, which occur several times in the stamps (nos. 19, 25, 27, 44–46, 51–54A). Λαμπρότατος corresponds to the Latin title of *clarissimus* and, while it had lost some of its importance in the sixth century, it still indicated very high rank indeed. It was, for example, accorded to consuls under Justinian. The title Σεβαστός was originally reserved for the emperor alone, and these stamp inscriptions seem to be the earliest evidence of its use for subordinate officials, although this became common practice in the ninth century.[69] No consistent relationship has been discovered between the inscriptions in the stamps on a single object. Table IV isolates these, and it is evident that although the same name may recur in two different stamps on the same object, for instance on no. 20, these repetitions do not occur in any regular pattern. Very often, however, the name inscribed in a stamp on one object recurs in the corresponding stamp on another. For example, the names in the round and cross stamps of no. 16 are found again in the round and cross stamps of no. 17. The name CICINNIC occurs at least seventeen times in the cross stamps from the reigns of Tiberius Constantine through Heraclius. Sometimes the repeated name figures on stamps that are identical too in all other respects. Nos. 27 and 28 have been mentioned above as sharing the secondary monogram in the long stamp; the name IWANNIC and the imperial bust in the same stamp are apparently also identical. Evidently, the stamp, originally used in the reign of Justin II, was still applied in the reign of Tiberius. The implication here is that both the person designated by the secondary monogram and the person

---

[68] W. Pape, *Wörterbuch der griechischen Eigennamen* (Braunschweig, 1863–1870), I, p. 691; II, pp. 1148, 1468.

[69] For λαμπρότατος, see E. Hanton, "Lexique explicatif du Recueil des inscriptions grecques chrétiennes d'Asie Mineure," *Byzantion*, IV (1927–1928), pp. 100–102; L. Bréhier, *Les institutions de l'Empire byzantin* (Paris, 1949), p. 103. For σεβαστός, G. Schlumberger, *Sigillographie de l'Empire byzantin* (Paris, 1884), p. 581.

called IѠANNIC held office under both rulers, and it becomes even more probable that the objects are separated only by a short time interval, i. e., that they belong respectively to the end of Justin's reign and to the beginning of that of Tiberius.[70] Again, on nos. 35 and 36, to quote one additional example among many, the long and cross stamps agree respectively as regards both their monograms and their name inscriptions (and the long stamps also in regard to the imperial portrait).

A name as common as IѠANNIC will recur throughout the entire series of Imperial stamps, but when a less usual name, such as CXOΛACTIKIC, appears in a single sequence of objects under Heraclius, it is very possible that members of the same family, if not actually the same person, may be meant. These relationships offer another way of bringing stamp groups together for purposes of dating. Where relationships among imperial portraits and monograms, secondary monograms, or corresponding stamps on different objects are lacking, the inscribed individual names can be used, if only with discretion. The occurrence of the same name in *corresponding* stamps—for example in the cross stamps of nos. 13 and 14, both from the reign of Justinian I—suggests a possible relationship between the two groups of stamps even though they differ in other respects. The occurrence of the same name in *different* stamps may also indicate a relationship between the objects concerned, provided the name is not a very common one; the name CXOΛACTIKIC, which is encountered first in the round stamp of no. 50 and the hexagon of no. 51, and then in the long stamp of nos. 55, 56, 58–66, 70 and in the cross stamp of nos. 72–74, thus helps to clarify and refine the order indicated by imperial portraits and monograms and by secondary monograms.

In summary, each of the five stamps on a silver object offers a means of dating the object so that whenever one is missing or worn and illegible, another may be used for this purpose. The imperial portraits and monograms serve to identify the reigns. The secondary monograms permit us to form groups within a given reign. The recurrence of identical stamps and individual names suggests associations *within* the groups formed on the basis of the secondary monogram, and may relate these groups one to another. Finally, certain broad limits of date may be defined by means of the changing shape or form of the cross stamp, and the two forms used for the secondary monogram. When all these methods, as illustrated in Tables I, II, III, and IV, are combined, a fairly consistent chronological sequence of silver stamps from the time of Anastasius I to Heraclius emerges. In Part III, the objects are arranged in this sequence, and the reasons for giving an object its particular place in the sequence become apparent from the analysis of its stamps.

---

[70] No. 29, also belonging to Tiberius, again repeats a stamp from the reign of Justin II, namely the hexagon. As was suggested above (p. 12), the system may not have been fully reorganized during Tiberius' brief reign.

C. IRREGULAR STAMPS

A number of silver vessels have stamps differing from those of the Imperial series and require, therefore, individual discussion. They fall into five separate categories: The stamps on one vessel are so inscribed as to be attributable to a definite locality, Carthage; five objects bear stamps similar to the Carthaginian stamps and with an indication of date though not of origin; two objects have stamps that can be assigned to Antioch; on a pair of plates there are stamps identifiable as Merovingian; three, or possibly four, objects bear stamps that may have developed at a later date from Imperial types. Three vessels have groups of stamps which, in each instance, are unique and have not been identified in any way.

A plate in the Galleria Sabauda, Turin, depicting a Nereid riding on a seamonster (no. 93), bears two stamps on the reverse. One stamp is square and, although badly defaced, appears to contain an alpha and omega in ligature; the other contains, in a rectangular frame, five lines of Latin inscription referring to the fifteenth year of the reign of Justinian, to the fifth indiction, to December, and to Carthage. It is thus dated in December 541.[71] Carthage, the capital of the Vandal Kingdom, fell to Belisarius in December 533,[72] and the stamps suggest a commemoration of this event.

Two stamps, slightly similar to the Carthaginian stamps in form, appear on each of five objects, nos. 94–98. Nos. 94, 96, 97 clearly show an eight-leafed rosette with Greek characters in the leaves and a rectangular stamp containing three lines of Latin inscription. The inscriptions in the rosettes are too indistinct to be deciphered completely, but those in the rectangles are sufficiently legible to be dated in the seventh century. The stamps on no. 95, an eagle signum in Kharkov, also belong to this group, but their inscriptions are still undeciphered; on no. 98 one of the stamps deviates somewhat from the others in that, instead of a rosette, it has an eight-pointed star, and the rectangular stamp has not been deciphered. This group of stamps is sufficiently large and consistent in form to suggest that it represents a kind of official control in silver that differed from, but was contemporary with, the Imperial system. Possibly, like the Carthaginian stamps, these represent a system used in another area.

A hanging lamp in Baltimore (no. 89), found at Hama in Syria, has, on the bottom, five stamps which were evidently applied after the object was finished. They clearly imitate the Imperial five-stamp group; their shapes are the usual ones (round, hexagonal, square, long, and cruciform) and they contain inscriptions and monograms that at first sight resemble those in Imperial stamps. An imperial monogram in the square stamp indicates a date in the reign of Phocas, but significant differences in each of the five stamps set

---

[71] Philip Grierson obtained the fullest reading of this inscription with the help of recent photographs and casts kindly provided by the Soprintendenza alle Gallerie del Piemonte. Grierson points out that Novel XLVII of Justinian decreed that all documents should be dated by the regnal year of the emperor, the name of the consul for the year, the indiction, the month, and the day. The consul in 541 was Basilius.

[72] Proc., *BV*, IV:iii:28; p. 234.

them apart from the Imperial series. These differences, which are listed in detail in the Catalogue,[73] suggest that the stamps represent another system of control, and the inscription ΘЄΟΥ[Π]ΟΛЄΟ[C] in the long stamp refers to the city of Antioch.[74] The stamps on the Dumbarton Oaks candlestick, no. 90, are similar to the stamps on the Baltimore lamp. The comparison of the individual stamps, made in the Catalogue, leaves no doubt that the stamps on both objects come from the same center and from the same period. The lamp was found with objects that are stylistically Syrian and have specifically Syrian inscriptions,[75] while the candlestick was found in Antioch. Thus the stamps may well indicate a control system set up in Antioch and based on the one that used Imperial stamps. The workmanship is crude in comparison with Imperial stamps and suggests provincial hands. But if the stamps reflect a local system at Antioch the controls there could not have functioned very efficiently or for very long since, among all the objects from Syria, only two have stamps of this kind. It is interesting to note that no. 98, a plate found with the "Hama treasure," also has stamps similar to, but not identical with, a more standard series (see *supra*, p. 19)

The plates from Valdonne (nos. 91 and 92), now in Paris, each bear five stamps undoubtedly inspired by Imperial types but very different from them. Since the plates were designed so that one could be fitted into the other, they are clearly a pair. Plate no. 91 has two cross stamps, two long, and one square, while no. 92 has two cross and three round. On no. 91 the cross stamps are simple, with a meaningless design, while on no. 92 they contain an illegible monogram. There are monograms also in the round stamps of no. 92. The square on no. 91 is inscribed with the name ARBALDO in Latin characters. The two long stamps of no. 91 contain identical busts in profile, with a palm branch. These stamps may be related to Merovingian coins of the mid-seventh century,[76]

[73] See also Alföldi and Cruikshank, "A Sassanian Silver Phalera at Dumbarton Oaks," *Dumbarton Oaks Papers*, 11 (1957), pp. 243–244.

[74] The name of the city was formally changed after the earthquake of A.D. 528: Mal., XVIII, p. 443; Procopius, *De aedificiis*, II: x, 2 (Loeb ed., 1940, p. 164: "... Ἀντιόχειαν, ἣ νῦν Θεούπολις ἐπικέκληται ..."). On the stamp the name is in the genitive (for the interchangeable use of omicron and omega compare, for example, the inscriptions in the cross stamps of nos. 41–43 and 54B–55).

[75] The lamp was found in 1910 with the "treasure from Hama," which also included nos. 13, 34, 89, 98. There is a strong probability that the "Hama treasure" is in fact part of the famous "Antioch treasure," including the "Chalice of Antioch," in the Metropolitan Museum of Art, and the smaller chalice, no. 80. No. 18, the chalice of St. Anne in Jerusalem, is alleged to have come from Kara, between Hama and Aleppo, which is also probably the actual find spot of the treasures of Hama and Antioch. For other pieces from the same location see Marvin Ross, "A Second Byzantine Silver Treasure from Hamah," *Archaeology*, III (1950), pp. 162–163. The problem of the discovery of these treasures is reviewed by J. J. Rorimer, "The Authenticity of the Chalice of Antioch," *Studies in Art and Literature for Belle da Costa Greene* (Princeton, 1954), pp. 161–168. While Mr. Rorimer argues that the two finds were separate, Bayard Dodge ("A New Explanation for an Ancient Treasure," *Al-Kulliya* [Journal of the American University of Beirut Alumnae Association (November, 1927)], in Arabic, pp. 34–44; and "The Chalice of Antioch," *Bulletin of the Near East Society*, III [1950], no. 5, pp. 3f., 6; no. 6, p. 10) recounts the finding of all the objects in one treasure. For other accounts see L. Woolley, in *Journal of Roman Studies*, XIV (1924), p. 281; and R. Mouterde, *Mélanges de l'Université Saint-Joseph*, XI (Beyrouth, 1926), pp. 361–367, especially pp. 363–365.

[76] M. Prou ("Les contre-marques mérovingiennes de la coupe de Valdonne (Bouches-du-Rhône)," *Revue Charlemagne*, I [1911], pp. 182–185) relates the profile head in the long stamp to portraits on Merovingian coins, in particular coins struck in Marseilles *ca.* 613–640. A. Héron de Villefosse, on the other hand (*Bulletin de la Société des Antiquaires de France* [1910], p. 256), has noted the branch

and all are crude in execution. Their chief importance lies in the fact that, though contemporary with the Imperial series, they belong to a different system and a different area, as do the stamps from Carthage and Antioch.

A Sassanian phalera in Dumbarton Oaks (no. 99), on the other hand, has three stamps which could be examples of a later development of the Imperial system itself. The stamps are disposed symmetrically on the smooth parts of the human face which decorates the front of the object. Hence the design must at least have been planned before the stamps were applied. Moreover, this is the only object with all its stamps on the front rather than on the reverse, and this suggests that they were applied after the mask was finished; possibly even by different hands. Two round stamps contain a standing, orant figure of a female saint circumscribed with her name which is, unfortunately, not entirely legible. The third stamp, a hexagon, contains a small bust of Christ and is inscribed with the trisagion: ἅγιος, ἅγιος, ἅγιος. The date of these stamps is discussed in an article in the *Dumbarton Oaks Papers* referred to in the catalogue. They have been assigned to the late seventh or early eighth century largely on the grounds of the religious element which is clearly present and which is evident also in stamps of the later Imperial series (nos. 45, 46, 77), as well as in those on the Baltimore lamp (no. 89) described above. Since a religious iconography appears likewise on coins of the late seventh century, a connection with the Imperial series—suggested also by the shapes of the stamps—should not be ruled out.

These stamps can be related to a group of five round stamps on a plate in the Hermitage (no. 100). The round stamp on the phalera resembles two of the stamps on the Hermitage plate which contain the standing figure of Christ with a crossed nimbus and one arm raised. The other three stamps on the plate contain a cruciform monogram. The recent cleaning of a plate in the British Museum, no. 78 (placed next to no. 77 which must be nearly contemporary), has disclosed stamps that clearly belong to the Imperial series, but among which there is also a round stamp with a cruciform monogram. The stamps on the plate are dated in the reign of Constans II and the relationship between this round stamp and the stamps on no. 100 above is additional reason for placing the latter in the seventh century, toward or after the end of the Imperial series. A bowl found in Zalesie in the Ukraine (no. 101) also has five stamps on the reverse, neatly fitted into the tips of the leaves of the design in areas smooth enough to show the stamps clearly. They were, therefore, applied after the design was finished, as were the stamps on the Sassanian mask. The outlines are effaced, but there seems to be an identical cruciform monogram in each and thus they too may be related to the stamps on the Hermitage plate (no. 100). The stamps on no. 102 are again cross-shaped. They are of crude execution and contain designs which appear to be imitations of cruciform

---

in front of the head which is found only on coins from the mint of Banassac at about the same period, *ca.* 650 (M. Prou, *Les monnaies mérovingiennes de la Bibliothèque Nationale* [Paris, 1892], pl. xxx: 13; A. de Belfort, *Description générale des monnaies mérovingiennes* [Paris, 1892], nos. 722, 733–748, 753, 754, 763, 770).

monograms without meaning. These stamps, and those on no. 101, suggest provincial imitation of more refined examples, such as those on no. 100, and they may reasonably be dated in the same period. No. 103, a ewer in New York, has no stamps but is included in the Catalogue because it has on the reverse five engraved circles containing monograms. When read in sequence, these yield a religious phrase and they were clearly incised after the vessel was finished. The choice of five circles with monograms is not likely to have been fortuitous and is, indeed, indicative of the influence of stamps of this kind in some provincial center.

No two objects in the group just discussed (nos. 99–102) have exactly identical stamps, but the relationships that do exist among them, and between them and the last stamps of the Imperial series, suggest that they may all be dated after the Imperial series. They could represent a system of control in silver that developed either in a different locality, or in the same locality as the Imperial system after the latter had died out. In contrast to the parallel series of stamps on nos. 94–98, this group lacks indications of imperial authority.

A few Irregular stamps cannot be convincingly associated with any of those already described and have not been closely dated. These are found on a plate from Cesena (no. 86), a dish in London (no. 87), and a bowl in New York (no. 88) that came from the same treasure as the inscribed ewer mentioned above (no. 103). A coin found with the Cesena plate suggests a relatively early date for its stamps which are of indefinite shape and contain letters not completely deciphered. The Chrism in the stamp on the dish in London also points to an early date. A hexagonal stamp containing a monogram on the bowl in New York, no. 88, is related in shape and type to similar stamps in the Imperial series, but, unlike the Imperial hexagon, this stamp does not contain an inscription. The bowl is dated on stylistic grounds in the fifth or sixth century.

PART II

THE QUESTION OF PROVENANCE AND CONTROLS

EXCEPT for the Carthage and Antioch stamps, and some of the stamps from the fourth and fifth centuries (nos. 81, 83), none gives direct indication of where it was applied or by whom. The date of the stamps is usually evident, particularly in the Imperial series, but the problem of their origin is also important for the study of artistic development in silver of this period. Since the great majority of stamps belong to the Imperial series, and since almost all the objects lending themselves to stylistic analysis have stamps of this kind, the following discussion will concentrate upon Imperial stamps. Earlier stamps and those of the Irregular group will be considered mainly in relation to the Imperial stamps. While there is no absolute proof that Imperial stamps were applied in Constantinople and only in Constantinople, both internal and external evidence favor this assumption.

A. CONCLUSIONS DRAWN FROM THE STAMPS

The earliest stamps on gold and silver bullion and the square stamps on bowls of the fourth and fifth centuries already point to a kind of official control in matters dealing with precious metals. In the case of bullion stamps, there are generally indications of where they were applied and these indications point to widely separated centers in Europe and the Mediterranean. Only one of the bowls (no. 83), however, has a stamp so marked, and in this case the place indicated is Constantinople. Two other stamps on these early bowls, nos. 81 and 82, have partially legible Greek inscriptions, pointing to an Eastern Mediterranean origin. No. 83 is dated in the fifth century and proves that the practice of stamping silver existed in Constantinople at that time. Moreover, the seated Tyche in the same stamp, undoubtedly Constantinople herself, is comparable to contemporary coin types, giving an imperial or at least an official character to the stamp. This was the forerunner of the later Imperial series with the emperor's bust or monogram, and the fact that it can so readily be assigned to the capital lends support to the argument that follows.

The presence of five Imperial stamps on an object indicates that they were applied by an especially designated group of officials, of whom there were five at one time; and, further, that these officials represented imperial authority in the capital itself, rather than elsewhere. In the first place, the persons whose names or titles are inscribed on the stamps must have held positions of some authority in the imperial service since their names were associated with the emperor's portrait and monogram. Indeed, the titles λαμπρότατος and σεβαστός, occurring several times in the stamps among the Christian names, represented officials of a certain dignity. Such a group of officials certainly existed in the highly centralized administrative organization of the capital, whereas it is more difficult to imagine equally imposing bodies of dignitaries functioning in provincial centers. Thus, if we assume that the stamps were normally applied under the direct supervision of these functionaries, the stamping most likely took place in Constantinople. The possibility that the stamps, though designating officials in Constantinople, were used on their behalf also in smaller localities will be considered below.

While there are, moreover, many sets of five stamps which theoretically could belong to different centers and different groups of officials, the fact that frequently one or more of the stamps on one vessel are repeated on another indicates that the groups did not operate in different places. In the Chart below, under A, the seventy-eight objects with Imperial stamps are listed by number so as to group together those with at least one identical stamp, and, instead of eighty-one separate sets of stamps (nos. 17, 54, and 55 each having two sets), about thirty-four groups are thereby established.[77] This number is further reduced if the thirty-four groups are related to each other by bringing together also all the secondary monograms common to them (Chart, B); thus related, the groups number only seventeen. Finally, if repeated inscribed names are taken into consideration as well (Chart, C), the separate groups are reduced to seven. If all these names were ordinary, like Ἀνδρέας (nos. 12–14), this last arrangement would prove very little, but the repetition of a name like

CHART

A. *Objects Grouped According to Repeated Stamps*

I 2 3 4 5 6 7 8–9 10 11 12–13 14 15 16–17 20–22 18 19 23 24 25 26 27–29 30–31 32–34 35–36 37–47 48–49 50–57 58–67 68–69 70 71 72–73 74 75–78

B. *Objects Grouped According to Repeated Stamps and Secondary Monograms*

I 2–3 4 5 6 7–13 14 15–29 30–31 32–36 37–57 58–67 68–69 70–71 72–73 74 75–78

C. *Objects Grouped According to Repeated Stamps, Secondary Monograms, and Inscribed Names*

I 2–4,6 5 7–14 15–29 30–31 32–78

[77] The following numbers are approximate because only too often stamps are lost or illegible. Some relationships may be considered tenuous, as, for instance, the repetition of an inscribed name that is very common. 54A and B are grouped together because they occur on the same object and for this reason were probably stamped in the same locality.

Σχολαστικίς (see *supra*, p. 18) does suggest persons in the same locality. This last method of grouping is particularly remarkable in that the different groups do not overlap in time but follow one another chronologically. These factors indicate that the stamps represent one group of officials in one place, rather than different groups in different places.

That there were not more than five men applying stamps contemporaneously is also implied by the nature of the stamps. The stamps are of only five different shapes, and on the great majority of objects each stamp contains a different individual name. Each one thus belongs to a different official. Where a name appears twice on the same object, it is a common name, such as Ἰωάννης (no. 16), and does not necessarily indicate that the same person applied more than one shape, although this may have happened. On the other hand, there could not have been more than five officials because this would mean that more than one person used the same shape of stamp. In that event, when two stamps of the same shape are found on the same vessel, the inscribed names might be expected to differ, but this is rarely the case. From the reign of Justinian, two stamps of the same shape on a vessel are generally identical and clearly belonged to the same official. Exceptions to this rule either belong to the period of preliminary organization under Anastasius I (when the question of five officials does not arise, since he used only four stamps and, apparently, a different system) or result from special circumstances.[77a]

Although the relationships between stamps on different objects point to a single group of five officials, and their imperial association and exalted rank relate this group to the capital, it might yet be argued that the stamps were made and applied in other centers also, as were coin dies. This is improbable, however, because the character of the Imperial stamp, with its changing individual name, implies that it was a guarantee by the person whose name was inscribed therein and that that person, therefore, applied his own stamp. If it had been used by some over-all authority in several centers, the individual names would no more have been required than they were on coins. Moreover, no mint-mark comparable to those on coins is found in the Imperial stamps[78] and this suggests that their especial character was enough to indicate where they were applied and by whom. What is more, the turnover in personnel was evidently frequent, for the names change constantly and the persons concerned cannot have been in office for more than two years at a time, more likely one.[79] Consequently, if the stamps had been applied in provincial centers as well as in Constantinople, these centers would have found it very difficult to stay up to date. Such a system would hardly have been practicable.

A kind of negative support for the above arguments is found in the Irregular group of stamps. It has been noted that several different kinds of stamps existed concurrently with the Imperial series, one set of which can be assigned to Carthage, another to Antioch. In the sixth and seventh centuries Carthage

---

[77a] Nos. 54, 78.

[78] With the possible exception of three stamps; *supra*, p. 15. See also *infra*, p. 32.

[79] See note 87.

was one of the few imperial mints to issue silver,[80] and if the Imperial stamping system extended to centers outside the capital, it should have included Carthage. As the Carthaginian stamps are very different from Imperial stamps, however, it is clear that this city was not included in the system, and the same logic is applicable where other irregular stamps are concerned. There is yet a third group of objects, silver without stamps, which should be taken into consideration also in a negative sense. Since this study is concerned with stamps it does not deal with the large number of objects having no stamps, each of which poses a problem of origin. Such objects were found with stamped objects, in the area encompassing the Mediterranean, Europe, and Russia, and frequently in the same hoards. A detailed account of these treasures and their places of discovery lies outside the bounds of this text. Nevertheless, it should be pointed out that many unstamped silver objects have been found in the famous treasures of Syria and many more in Europe, especially in Italy and Southern France. Equally, objects of Sassanian origin and others of obviously local workmanship have been found along with stamped silver in hoards from the South of Russia. The large number of unstamped objects from those areas where stamped silver has been found makes it the more unlikely that the use of stamps was very widespread. It indicates, rather, that the stamps distinguish a small group of objects of a particular kind and most probably from a particular place. All of these observations point to the conclusion that the use of Imperial stamps was confined to Constantinople.

B. EXTERNAL EVIDENCE

Contemporary references to the stamps on silver, together with what is known of the economic history and administrative organization of the Empire in the sixth and seventh centuries, support the conclusions drawn from the stamps and throw further light not only on their provenance, but also on their purpose and their history. Smirnov was the first to draw attention to a reference to five stamps on silver of the seventh century from Constantinople, and to point out that these stamps indicated the superior quality of the metal.[81] He referred to a legend in the life of John the Almoner, Patriarch of Alexandria in the early seventh century (d. A.D. 616). Several versions of this story exist; in the later versions, a boat returns to Constantinople from England with its cargo of tin miraculously changed to "silver of the best quality with five stamps."[82] In an earlier version, written by actual contem-

---

[80] Wroth, I, pp. xvi, lxxv–lxxvi, ci; Grierson, *Num. Chron.* X, p. 61. A vivid description of the wealth at Carthage under the Vandals of the sixth century is given by Procopius, *BV*, IV:iii:25ff.; IV:iv:3f.; IV:vi:6–9. Little is known about mines in Carthage in the Byzantine era; presumably much of the silver was imported as in Roman times. See A. Héron de Villefosse and H. Thédenat, "Les trésors de vaisselle d'argent trouvés en Gaule," *Gazette archéologique*, IX (1884), p. 234; Walters, p. x; M. Rostovtzeff, *The Social and Economic History of the Roman Empire*, II (Oxford, 1957), pp. 690, 691, notes 101, 102; for Vandalic treasures, see also Jacques Heurgon, *Le trésor de Ténès* (Paris, 1958), p. 15, note 1.

[81] Smirnov, p. 507.

[82] Fr. Combefis, *Historia haeresis monothelitarum* (Paris, 1648), col. 641 A.

poraries of John the Almoner, the story takes place in Alexandria and there is no mention of five stamps.[83] The transference of the location from Alexandria to Constantinople evidently came about later, and it may be significant that the descriptive phrase concerning the five stamps is present only in the versions written after this transfer.

A second reference to five-stamped silver as a proof of quality comes from the life of Theodore of Sykeon, a text written in the time of Heraclius.[84] According to this story, St. Theodore sent his archdeacon to Constantinople to buy a chalice-and-paten (the word is in the singular, as it is in Greek today, to signify both vessels: δισκοποτήριον). This the archdeacon did, and he brought it back to the monastery. Before Communion the next day, he carried it into the vestry to show it to the Saint. When St. Theodore objected that the piece was defective, the archdeacon assured him that it was of very good quality and bore the five-sealed proof (πεντασφράγιστον αὐτῶν δοκιμήν). The Saint agreed that it was indeed beautifully worked and that the worth of the silver was evident from the stamps on it (ἐκ τῶν ἐπικειμένων σφραγίδων ἡ τοῦ ἀργύρου δοκιμή), yet he insisted that it was defiled. Then the archdeacon chanted an invocation and the Saint prayed and filled the chalice, after which it turned black. Only when it was put away did it turn silver again. Thereupon it was returned to Constantinople, where it was discovered to have been used for profane purposes.[85] This story admirably illustrates the purpose of the stamps and relates them without question to Constantinople.

While pointing to Constantinople as their place of origin, the stamps also give an indication of the type of organization that applied them. The identity of all the officials connected with the stamping of silver has not been discovered, but something of their function is indicated by the stamps, and when this is related to what is known about the Empire's financial administration in the sixth and seventh centuries a certain correlation is revealed.

The stamps of the Imperial series suggest that at least six persons were involved, the five whose individual names and titles occur in the five stamps and a sixth to whom belonged the secondary monogram. The first of the five stamping officials, he who placed his name in the round stamp, presumably was responsible to the emperor whose portrait he used. Similarly, in the square and hexagon the names were linked to the emperor's monogram; but the individual whose name occurs in the long stamp with the secondary monogram and emperor's portrait must have been responsible to the owner of the secondary monogram as well as to the emperor. This suggests that he was less important

---

[83] H. Delehaye, "Une vie inédite de Saint Jean l'Aumonier," *Analecta Bollandiana*, XLV (1927), p. 32.

[84] Theophilus Ioannou, *Mnemeia Agiologika* (Venice, 1884), p. 399, para. 42; E. Dawes and N. H. Baynes, *Three Byzantine Saints* (Oxford, 1948), p. 117f. I owe these references to Prof. E. Kitzinger.

[85] Two other sources concerned with silver are relevant in this context, though the five stamps are not mentioned. Theophanes relates that in the early ninth century, when Nicephorus carried off the treasure of the Khan of Bulgaria, he had his stamps put upon it, "thereby making it his own property" (Theoph., p. 490, 23–25). This happened considerably later than the period under discussion, but it is revealing that there was such a thing as an Imperial stamp placed on treasure. Theophylactus Simocatta, in the late sixth century, tells a story which resembles that of St. Theodore (I:xi [Bonn ed., 1834, pp. 53–57]. Dr. C. Mango brought this reference to my attention).

than the other officials. The official using the cross stamp did not have the privilege of the emperor's monogram or portrait, but was responsible mainly to the owner of the secondary monogram.[86] It has been noted that the secondary monogram changes more frequently than does that of the emperor, but not as frequently as do the inscribed names. The person to whom it belonged was evidently in office for a longer period of time than the individual signatories.[87] He did not stamp the silver himself, but had two of the five stamping officials (those using the long and cross stamps) under his authority. He must have been a person of high position. Among the principal administrative officials in the government, the one concerned most directly with the silver trade was the *comes sacrarum largitionum.* As administrator of the Imperial Largesses, the central treasury of the Empire, this dignitary was in charge of state factories, trade, and mines. He did not, as a rule, remain in office for any length of time; but there were exceptions, the most notorious being Peter Barsymes, who, by favor of Theodora, was *comes sacrarum largitionum* twice in the reign of Justinian, both times for several years.[88] Table V gives a list of the known names of *comites sacrarum largitionum* in the sixth and seventh centuries with the date of their office and the texts that refer to them.[89] The list is by no means complete, for there are large gaps throughout the entire

[86] This hierarchy conforms to the rules of the hereditary *corpora* described on p. 43 and in note 94.

[87] In the fifth century, the period of office decreed for the assistant masters of the Sacred Largesses, the Privy Purse, and the Sacred Imperial Bureaus was one year: *Cod. Theod.,* VI:xxx:21. See also p. 37.

[88] The dates are not certain: see Table V. The Edict of 559 (*Ed. Just.,* XI) calls him *comes sacrarum largitionum twice,* but Procopius speaks of his promotion direct from *officialis* to Prefect. If this is correct, the Petrus of 542 (*Ed. Just.,* VII:vi) must be a different man and Barsymes' second tenure fall in the early 550's. On the other hand, Grierson would place Barsymes' first period of office in the year 539.

[89] This list of *comites* was compiled largely by Dr. John Kent. It represents the latest study in the subject and is the most thorough. There remain, however, many uncertainties as to the identity of some of the officers and particularly as to their dates. For the dates of Peter Barsymes, see note 88. Stein (*BE,* p. 434, note 1) mentions "Elie, patrice et comte des largesses sacrées en été 528" giving the date according to Malalas (XVIII, p. 441, 8–12); but Theophanes (p. 186, 8–13), who refers to the same event as Malalas, gives the year A.M. 6025 (A.D. 532/3). In Table V, Dr. Kent has favored the earlier date. Evagrius implies that Magnus was *curator* of one of the imperial *domus* (see Excursus p. 37), while Corippus says that he was *comes sacrarum largitionum.* Anastasius was killed by Phocas before the latter's own fall, i.e. in 610, although Theophanes gives the year 6101 (A.D. 608/9); the names of his associates in conspiracy, however, show him to be identical with the Athanasius mentioned in the *Chronicon Paschale,* A.D. 605. Finally, three more names are known of men who assumed the title of *comes sacrarum largitionum* in the sixth century: Ephremius (524/5), Constantinus (528/33), and Cratinus (533). Kent believes, however, that these men bore the title only in an *honorary* capacity (p. 37). Prof. George Ostrogorsky kindly discussed some of these problems with me and made most helpful suggestions; but it was not possible to pursue this topic further in the present context. For earlier investigations of the office of the *comes sacrarum largitionum,* see F. Grossi-Gondi, in *Dizionario epigrafico di antichità romane* (ed. Ettore de Ruggiero, 1900), II, 1, pp. 487–493; O. Seeck, "Comites," in Pauly-Wissowa, *Real-Encyclopädie,* IV (Stuttgart, 1901), cols. 671–675. See also Daremberg and Saglio, *Dictionnaire des antiquités grecques et romaines,* II (1908), pp. 876–877; Bury, pp. 80–90 and *passim; idem, History,* I, p. 51; A. E. R. Boak and J. E. Dunlap, *Two Studies in Later Roman and Byzantine Administration* (New York, 1924), pp. 21, 179, 224; F. Dölger, *Beiträge zur Geschichte der byzantinischen Finanzverwaltung, besonders des 10. und 11. Jahrhunderts...* (*Byzantinisches Archiv,* 9) (Munich, 1927), pp. 16, 27, note 4; *idem, Regesten der Kaiserurkunden des oströmischen Reiches,* I, *Regesten von 565–1025* (Berlin, 1924), p. 6 (A.D. 575–6); R. Guilland, "Le consulat dans l'Empire byzantin," *Byzantion,* XXIV (1954), p. 552; E. Hanton, "Lexique explicatif du Recueil des inscriptions grecques chrétiennes d'Asie Mineure. Titres byzantins," *Byzantion,* IV (1927–28), pp. 53–136, esp. p. 97; G. Ostrogorsky, *History of the Byzantine State* (New Brunswick, N. J., 1957), p. 89; L. Bréhier, *Les institutions de l'Empire byzantin* (Paris, 1949), pp. 95, 106; Stein, *BE,* pp. 213–214.

period. Similarly, Table III shows the secondary monograms and there are omissions in this list also, since not all the stamps have been preserved. Some of the names are common ones. Nevertheless, there is enough correlation between the two lists to lend strong support to the suggestion that the secondary monogram belongs to the *comes sacrarum largitionum* in office at the time the object was stamped. John the Paphlagonian was *comes sacrarum largitionum* in 498. It was he who was largely responsible for the reforms in the domain of finance under Anastasius and probably for instigating the stamp system as well.[89a] Among only five sets of stamps from the time of Anastasius, the monogram IѠANNOV occurs twice. Peter Barsymes has already been mentioned; he was Justinian's favorite from 540 to about 559 and when he was not Count of the Sacred Largesses he held the even more powerful office of Praetorian Prefect. He was responsible for the reorganization of the "imperial monopolies," especially in the silk trade, and by means of "shameless traffic in the magistracies and...scandalous speculation in corn" he filled Justinian's treasuries.[90] It is easy to believe that it was this same Peter who was responsible for the monogram on seven of the fourteen sets of stamps belonging to Justinian. The name IOVΛIANOV occurs in the monograms, and also in the list of *comites* under Justinian. One Theodorus Petri evidently held this influential post in the reign of Justin II, and the monogram Theodorus occurs in seven of the eight sets of stamps from the same reign.[91] Finally, Athanasius was a *comes sacrarum largitionum* and was killed by Phocas in 605; his monogram occurs in the stamps of Phocas. No names of *comites sacrarum largitionum* during the reign of Heraclius are known. From the reign of Anastasius through the reign of Phocas, only eleven names have been found in texts and there are fifteen different secondary monograms for the corresponding period. Out of these, five correspond in sequence and in time. Considering the number lost on either side, this is a substantial proportion. The closeness of the relationship gains added support if the list of monograms is compared to similar lists of the names of two other prominent officials, the Praetorian Prefects,[92] or the Masters of Offices.[93] It is apparent that no relationship exists between these two lists

[89a] See *infra*, p. 32 and note 101.

[90] C. Diehl, in *The Cambridge Medieval History*, II (Cambridge, 1913), p. 42; for monopolies, see note 94.

[91] See nos. 20–26. Although the combination of letters in the monogram could equally well spell the name ΔѠPOΘEOV, it should probably read ΘEOΔѠPOV, for the letter Θ in the center, rather than one of the letters on the arms of the cross, is likely to be the initial letter of the name (compare the secondary monogram of no. 58 and the monogram of Theodora on the capitals of St. Sophia, *supra*, p. 16). In the monograms on nos. 20–26, the position of the P in the name is not always clear, for it becomes confused with the O of the 8. In the long stamp of no. 25, a P shows clearly below the V; so presumably the O may be derived from the shape of the central Θ. This difficulty was resolved in a more satisfactory way for the monogram in the long and cross stamps of nos. 58–67.

[92] A list of Praetorian Prefects is to be found in Stein, *BE*, Excursus A, pp. 781–786, and W. Ensslin, "Praefectus Praetorio," in Pauly-Wissowa, *Realencyclopädie*, XXII² (Stuttgart, 1954), cols. 2495–2501.

[93] Boak and Dunlap, *Two Studies in Later Roman and Byzantine Administration*, pp. 150–151. Complete lists of other major dignitaries of this period, the Counts of the Privy Purse, the Quaestors, or the City Prefects are not available. It does not seem likely, however, that a comparison between the list of monograms and the names of these officials would prove rewarding. For a study of the office of the Privy Purse and a few names from this period, see F. Grossi-Gondi, in *Dizionario epigrafico di antichità romane* (ed. de Ruggiero), II, 1, p. 497; Seeck, "Comes rerum privatarum," in Pauly-Wissowa,

and the list of monograms, except in one or two instances where the Count of the Sacred Largesses also assumed another office. So it is that the last factor in dating the stamps is the identification of the owner of the secondary monogram. When he cannot be identified, the stamps may tentatively be dated according to their relationship to the general sequence of stamps that are dated. The Stuma paten (no. 27), for example, may be placed in 577–578 because its stamps belong to the reign of Justin II (565–578) and succeed stamps assigned to the period of office of Theodorus Petri (577). The significance of the secondary monogram is described in the Catalogue wherever pertinent. The reader is reminded, however, that the list of *comites sacrarum largitionum* is short and that some of the dates are uncertain. The attributions of the monograms and the dates assigned to silver objects on these grounds alone cannot be considered final.

The likelihood of a connection between the stamps and the office of the *largitiones* is enhanced by a more detailed study of the office. An Excursus, contributed by Dr. John Kent, provides a history of the office and a description of its functions and organization. Dr. Kent throws valuable light on the relationship between the stamps and the *largitiones*.[94] The title *comes sacrarum*

Real-Encyclopädie, IV (Stuttgart, 1900), cols. 664–670; Stein, *Studien*, pp. 176–186; *idem*, *BE*, pp. 423–425, 433; L. Bréhier, *Les institutions de l'Empire byzantin* (Paris, 1949), pp. 96, 256. The office ran parallel with the office of *comes sacrarum largitionum* and died with it toward the end of the sixth century or the early seventh (Bréhier, *op. cit.*, p. 106 f.; Bury, p. 19 f.; Stein, *loc. cit.*; Boak and Dunlap, *op. cit.*, p. 224). The Quaestors did not have much to do with the management of traffic in precious metals, and the few names that come readily to hand bear no relation to the list of monograms: Bréhier, *op. cit.*, pp. 95, 107; Stein, *Studien*, p. 186; *idem*, *BE*, pp. 246, 406, 433; Boak and Dunlap, *op. cit.*, p. 179. The City Prefect was the dignitary most closely concerned with the guilds in the city, and, in the ninth century, was most immediately responsible for the guild of silversmiths: see *Le Livre du Préfet*, chap. ii (ed. Jules Nicole [Geneva, 1893], pp. 22–24); Bréhier, *op. cit.*, pp. 186–192, esp. p. 189. The names of City Prefects in the sixth century, however, do not correspond to the list of monograms: *Nov. Just.*, XXII, p. 186; XLIII, p. 269, LXIII, p. 334; LXIV, p. 336; LXXIX, p. 390; LXXXII, p. 402; CXXV, p. 630; CXXXIV, p. 676; CXL, p. 701; Proc., *Anec.*, ix: 37; Stein, *Studien*, p. 186.

[94] Further research in this direction should prove highly rewarding. Dr. Kent's description of the organization of the department, for example, reveals a group of workmen bound to the state by hereditary ties. This factor would explain the recurrence of names in the stamps over long periods (p. 17) and the migration of the same name through different shapes of stamps. The fact that there are titles of rank among these names supports Dr. Kent's account of the privileges accorded to the *barbaricarii*, the workers in precious metals (p. 44), and probably also to the *argentarii comitatenses*, the holders of the parallel office, under whose authority Dr. Kent suggests the silver was stamped (*ibid.*). Dr. Kent mentions also the "twin factories at Antioch and Constantinople... directly administered by a section of the palatine *scrinium ab argento*" (*ibid.*). We already have official stamps from Antioch with a distinctive character, and it seems evident that Imperial stamps represent the office in the capital. Further, the office of the *sacrae largitiones* was responsible for the organization of the textile mills, including the garment, linen, and canvas mills, the purple dye works, and especially the so-called "monopoly" of silk; and on silk, at least in a later period, stamps were used to facilitate imperial control (*Le Livre du Préfet*, viii:9; p. 37 f.). Thus the stamps on silver afford a precedent for this practice in another branch of the *largitiones*. This "monopoly" of silk, moreover, seems to be another innovation by Peter Barsymes who was, as we have seen, responsible for innovations in silver stamps. According to Procopius, Peter Barsymes "... set up a great number of what are called 'monopolies' and sold the welfare of his subjects to those who wanted to operate these abominations, and thus, on the one hand, he carried off a price for the transaction, and, on the other hand, to those who had contracted with him he gave the privilege of managing their business as they wished.... But when these sovereigns had brought most of the merchandise under the control of the monopolies, as they are called, and every single day were strangling those who wished to buy anything, and only the shops where clothing is sold were left untouched by them, they devised this scheme for that business also...." (Proc., *Anec.*, xx:5; xxv:13). For these monopolies, see *Cod. Just.*, XI:viii, ix; cf. Kent's Excursus, p. 42 f. and R. S. Lopez, "Silk Industry in the Byzantine Empire," *Speculum*, XX (1945), pp. 1–42.

largitionum was given up sometime during the reign of Heraclius, and the duties of the office were transferred to, or divided among, persons with other titles.[95] Imperial stamps in the reign of Heraclius continue to show a secondary monogram, but who assumed this part of the office of the Sacred Largesses has not been determined. Toward the end of the Imperial series the stamps show irregularities for which the reorganization of financial controls may have been responsible. The disintegration of the office of the *comes sacrarum largitionum* may also have caused the abandonment of this type of Imperial stamp, and during the subsequent reorganization of the department of finance new stamps, e.g. those of nos. 99–102, may have been substituted.[96]

The *comes sacrarum largitionum* controlled not only stamps but coins also. It is not surprising, therefore, that certain relationships existed between the use of silver in trade and its use in the imperial mints. Indeed, the stamps have frequently been compared to coins which also have the emperor's effigy and which were certainly regulated by a strongly centralized administrative organization. The term ἀργυροπράτης could refer either to the money changer or to the silversmith.[97] A comparison between the use of silver in imperial mints and its use in trade points to a connection between the controls of the metal instituted for both purposes. Silver was not plentiful in the Empire and the output of silver coins was consequently small relative to that of gold or bronze. Its use was actually restricted to the mints of Constantinople, Carthage, Rome, and Ravenna.[98] It is, therefore, particularly in these areas where silver for making coins came under imperial supervision that similar supervision might be expected to have extended to other uses of the metal. That Constantinople was a major center for silver trade is well known, and Justinian lavished the precious material in wonderful abundance on the decoration of St. Sophia.[99] Constantinople, therefore, would have been a logical area for silver controls. The wealth of silver in Carthage has already been mentioned, and the stamps on the Turin plate are evidence of some kind of official control; but since they differ from those of the Imperial series, the control evidently took a different form. On the other hand, no silver coins from other major centers, such as Antioch, Alexandria, or Salonika, have been found.[100] Correspondingly,

---

[95] Excursus, p. 37 f.

[96] See *supra*, p. 21 f.

[97] The archdeacon of Sykeon (p. 27) carried out his transactions in Constantinople with the ἀργυροπράτης. This person, in turn, referred the problem of the chalice to the ἀρμαρίτης and the ἀργυροκόπος. The ἀρμαρίτης was concerned with the legal side of the dispute, for he was the official scribe and keeper of official documents (*Ed. Just.*, IX: ii: 1). Ἀργυροπράτης and ἀργυροκόπος are equivalent to the Latin terms *nummularius* and *argentarius* and both could mean the banker or tester of coins or the silversmith; see, under the relevant words, H. G. Liddell and R. Scott, *A Greek-English Lexicon* (Oxford, 1925) and C. B. Hase, W. and L. Dindorf, *Thesaurus Graecae Linguae* (I, pt. 2 [Paris, 1831–1856]); J. G. Platon, *Les banquiers dans la législation de Justinien* (Paris, 1912), p. 4.

[98] Wroth, I, p. lxxvi. The large output of silver coins from Constantinople did not start until the seventh century (see *infra*, p. 32f.).

[99] As described by Paul the Silentiary: Lethaby and Swainson, *passim*. The wealth of silver in Constantinople is described by H. Graeven, "Ein Reliquien-Kästchen aus Pirano," *Jahrbuch der Kunsthistorischen Sammlungen des allerhöchsten Kaiserhauses*, XX (Vienna, 1899), pp. 6, 7.

[100] All silver in Egypt had to be imported: A. C. Johnson and L. C. West, *Byzantine Egypt: Economic Studies* (Princeton, 1949), p. 117.

only two stamped silver objects have been traced to Antioch and none to the other major centers.

Moreover, as we have seen, the first organized system of stamps was instituted by Anastasius, and it can hardly be coincidence that this Emperor was also responsible for the most far-reaching monetary reforms since Constantine the Great.[101] Among these reforms, which placed the treasury on its feet, was the institution on coins of the mark of value in Greek letters. The use of Greek lettering on the coins recalls the change from Latin to Greek inscriptions on the silver stamps of Anastasius; but if there is a connection between stamps and coins, it is all the more noteworthy that the stamps do not show the device of the mint. As was suggested above, the mint mark was not required on the stamps of Anastasius because they came from only one locality, Constantinople. The monetary reforms of Anastasius were elaborated by Justinian who established a system that endured, virtually unchanged, well into the seventh century,[102] and it was this same Emperor who established the five-stamp control on silver which lasted until the reign of Constans II.

Finally, an event occurred in the reign of Heraclius pertinent to the history of silver stamps. When Heraclius was embroiled in the Persian Wars, he drained the treasury and by A.D. 621 was in considerable financial distress. The personality of this Emperor was strong enough to inspire in Constantinople, at this critical moment, an action by the church and the populace that can be considered psychologically extraordinary; it is told in several sources[103] that for this emergency he called in all the treasure from all the churches in the capital. The sum collected must have been immense, for the wealth of the churches at this time was famed and their treasure allowed Heraclius to conduct a successful war that lasted for seven years. Apparently the Emperor had already tried to collect treasure in Egypt when the Persians attacked Alexandria in 615, but on this occasion had not been successful.[104] It was in 615, however—this same year of financial difficulty—that a new silver coin, the *hexagram*, weighing over six scripula, was first issued in Constantinople.[105] The *hexagram* continued to be coined throughout the reign of Heraclius and during the three following reigns. The fact that it first appeared in a year when the Emperor was in great financial need, and that it continued to be minted in

[101] Sabatier, I, pp. 25f., 151; R. P. Blake, "The Monetary Reform of Anastasius I and Its Economic Implications," reprinted from *Studies in the History of Culture*, February 1942 (American Council of Learned Societies Devoted to Humanistic Studies. Conference of the Secretaries of Constituent Societies), pp. 84–97; Stein, *BE*, pp. 192–198; Ph. Grierson, "The Currency Reform of Anastasius," *Atti dello VIII Congresso internazionale di studi bizantini, Palermo, 1951*, pt. 1 (*Studi bizantini e neoellenici*, VII [1953]), p. 374f.

[102] Wroth, I, pp. xiii, xv. Major financial reforms occurring in the seventh century brought with them changes in the monetary system, for which see *infra* and Wroth, I, p. xxviii. For Justinian's financial policy and reforms, see Bury, *History*, II, pp. 348–359; Stein, *BE*, pp. 422–427.

[103] Nicephorus, *Opuscula historica* (ed. de Boor, Leipzig, 1880), p. 15; Georgius Monachus, *Chronicon*, IV:ccxxvii:10 (*PG*, CX [1863], col. 829). A. Pernice, *L'Imperatore Eraclio* (Florence, 1905), p. 102, cites other textual sources. It is true that Nicephorus, *op. cit.*, p. 15, says that Heraclius took away the treasure and, p. 22, that he returned it. This can hardly be a literal statement; as Pernice observes, Nicephorus probably meant that it was not taken without assurance of later payment with interest.

[104] Pernice, *op. cit.*, p. 77f.

[105] Wroth, I, p. lxxvi.

considerable quantity when he was successful in procuring silver treasure in Constantinople, may have been one reason for the disappearance of stamped silver vessels. The silver coin was required, in addition to gold, to pay the troops, and it was found to be so valuable in this respect that there must have been a corresponding drop in the use of silver for manufacturing purposes and trade. Certainly, for a brief period following the collection of the treasure in 621 and until the immediate danger was over, all procurable silver would have been used for coinage rather than for silver vessels. Objects from the period after 629 indicate that silver manufacture was not abruptly stopped, but while the stamping system lingered on, it is evident that under Constans II, at least, the controls were more loosely applied.[106] Moreover, the treasures of the church would eventually have had to be replenished; so the demand for silver in the capital must have been greater than ever before. External trade would have correspondingly lessened. Most of the stamped objects were found outside Constantinople[107] and must, therefore, have been exports; thus it is not so surprising that none have survived from the second half of the seventh century. Finally, as more silver was used for coins and less for vessels, the elaborate stamping system fell into disuse.

The question of trade raises the problem of the migration of silver objects and it is revealing, indeed, to consider the area over which silver with stamps has been found. This is indicated in the Distribution Map. Each known place of discovery is marked, but without any indication of the number of objects found, for this would be misleading in the instances of the chance preservation of large hoards like the Cyprus finds. It has been pointed out[108] that silver with stamps has been found in the area of trade routes radiating from Constantinople. Comparatively few stamped objects come from the Western Mediterranean, a fact unfavorable to the assumption of a Western origin for the stamps, while the large number of objects found in Russia, along the river routes from the Black Sea, points to the markets of Constantinople as a most logical source.

The great distance travelled by silver objects in trade is also illustrated by the Map. Frequently valuable objects were broken up and used for currency en route, but if they survived the journey they might then have been decorated or redecorated by local craftsmen. The changes made in the decoration of the rim of the plate of Paternus (no. 2) may be an example of this. We noted above (p. 2f.) that the stamps were applied to an object before it was decorated, but after the silver was cut out and partially fashioned. This means that even within Constantinople there may well have been a division of labor; the men who shaped the vessels might not necessarily have been the same as those who finished them. Sometimes the vessel might not have been decorated until several years after it was stamped: a plate from the Lesbos treasure, no. 32, with a crude niello cross on the obverse, is identical in size and in every detail

---

[106] See *supra*, pp. 8, 12.

[107] See *infra*.

[108] Matsulevich, *Byz. Ant.*, p. 61; Kitzinger, "The Sutton Hoo Ship Burial. V: The Silver," *Antiquity*, XIV (1940), p. 50.

of decoration with another plate from the same treasure, no. 40. Yet no. 32 has stamps from the reign of Phocas and no. 40 from the reign of Heraclius. As the other six objects from this treasure (nos. 41, 42, 43, 48, 49, 50) also belong to the reign of Heraclius, it seems probable that the first plate was decorated at the same time as the others, though it had been stamped some years before. Further, in a case where an object has two sets of stamps, as has no. 54, some time may have elapsed between their application. Since the inscription in the square stamp has changed, there was time enough for a change of at least one of the officials concerned; and, since the decoration was completed after the second set of stamps, the first set, at any rate, does not afford an accurate clue to the date of the vessel. At times an old vessel may have been returned to the central offices, perhaps in payment of debt, or simply to be redecorated.[108a] Before it was resold, or renovated, a second set of stamps may well have been applied. Whatever the reason for the existence of dual sets, it is evident from these examples that there was an organization of artisans engaged in the production of objects which were roughly shaped and stamped, but which may or may not ultimately have been decorated in the same workshop. Indeed, a comparable workshop had existed at an earlier period for the garland sarcophagi that were shipped in a semidecorated condition, to be finished locally before being sold to the ultimate owners.[109] The same could have held true for the silver objects which admittedly travel more easily than sarcophagi. In any case, we must reckon with a "production line" involving several distinct phases: the crude metal was received and refined by members of the *largitiones*, its use in coin or vessels being determined in this office. The vessels were then cut into preliminary shapes, but before they could leave the imperial offices Imperial stamps of guarantee were applied. Presumably a vessel might then be sold unfinished, as it was, or worked in the official atelier and sold as a finished object. As happened in other departments belonging to the *largitiones* (p. 43), the factories were no doubt permitted to trade on their own account so long as they met the requirements of the state. In this event, the stamps would also have signified imperial permission to trade. Finally, a silver object might be returned to the imperial offices, probably in payment of debt or tribute, and then be tested and stamped again, as witness the objects with two sets of stamps.

In summary, a study of Imperial Byzantine stamps leads to the conclusion that they were applied by a single group of officials in Constantinople, and that they were not used in other centers of the Empire. Stamps used in centers outside the capital were sometimes similar to, but clearly did not belong to,

[108a] In the reign of Justin II, Corippus relates that during the celebration of Consular games the Emperor distributed old silver plates engraved with new inscriptions and reliefs, and that each plate was filled with gold (Corippus, IV, 103 ff., 142 ff.). Cf. also the inscription on the plate of Paternus (no. 2) referring to a "renovation." I am most grateful to Mr. Thomas Cole who discussed with me some of the ambiguities of the passage in Corippus and who also helped in the transcription of some of the inscriptions in the Catalogue.

[109] J. B. Ward Perkins, "Roman Garland Sarcophagi from the Quarries of Proconnesus (Marmara)," *The Smithsonian Report for 1957* (Washington, 1958), pp. 455–467; *idem*, "Four Roman Garland Sarcophagi in America," *Archaeology*, XI, 2 (1958), pp. 98–104.

the Imperial series. Contemporary texts and examination of the financial administration of the Empire in the sixth and seventh centuries support the conclusion drawn from the stamps. Byzantine silver objects with Imperial stamps of the sixth and seventh centuries are thus documented as coming from Constantinople. In any study based on these conclusions, however, two reservations should be borne in mind: first, though the objects were stamped in Constantinople, they were not necessarily decorated there. Some Byzantine silver objects with Imperial stamps show a provincial crudity of style, and many authorities believe, on convincing grounds, that the stamped objects found among the silver treasures of Syria belong to Syrian workshops and exhibit distinctive Syrian styles. Indeed, a silversmith in the provinces could order the finest silver from the capital, roughly cut into the desired shape and guaranteed in quality by the stamps on the reverse, and then decorate it to the satisfaction of his clients at home. Second, although the stamps provide a *terminus post quem* for the date of an object, in at least one example the object was not decorated until several years after it had been stamped.

EXCURSUS: The *Comes Sacrarum Largitionum*[1]

by

J. P. C. Kent

Assistant Keeper, Department of Coins and Metals, British Museum

The great financial department of the *sacrae largitiones* was not the work of any one imperial reformer, but an institution that can be traced back at least to the second century—to the development in Rome of the *summae rationes*. The function of the latter was the unification of the many procuratorial accounts, and in spite of periodic efforts, for example under Septimius Severus, to maintain the distinction between public monies and imperial domains, the tendency throughout the third century was for all finances other than those of the Praetorian Prefects to be dealt with by the one central office. It is to this omnicompetence of the *summae rationes* and its head, the *rationalis*, that the *sacrae largitiones* was to owe the miscellaneous character of its duties and sources of revenue.

Not until the fourth century was far advanced were the public and domain accounts once more separated. The reversion to this policy can be detected, however, by the time of Diocletian, under whom we see that the *summae rationes* has developed a twofold staff—the *res privata* and the *summae rationes* (or *res summa*) par excellence, each administered by a *magister* responsible to the *rationalis*. In the late third and early fourth centuries we find the same

---

[1] This excursus is based on J. P. C. Kent, *The Office of Comes Sacrarum Largitionum* (1951), a dissertation presented to the University of London for the degree of Ph.D.

duality between *rationalis* and *magister* at diocesan levels, both ultimately responsible to the same official at the capital.[2]

Though for minor officials the title of *magister* survived at least until the reign of Justinian, its use in the central offices cannot be shown to have outlasted that of Constantine I. The replacement of the formulae *summae rationes* and *rationalis* by *largitiones* (not at first *sacrae*) and *comes* took place by 342. Development was not quite in step in the Eastern and Western parts of the Empire, but there is no evidence which enables us to attribute the step to Constantine himself rather than to his sons. It marks a stage in the militarization of the formerly servile *officia*, and their transformation from the sedentary staffs hitherto encountered to the mobile palatine *officia* of the late fourth century. This change does not seem at first to have affected the actual status of the officers at their head. Certainly in the East the earliest *comites largitionum* remained *perfectissimi*, of the same grade as *rationales summarum rationum* had been since the early third century.[3]

The Western policy attested under Constans of creating a cognate *comes rei privatae* was not followed by Constantius II. Though his *rationalis rei privatae* was integrated into the *comitatus*, his inferior status was maintained by his exclusion from the *consistorium*, and not until almost the end of Julian's reign did the emperor revive the *comitiva rei privatae* for his friend Elpidius. Both offices were by now senatorial, and underwent the usual hierarchic rise; to *spectabilis* in 372, and to *illustris* in about 396. They were not, however, strictly co-ordinate officials. Their origins in the unified *summae rationes* resulted in the *largitiones* retaining control of state land other than that directly administered, and it was not until the fifth century that revenue from this source was transferred to the *res privata* in the west, and a true dichotomy of function established between the two departments.[4]

By the advent of the sixth century the *sacrae largitiones* was declining in importance. In the West its *comitiva* was combined with a *primiceriatus*, probably that of the *sacrum cubiculum*, and Cassiodorus bids the holder console himself with the double office 'etsi quid tibi de antiquo privilegio usus abstulit'. In the East too the decline was substantial. The tendency of much revenue to become customary in amount will have reduced income, and the abolition in 498 of the *collatio lustralis*, probably a whole third of the *largitiones'* budget, must have struck a heavy blow at its importance. This was the more severe because the revenue from imperial estates, which Anastasius diverted in re-

[2] For *magistri*, see Dessau, No. 1347; *Cod. Just.*, III:xxii:5, A.D. 294; Lactantius, *De mortibus persecutorum*, vii (*PL*, VII [1844], col. 205); *CIL*, III, 18, 12043; *Cod. Theod.*, X:i:4, A.D. 320; Athanasius, *Apology to Constans*, X (ed. Szymusiak, Paris, 1958, p. 99); B. P. Grenfell and A. S. Hunt *The Amherst Papyri*, pt. II (London, 1901), no. 138; *Aegyptische Urkunden aus den Koeniglichen Museen zu Berlin, Griechische Urkunden*, III (Berlin, 1903), no. 927 = L. Mitteis and U. Wilcken, *Grundzüge und Chrestomathie der Papyruskunde*, I, pt. 2, *Chrestomathie* (Leipzig-Berlin, 1912), no. 178.

[3] The earliest *comites largitionum* are the eastern officials Nemesianus *v. p.* (*Cod. Theod.*, XI:vii:5, A.D. 345) and Domitianus *ex comite largitionum* in 354 (Amm. Marc., XIV:vii:9). Constans' finance system was styled *largitiones* by 349 (*Cod. Theod.*, IX:xvii:2; IX:xxi:6).

[4] Early western *comites rei privatae* include Eusebius (*Cod. Theod.*, X:x:6, A.D. 342; Amm. Marc., XV:v:4, 13), Eustathius (*Cod. Theod.*, X:x:7, A.D. 345), Orio (*Cod. Theod.*, X:x:8, A.D. 346; X:xiv:2, A.D. 348). For the comitatensian *rationalis* see Amm. Marc., XV:iii:4, 5; XXII:iv:9.

compense to the public account, passed through a new officer, the *comes sacri patrimonii*. *Patrimonium* and *largitiones* in consequence remained closely linked, and by the second half of the sixth century the former seems to have dissolved into several *domus* under *curatores*. A further weakening of the position of the *comes sacrarum largitionum* was the creation, early in the sixth century, of a special βασιλέως ταμίας for dealing with out-payments of money from the treasury. By the early seventh century this officer emerges as the *sacellarius*, and with his subsequent history we are not concerned.[5]

Tenure of high office in the late Roman Empire was generally of very short duration. For the period between about 350 and 430, for which we have the fullest information, surviving names show an average tenure of less than three years, and a complete list would probably reduce it to below two years. There are several cases of specially competent or privileged persons holding office for three years and more, thus emphasising the brevity of the normal period of tenure.

Peculiar to the sixth century, in the light of our present knowledge, was the creation of honorary *comites sacrarum largitionum*. The earliest is Ephremius, *comes orientis* in 524–5, but two more, Constantinus and Cratinus, *magister libellorum* (528–33) and *antecessor urbis* (533) respectively, are known from Justinian's Code, and such officers must be carefully distinguished from effective holders of the rank. Under Justin II there is some evidence that Magnus doubled the office of *comes sacrarum largitionum* with that of *curator* of an imperial *domus*. We cannot say whether this was by now normal. One of the supporters of Maurice killed in 602 was Constantinus, ex-Praetorian Prefect and 'Logothete and Curator of the Estate of Hormisdas' (an imperial *domus*), and while such an expression does not exclude the possibility of his being a *comes* of the same type, there can be no certainty.[6]

In the end the disappearance of the *sacrae largitiones* was due to its absorption by the vast finance system of the Praetorian Prefecture. Even in its heyday the budget of the *largitiones* was probably not more than a third of that of the Prefecture, and in its decline its functions must have seemed increasingly trivial and vestigial. Meanwhile the inflated finance bureaux of the Prefect of Oriens were themselves undergoing modification. Shortly after 540 we meet for the first time a division of his *scrinia* into three groups; the ἰδική and γενική τραπέζαι and τὸ στρατιωτικόν. The specifically military function of the latter is clear, and is reflected in the specific exclusion of debts to its account from the periodic remissions of tax arrears. The distinction in the sixth century between the other two is obscure, one of the few references being

---

[5] Cassiodorus, VI:vii. For the *collatio*, see *infra*, note 8. *Comes sacri patrimonii*: *Cod. Just.*, I:xxxiv; Lydus, *De magistratibus* (Bonn ed., 1837), II:27 (eastern); Cassiodorus, IX:xiii; *Nov. Just.*, LXXV = CIV, A.D. 537; *Regesta pontificum romanorum*, I (ed. Jaffé-Wattenbach, Leipzig, 1885), nos. 961, 971, 997, 1013 (western). The *patrimonium* remained as a separate account long after the disappearance of its *comes*.

[6] Ephremius: V. Chapot, "Antiquités de la Syrie du Nord," *BCH*, XXVI (1902), p. 166; Stein, *BE*, p. 241, note 1. Constantinus and Cratinus: *Cod. Just.*, I:xvii:2 = *Const. Tanta* (*Corpus Iuris Civilis*, I, *Justiniani Digesta* [ed. Mommsen and Krueger, Berlin, 1928, p. 17]); *Const. Summa* (*Cod. Just.*, p. 2). Constantinus: *CP*, *sub anno* 602.

the (mistaken) statement of Evagrius that the *collatio lustralis* of old was paid to the account τῶν καλουμένων εἰδικῶν σκρινίων. Presumably they dealt with the cash land-tax that Evagrius thought replaced it. A *comes largitionum* is last attested under Phocas: the Logothete of the γενικόν is not explicitly named until Justinian II. Yet, under the Byzantine system the γενικόν dealt with mines and trade taxes, and clearly absorbed most of the functions of the *largitiones*. The earliest attested independent logothete of high rank is 'the most glorious patrician Theodosius' in 626. Seals record γενικοὶ κομμερκιάριοι from the latter part of the reign of Heraclius, and the evidence seems sufficient to infer that by the middle of his reign that emperor had broken down the inflated Prefecture into its component *logothesia*, and divided among them the remaining functions of the degenerate *largitiones*.[7]

The *comes sacrarum largitionum* had no financial policy of his own: the order to pay taxes to his treasury was contained in the Praetorian Prefects' indiction. Even his powers of gathering his own income were severely restricted. His main interest lies, consequently, less in the taxes which accrued to his treasury and the disbursements which fell on it, than in the supervisory duties which he exercised over various groups of state factories, trade and mines. The direct taxes, as we shall see, came to the *largitiones* in order to finance specific expenditure. The indirect taxes and administrative duties testify to the department's origin in the numerous procuratorial accounts of the early empire, and are part of its very nature. It was surely a symptom of decline when the *siliquaticum*, the revived sales-tax of the fifth century, was allocated to the Prefects' *arca* and not to the Count's *thesaurus*.

From the time of Constantine I until its abolition in 498 the biggest single source of revenue to the *largitiones* was the *collatio lustralis* (χρυσάργυρον πραγματευτικόν). As its name shows, it was collected in cash and had originally a five-yearly incidence. There is no evidence that it was particularly heavy, but its origin in the hated urban *capitatio* led to workmen liable to it being assessed in terms of some arbitrary monetary value. Consequently, solvent or not, they were still called on to pay, and our sources are full of the hardships this provoked. The tragedy which Timotheus of Gaza is said to have written on the theme of this tax savours perhaps of melodrama, but it certainly inspired what must be one of the last recorded endowments of a citizen to his town. No doubt things were better after 410, when Theodosius II authorised its payment 'sub parva et minima contributione'—the monthly instalment plan we find used by a trade guild in Egypt some twenty years later. Along with the other direct taxes, the collection of the *collatio* was originally the responsibility of the *curia* of each city, but by the end of the fourth century this had been transferred to *mancipes* derived from the body of *negotiatores* itself. There is little doubt that this quinquennial tax was designed to meet the burden of the quinquennial donative which late Roman emperors were expected to pay their armies, and it is indeed

---

[7] For the *logothesia* see G. Millet, "L'origine du logothète général, chef de l'administration financière à Byzance," *Mélanges d'historie du moyen âge offerts à M. Ferdinand Lot* (Paris, 1925), p. 563 ff.

38

likely that the *largitiones* derived its name from the technical use of the word in late Latin to mean 'military donative'.[8]

The supervisory duties of the *comes* over the government textile factories (*gynaecea*) with the consequent function of providing military uniforms is the natural origin of the land-tax *militaris vestis*. At least down to 374 actual garments in the stipulated numbers and of the required quality had to be found for the treasury, but the 'adaeration' of this tax, which the collectors must have practised with individuals and even communities from the first, was complete by the end of the fourth century when the troops received a cash allowance in lieu of uniform. With all the supervision in the world, 'uniforms' produced by taxation must have been a heterogeneous lot, and there is more than a hint that they tended to lie unused in treasury warehouses.[9]

Other land taxes of the *largitiones* were miscellaneous in character. Most important were the *titulus auri comparaticii* and the mysterious *bina et terna*. The former seems to have been a simple land-tax for the purpose of financing the purchase of gold, an important feature of late Roman finance. The origins of the latter are obscure. In East and West alike, however, certain minor land-taxes, of which this is an example, were paid to the *largitiones* in the fifth and sixth centuries. With them can be classed the *gleba senatoria* and the other supertaxes paid by the estates of senators and other members of the hierarchy. It is doubtful whether the revenue they yielded was very substantial. The senatorial burdens at least were abolished by Marcian on his accession, and his finances were on a notably sound footing.[10]

A more characteristic source of revenue was constituted by the so-called 'voluntary' payments. These were twofold: the *oblatio senatoria* of the Roman Senate, made on a grand scale at the quinquennial celebrations and more modestly with the renewed *vota* of each New Year. The corresponding curial burden was the *aurum coronarium*, whereby the government was 'given' gold crowns, images of Victory, and the like, on all occasions of public rejoicing, such as imperial accessions and anniversaries, military successes, remissions of tax arrears, et cetera. But in spite of efforts to ensure that it fell directly on landed proprietors, the city councils financed the burden with a super-tax (στεφανικόν) on the community at large, and since the fiction of its voluntary character remained, it had to be excluded from the indiction and could not be effectively controlled. By the sixth century it appears that, like many other

---

[8] The main texts on the *collatio* are: Zosimus, *Historia* (Bonn ed., 1837), II:xxxviii:3; Evagrius, III:xxxix; Zonaras, *Epitome Historiarum* (Bonn ed., 1897), XIV:iii:11; Libanius, *Orationes* (Teubner ed., III, 1906), XLVI (*contra Florentium*):xxii; *Cod. Theod.*, XIII:i, *passim*; *Novellae Theodosii II*, XVIII (*Nov. Theod.*, p. 44); *Cod. Theod.*, VII:xx:3, A.D. 326; Vitelli, Norsa, etc., *Papiri greci e latini*, VIII (Florence, 1927), no. 884; St. Basil, *Epistolae*, LXXXVIII (*PG*, XXXII [1886], col. 470); Cassiodorus, II:xxvi, xxx; Mal., p. 398; Chronicle of Edessa (ed. Ludwig Hallier, in O. Gebhardt and A. Harnack, *Texte und Untersuchungen zur Geschichte der altchristlichen Literatur*, IX [Leipzig, 1893]), LXXIV (cf. Stein, *BE*, p. 204, note 1).

[9] For *militaris vestis*, see especially *Cod. Theod.*, VII:vi, *passim*; *Scriptores Historiae Augustae*, *Severus Alexander* (Loeb ed., II, 1924), XL:3.

[10] *Aurum comparaticium*: *Cod. Theod.*, VII:vi:3 = *Cod. Just.*, XII:xxxix:2, A.D. 377. *Bina et terna*: Cassiodorus, III:viii; VII:xx–xxiii; cf. *Novellae Maioriani*, VII:16, A.D. 458 (*Nov. Theod.*, p. 171). *Gleba*: O. Seeck, "Collatio glebalis," in Pauly-Wissowa, *Real-Encyclopädie*, IV (Stuttgart, 1901), cols. 365–367.

dues, it had become a customary payment, perhaps made annually, and in this form it continued into Byzantine times.[11]

The revenue from emphyteutic and patrimonial land, originally classed as 'commoda largitionum', passed to the *res privata* as early as 379, but the control of civic *vectigalia* continued to provide both an income and an administrative problem. An early solution of the problem of municipal expenses provided that the *largitiones* should refund one third of the civic revenue for this purpose, and this regulation, revived by the time of Justinian, was supplemented by the periodic allocation of specific *vectigalia* for specific civic purposes.[12]

The *largitiones* also enjoyed several miscellaneous sources of revenue, such as the *aurum tironicum* paid by landowners in lieu of the provision of recruits. Cash fines were paid to the *largitiones* until well into the fifth century, whereas confiscated land and goods entered the *res privata*. We do not know the date of the reform, evident from the practice of the Justinian Code and Novels, which gave fines also to the latter, though there is a slight indication that Justinian himself may have been responsible.[13]

Although policy fluctuated, two major phases can be detected in the methods employed to collect *largitionales tituli*. Under the first system which operated down to the comprehensive reforms of Valentinian I and Valens in 364–5, officers styled *largitionales civitatis* were responsible for the collection of taxes from the treasury of each city (initial exaction was of course in civic hands) and their transport to the *comitatus*. The exaction of arrears was the task of the provincial *rationalis* and his *officium*. Bulky goods of no great urgency, such as textiles, travelled by ship or requisitioned vehicle, but fragile materials, particularly those destined for imperial use, were authorised to use the *cursus publicus*. Under no circumstances might the transport of bullion be delayed. There was of course much abuse to be put down: joy-riding on the *cursus publicus*, pilfering of coin en route to the treasury.[14]

Valentinian I and his successors aimed to prevent the central treasuries becoming powers in the provinces, and to this end withdrew all part in the exaction of taxes and arrears from *palatini*, vesting it all in the *officia* of provincial governors, particularly those of the diocesan vicars. The big increase in financial

---

[11] *Oblatio*: Symmachus (ed. O Seeck, *Monumenta Germaniae Historica, Auctores Antiquissimi*, VI, 1), *Epistulae*, II:lvii; *Relationes*, xiii, xxx; *Cod. Theod.*, VI:ii, *passim*. *Aurum coronarium*: *Cod. Theod.*, XII:xiii, *passim*; Themistius, *Orationes* (ed. Dindorf, 1832), III:40c; Amm. Marc., XXVIII:vi:7.

[12] *Res privata*: *Cod. Theod.*, V:xv, *passim*; *Novellae Marciani*, III, A.D. 451 (*Nov. Theod.*, p. 188). *Vectigalia*: Amm. Marc., XXV:iv:15; C. G. Bruns, *Fontes juris romani antiqui* (7th ed., Tübingen, 1909), no. 97; *Cod. Theod.*, XV:i:18, A.D. 374; IV:xiii:7, A.D. 374; V:xiv:35, A.D. 395; *Novellae Valentiniani III*, XIII, A.D. 445 (*Nov. Theod.*, p. 95); *CIL*, nos. 7151, 7152; *Cod. Just.*, IV:lxi:13, A.D. 431.

[13] *Aurum tironicum*: *Cod. Theod.*, VII:xiii:2, A.D. 370, and 13, A.D. 397; Amm. Marc., XXXI:iv:6; Socrates, *Historia ecclesiastica*, IV:xxxiv (ed. R. Hussey, Oxford, 1853, II, p. 562); Sozomen, *Historia ecclesiastica*, VI:xxxvii (ed. J. Bidez and G. C. Hansen, Berlin, 1960, p. 297); Synesius, *Epistolae*, LXXIX (*PG*, LXVI, 1864, col. 1445); Anonymus, *De rebus bellicis*, V (ed. E. A. Thompson, Oxford, 1952, p. 96). Fines: *Cod. Theod.*, IX:xvii:2, A.D. 349; XI:xxx:25, A.D. 355 = *Cod. Just.*, VII:lxii:21; *Novellae Theodosii II*, XXV, A.D. 444 (*Nov. Theod.*, p. 65), etc.

[14] *Largitionales*: *Cod. Theod.*, VI:xxxv:3, A.D. 352. For this and the following paragraph, see also J. P. C. Kent, "Gold Coinage in the Later Roman Empire," *Essays in Roman Coinage Presented to Harold Mattingly* (Oxford, 1956), p. 190 ff.

duties involved changes in the structure of provincial *officia*, which acquired two accounting branches, dealing respectively with the affairs of the Prefects' *arca* and those of the *largitiones*. Speedy and effective action was ensured by the dispatch of two *palatini* into each province in each indiction, with the task of demanding delivery of taxation material by the governors to the diocesan *thesauri*, and preparing provisional and final statements of payments and arrears. Collection of the latter remained for long the responsibility of a new officer, the *comes titulorum* (*largitionum*, *thesaurorum*, etc.), appointed on a diocesan basis in the East, and with rather wider circumscriptions in the West. He still worked through the medium of the provincial *officia*, and this practice continued into the sixth century, after the *comites* had disappeared and been replaced by palatine *scriniarii*. Towards the end of the fourth century the *largitiones* was rendered independent of the *cursus publicus* and the need to requisition, by the provision of a transport corps (*bastaga*). The problem of pilfering was dealt with by the extension to taxes of a system applied to the rents of the *res privata* since the time of Constantine I. Provincial governors were, after 365, forbidden to accept coin without melting it down and subjecting it to tests for weight and purity. Any deficiency was required to be made up by a charge called *obryza*. Thus tested for weight and fineness at every stage, bullion finally arrived at the *comitatus* in refined bar form, and from 368 the new standard of imperial fineness was expressed on the gold and silver coinage by the symbols OB (*ryzum*) and P(*u*)S(*ulatum*) respectively.

Of the indirect taxes of the early empire, only *portoria* survived the financial upheavals of the third century to remain an important source of revenue to the *largitiones*. Trade with tribes or nations beyond the Roman frontier had always been severely restricted, with the three objects of maintaining security from spying and surprise attack, the prevention of the passage of strategic materials (gold, iron, etc.) to potential enemies, and the facilitation of the collection of customs. All frontiers were therefore furnished with a few organised and closely controlled points of intercourse with those beyond, all passage or commerce elsewhere being illegal. From the fifth century such centres were policed by soldiers under the supervision of *curiosi* selected from the *agentes in rebus* of the *magister officiorum*, but by a characteristic anomaly were responsible not to him but to the *comes sacrarum largitionum*.[15]

Once diverted through an authorised commercial centre, customs were collected by curials with the time-honoured title of *conductores*. The form of the triennial auction of contracts lasted into the sixth century, and with the government annexation of civic *vectigalia* had to be done port by port and tax by tax. In fact, the government recognised the state of affairs which had

---

[15] Foreign trade at restricted points: Cassius Dio, *Roman History*, LXXII:xi:3; xv (Loeb ed., 1929, IX, pp. 12 ff., 34); Dessau, no. 775; Themistius, *Orationes* (ed. Dindorf, 1832), X:135C (Danube); Petrus Diaconus, *Liber de locis sanctis* (*Corpus Scriptorum Ecclesiasticorum Latinorum*, XXXIX, p. 116: "India," i. e. India, South Arabia, and Ethiopia); Petrus Patricius, frag. 14, in *FHG*, p. 189; *Cod. Just.*, IV:lxiii:4, A.D. 408–9; Menander Protector, *Historia*, frag. 11, in *FHG*, p. 212 (Persia). *Curiosi*: *Cod. Theod.*, XI:vii:17, A.D. 408; VI:xxix:10, A.D. 412; Ioannes Chrysostomus, *Epistolae ad Innocentium*, I (*PG*, LII [1862], col. 532).

effectively prevailed since the second century, that the duty of *conductor* was now no more than a liturgy, and furnished the incumbent with some temporary immunities from civic duties, and an *officium* at first from the imperial *familia*, but later militarized, and even sometimes containing actual soldiers. In the East, the high rate of $12^1/_2\%$ resulted in the term *octavarii* being applied to the farmers, and this obtained at least until about 600. When times were good, there is no doubt that the farmer was able to profit substantially from his undertaking. Though the idea of directly collecting *vectigalia* by imperial officials is first mentioned as one of the lunacies of Caligula, there is no evidence for its application before Justinian. Procopius records the establishment of salaried officials at Hieron and Abydos, paying their takings into the treasury, as one of his many evil deeds. There is no sign of a farming system after the sixth century, and it it is probable that Heraclius swept away its last traces when he established his γενικοὶ κομμερκιάριοι along with his new finance organisation.[16]

State-owned mines and quarries belonged to the *res privata*, but the *metallicus canon* paid by their hereditary workmen was owed to the *largitiones*. Supervision was in the hands of curial procurators, a not unprofitable job if our sources are to be credited. Several mines were used as penal settlements. Even privately owned *metallica loca* came under strict state control. They were not entered in, nor transferable to, the ordinary taxation registers, and had obligations to the *largitiones* only. Inhabitants of such land were hereditarily bound to work the deposits, and owners liable to ensure fulfilment of fiscal dues. Quarries paid 10% of their products to the state; the government had a right of pre-emption of gold, and very likely of other metals also. Itinerant gold prospectors constituted a difficulty which the government met by demanding the purchase of a licence, and the sale to its officials of all produce. In Illyricum, where mining was an important source of revenue, a special *comes metallorum* was appointed, and as the κόμης τῆς λα[το]μίας he survived into the Byzantine period.[17]

The notorious monopolies that are said to have enriched the *largitiones* under Justinian have no place before his reign. Such monopolies as existed were for the most part fortuitous, and, with the exception of salt, were suppressed by Leo I in 473. Complementary legislation ten years later under Zeno aimed at

---

[16] *Conductores*: *Cod. Just.*, V:xli:1, A.D. 213; X:lvii:1, A.D. 287–293; *Cod. Theod.*, XII:i:97, A.D. 383; XI:xxviii:3, A.D. 401. *Octavarii*: H. Grégoire, *Recueil des inscriptions grecques chrétiennes d'Asie Mineure*, I (Paris, 1922), no. 10; *Cod. Theod.*, IV:xiii:6, A.D. 368 = *Cod. Just.*, IV:lxi:7; *Cod. Theod.*, IV:xiii:8, A.D. 381 = *Cod. Just.*, IV:lxi:8; *Cod. Just.*, IV:xlii:2, A.D. 459–465; Sophronius Monachus, *Narratio miraculorum SS. Cyri et Ioannis* (*PG*, LXXXVII, 3 [1865], col. 3424). Caligula: Suetonius, *De vita caesarum, Caligula* (Loeb ed., I, 1935), XL. Justinian: Proc., *Anec.*, xxv:1 ff.; H. Grégoire, *op. cit.*, no. 4. Commerciarii: G. Millet, "Sur les sceaux des commerciaires byzantins," *Mélanges offerts à M. Gustave Schlumberger*, I (Paris, 1924), p. 303 ff.

[17] Mining regulations: *Cod. Theod.*, X:xix, *passim*; I:xxxii:5, A.D. 386 = *Cod. Just.*, XI:vii:4; *Notitia Dignitatum* (ed. O. Seeck, Berlin, 1876), *Or.*, XIII:11; Firmicus Maternus, *Mathesis* (Teubner ed., 1897), III:xii:10. *Damnatio ad metalla*: E. G. Hardy, *Pliny's Correspondence with Trajan* (London, 1889), p. 127. Quarries: *Cod. Theod.*, X:xix:8, A.D. 376; X:x, A.D. 382 = *Cod. Just.*, XI:vii:3. Gold prospecting: *Cod. Theod.*, X:xix:3, A.D. 365 = *Cod. Just.*, XI:vii:1; *Cod. Theod.*, X:xix:12, A.D. 392 = *Cod. Just.*, XI:vii:5; Amm. Marc., XXXI:vi:6.

breaking up trading rings and restrictive practices, and though the Ostrogothic kingdom issued licences to engage in specific trades under the name of *monopolium*, there is no trace of such a system in the East. Justinian maintained the anti-monopolistic legislation of his predecessors and, apart from the imperial purple dye being made available to the public, there is little to suggest that the so-called monopolies of Procopius were anything more than the mere cornering of various commodities by wealthy men with the bought connivance of a corrupt government, or that they extended beyond Constantinople. The strict control of the trading *corpora* seems only to be in its infancy under Justinian.[18]

One of the special duties of the *largitiones* was the supervision of a large group of factories and workmen. These seem to have originated partly in bodies of imperial slaves and freedmen, partly in free workers, all or part of whose services had been requisitioned by the government. The establishments falling within this category were the mints (*monetae*), textile and garment mills (*gynaecea*), linen and canvas mills (*linyfia*) and purple dye works (*bafia*). They must not be considered solely as government factories, because so long as they fulfilled state requirements there was no doubt of their right to work on their own account—their workers were subject to *collatio lustralis*—nor of that of their head to negotiate private contracts. There were of course certain restrictions. Just as the arms factories might produce for the general public knives but not swords, so the textile workers might not supply cloth of the imperial purple shade, or garments resembling those worn by the emperor.

The workmen of these establishments were constituted into hereditary *corpora*, bound *nexu sanguinis* to the *largitiones*. They could abandon their calling only with the approbation of the emperor himself, and then only by the sacrifice of family and property. Subject to the S. C. Claudianum, women who married them descended to their degraded status, while their own womenfolk could not marry outside the *corpus*. For a long while they were forbidden to acquire dignities, and though in practice skilled workers came to have a more enhanced position, assignment to the mints and textile factories was used in the fourth century as a humiliating punishment, where convicts might work in chains.

Provision of raw materials for government work at these factories was a tax which fell on specific bodies and localities. The *corporati* of Carthage, for example, jointly maintained the supply for the city's *gynaeceum*. Ensuring the production and delivery of the government quota was the responsibility of the *procurator*. These managers of state factories, like other minor posts under the *largitiones*, were appointed subject to certain strict rules. Adequate sureties had first to be found, and on leaving office they were required to deposit all official papers and accounts at the appropriate provincial *thesaurus*, and present a copy to their successors. Failure to observe these regulations meant loss of dignity—such *procuratores* held rank as *perfectissimi*—and liability to torture

[18] Monopoly legislation: *Cod. Just.*, IV:lix, *passim. Monopolium*: Cassiodorus, II:iv, xxvi, xxx. Justinian's monopolies: Proc., *Anec.*, xx:5, xxv:13, xxvi:19.

until the accounts were balanced. Conviction for overt fraud meant prohibition against seeking any further office on pain of death, but the financial risks of such posts led to their occasional appearance in the lists of those whose treasury debts were from time to time remitted. There is no doubt that the output, as well as the accounts of the factories, was deposited in the provincial *thesauri*.[19]

One group of specially skilled workmen was exempted from the humiliating status of the others, the *barbaricarii*. These were workers in the precious metals, men skilled in their use as ornaments, and able to manufacture the highly ornate ceremonial armour worn by the emperor, and the great gold brooches that constituted one of the insignia of high ranking officers. In the West, these workmen were grouped in factories, differing from the others only in their relatively exalted status. From the time of Valens in the East, however, though remaining in their twin factories at Antioch and Constantinople, they were directly administered by a section of the palatine *scrinium ab argento*, and were not classed with the other state employees.[20]

The Eastern *largitiones*, among its large staff of clerks dealing with questions of taxation and administration, included two departments with technical branches, dealing respectively with gold and silver. The first was the *scrinium aureae massae*, the recipient of the tested gold bars in which alone the government would accept cash taxes after 365. Apart from a small clerical staff, the department mainly consisted of two technical branches; *aurifices solidorum*, and *sculptores et ceteri aurifices*. The concentration of gold coinage at the *comitatus* in and after 368 to the exclusion of the provincial *monetae publicae* is a phenomenon explicable by the structure of this *scrinium*, and its continuance is demonstrated by the occurrence of the relevant laws in the Justinian Code and the presence of officials styled *pal(atinus) s(a)c(rarum) l(argitionum) et monitarius auri* in sixth-century Ravenna. The *ceteri aurifices* must be considered as *barbaricarii* working in gold as opposed to silver, and this dichotomy even within the one *officium* is interesting evidence of the minuteness governing all aspects of late Roman organisation. The second was the *scrinium ab argento* (if we accept, what seems beyond doubt, that its composition in the published versions of the Justinian Code has become transposed with that of the *scrinium a pecuniis*). Here again we find two divisions: *argentarii comitatenses*, and *barbaricarii*. The latter we have already considered. The former I believe to have included those responsible for the coinage of comitatensian silver, a negligible function by the time of Justinian, and in all probability the officials responsible for the stamping of silver with marks indicating its sterling character.[21]

The release of such officially stamped silver to the public we now see to be an innovation of the reign of Anastasius. If, as we can hardly doubt, the *largitiones* charged a fee for hall-marking silver brought to its smiths, or for issuing already

---

[19] State factories and personnel: *Cod. Theod.*, X:xx, *passim*.

[20] *Barbaricarii*: Donatus, *Interpretationes vergilianae*, Aeneid, XI:777 (Teubner ed., II, 1906, p. 529); *Cod. Theod.*, XIII:iv:2, A.D. 337; X:xxii:1, A.D. 374; *Cod. Just.*, XII:xxiii:7, A.D. 384.

[21] For the *officium*, see *Cod. Just.*, XII:xxiii:7, A.D. 384; *Notitia Dignitatum* (ed. O. Seeck, Berlin, 1876), *Occ.*, XI:88; *Or.*, XIII:22.

authenticated silver from the treasury, the repute of such silver and the *bona fides* of the marks must have been ample compensation. It has been shown that of the five different shapes of stamp used in the later years of Anastasius, four normally are marked with the Emperor's portrait or monogram, presumably in order to give that guarantee of sacred authenticity carried by the coinage, and to discourage imitation. In these stamps, as well as in the normal set of five stamps instituted by Justinian, occur also the individual names and monograms of officials; among them, in all probability, were the stamps of the *comes sacrarum largitionum* himself, the *primicerius* of his *officium*, and the *primicerius* of the *scrinium ab argento*. Together the five stamps served to authenticate the quality of the silver, and perhaps also to signify that the appropriate dues had been paid. Imperial stamps show that this system was maintained at least down to c. 650. It would seem that the end of the stamp system and the dissolution of the *largitiones* were connected. Yet the demand for authenticated silver plate must have survived the loss of the eastern provinces and the resumption of a substantial silver coinage; the interaction of the demand for plate and the circulation of a copious silver currency is something which remains to be evaluated. It may well be that for a while the skilled metal workers who remained to the empire were able to satisfy the reduced demand by melting down the new coins.

PART III

CATALOGUE OF STAMPED OBJECTS

EXPLANATORY NOTE

In the Catalogue of stamped silver objects it was intended that for each entry there should be illustrations of the object itself, of its stamps, and of casts made from its stamps wherever this would be helpful. Photographs of the casts are sometimes easier to read than photographs of the actual stamps because in the latter discoloration of the silver may impair legibility. In addition, each entry was to be accompanied by drawings to facilitate the reading of monograms. This intention has been largely fulfilled, but the quality of the illustrations varies, and in a few instances the stamps were so illegible as to make any attempt at transcription futile.

Since it has not always been possible to study the objects at first hand or to secure good photographs or casts, the following method has been adopted: In each instance it is stated whether the readings of the stamps were taken from the object itself or from reproductions. Unless indicated otherwise, the readings given are those of the author. Frequently it has been necessary to rely on the interpretations of other writers, particularly Rosenberg and Matsulevich, and where these authors disagree the reading that seemed the most reasonable according to the reproduction has been chosen, or else the reading was confined to what was readily visible in the reproduction. This method may seem arbitrary, but it must be emphasized that the disputed points concern only minor variations in the spelling of an inscribed name or the clarity of certain letters in an inscription or monogram. They do not significantly affect the conclusions drawn in the text.

Further, standard letters have been adopted in transcription. The lettering of the inscriptions is so small and the stamps are so frequently excessively worn that it is usually difficult to distinguish the exact form of a letter. The alpha, for example, appears in three forms: A, A, A; or, the epsilon: E and Є. The distinctions are rarely clear, however, and accurate reproductions were, therefore, not feasible.

No attempt has been made to give the actual sizes of the stamps in each case, or to indicate the relationship between the stamps and their enlarged reproductions. It was decided always to reproduce the clearest available photographs of the stamps regardless of variations in the sizes of the enlargements. The dimensions of Imperial stamps are reasonably uniform. For nos. 44 and 46 the reproduction is to scale; for no. 45 it is double. These examples set a standard measurement for Imperial stamps. Dimensions of Irregular stamps do not vary greatly, and can be ascertained from the dimensions given for the whole object or, in some instances (nos. 74, 82), from the scale which is provided. The size of the illustration of the stamps determined the space available for the reproduction of the objects themselves.

Finally, cross references to corresponding names and monograms in the stamps on different objects are given where they seem to be useful; for a full synopsis of related features on different stamps, Tables I–IV should be consulted.

CATALOGUE

OBJECTS WITH IMPERIAL STAMPS FROM THE REIGN OF ANASTASIUS I, A.D. 491–518

a. *Trulla* with Nilotic Relief

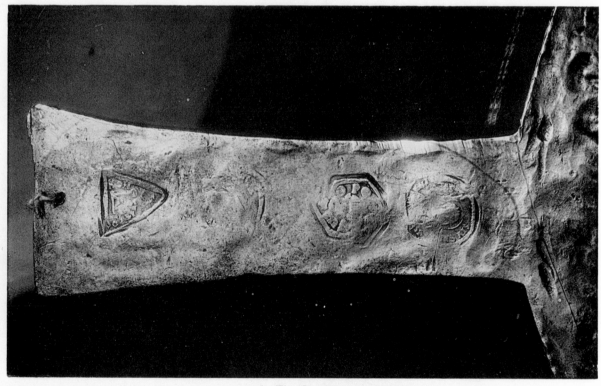

b. The Stamps

No. 1. *TRULLA* WITH NILOTIC RELIEF

THE HERMITAGE, LENINGRAD; acc. no. W. 2

DESCRIPTION: *Trulla* with Nilotic scene in relief (fig. a). Nilotic motifs decorate the rim; incised vases surround the central disc in which two erotes, midst fishes and lotus plants, play beside a Nilometer. The handle is decorated with a figure of Poseidon standing with one foot on a dolphin and holding a fish and a trident.

Wt. 958.4 gr.; diam. 24.5 cm.; diam. of footring 11.2 cm.; ht. 8.4 cm. (Matsulevich).

PLACE OF DISCOVERY: Bought in 1859 in Perm (renamed Molotov in 1942).

CONTROL STAMPS: Four stamps on handle — two round, one hexagonal, one triangular (fig. b). It is difficult to judge whether the stamps were applied before or after the handle was decorated, but since the clearest stamp, the triangle, is found in the hollow formed by the head of Poseidon on the obverse, it seems unlikely that it was stamped after the relief was formed; and, indeed, the other stamps appear to have been worn down when the handle was beaten and polished. The readings were taken from cast and photograph:

O   Bust, type 1; inscribed DN A[N]AST[A]‖SIVS PP AVG.

O   The same?

O   Monogram of box type (p. 6), almost indistinguishable; inscribed [Θ]ЄѠ ΔOPO[V]?

△   Small cross; worn, box-type monogram which Rosenberg tentatively read ΔIOMIΔOV (the reading seems doubtful since there is no sign of a M); inscribed KON[CT‖AN]TIOC?

DATE: Anastasius I, A.D. 491–518 (p. 6).

Principal References: Rosenberg, pp. 630–631; Matsulevich, *Byz. Ant.*, p. 6f., no. 11, pp. 75–79, figs. 9–11, pl. 16; C. Picard, *BCH*, LXXVI (1952), pp. 82, 83.

Source of Illustration: The Hermitage.

No. 2. THE PLATE OF PATERNUS

THE HERMITAGE, LENINGRAD

DESCRIPTION: Large paten with design of vine, birds, and chalices around the rim (fig. a). In the center a monogram of Christ with the letters A and ω inscribed on either side; surrounding this, within the rim, the inscription:

+ EX ANTIQVIS RENOVATVM EST PER PATERNVM
REVERENTISS(imvm) EPISC(opvm) NOSTRVM AMEN*

Wt. 6224 gr.; diam. 61 cm.; diam. of footring 31.8 cm.; ht. of footring 1.8 cm. (Matsulevich).

PLACE OF DISCOVERY: Found in 1912, in Malaia Pereshchepina, Government of Poltava, South Russia, with nos. 30, 31, 73, 79.

CONTROL STAMPS: Four stamps on base of dish – two round, one hexagonal, one triangular. It is difficult to judge whether they were applied before or after the plate was decorated. The readings were taken from the object:

O (fig. b) The bust, in three-quarter face, wears a helmet (see pp. 7, 9); inscribed DN ANASTA‖SIV[S] PP AVG.

O (fig. c) Bust type 1; inscribed MH‖NNA (p. 6).

O (fig. d) Monogram of Anastasius or Justinian, type b; inscribed ΞΕΝΟΦΙΛΟV. Relative position of monogram and inscription to the hexagonal frame differs from that usually found in the Imperial series; normally the inscription is divided by the monogram, and the latter's vertical axis intersects angles rather than sides of the hexagon (cf. also nos. 5, 9, 72, 73).

△ (fig. e) Small cross; box-type monogram that reads IωANNOV and is also found in the corresponding stamp of no. 3; inscribed KOMI‖T[AC].

DATE: Anastasius I, A.D. 491–518 (p. 6). The secondary monogram may refer to John the Paphlagonian, *comes sacrarum largitionum* in A.D. 498 (p. 29, Table V).

Principal References: Rosenberg, pp. 632–633; Matsulevich, *Byz. Ant.*, p. 5, no. 6, p. 101 ff., figs. 21, 22, pls. 26, 27; *Byz. Art, 1958*, no. 28.

Source of Illustration: Victoria and Albert Museum, reproduction courtesy of the Hermitage Museum and of Mr. John Beckwith.

* Paternus has been identified with a dignitary of that name who was Bishop of Tomi in the first quarter of the sixth century. On the evidence of the stamps, the plate was made in Constantinople. Changes were subsequently carried out in the decoration of the rim; but these, according to Matsulevich, are not the "renovation" to which Paternus' inscription refers. See also *supra*, p. 33 f.

a. The Plate of Paternus

b. Round

c. Round

d. Hexagonal

e. Triangular

The Stamps

Ornamented Bowl, with reverse of Central Fragment
showing Stamps

No. 3. ORNAMENTED BOWL

THE MUSEUM OF THE HISTORY OF THE LATVIAN SSR, RIGA

DESCRIPTION: Fragmentary bowl with ornamented rim. The central part, including the footring, has become detached (see fig.).

Wt. 253.30 gr.; diam 17 cm.

PLACE OF DISCOVERY: Voronia, Lake Peipus.

CONTROL STAMPS: Four stamps – two round, one hexagonal, and one triangular. The photograph does not indicate whether the stamps were applied before or after the decoration of the plate. The readings were taken from the photograph:

O Bust, type 1 (the nimbus is not clearly distinguishable, but its absence would be unusual in a stamp of this period; see p. 9); box-type monogram appears to be identical with that in the second round stamp and in the triangle, and similar to the monogram in the triangle of no. 2; it reads IⲰANNOV; inscribed ICAK‖IOV.

O Bust very worn; monogram as above; inscribed ⲐⲰ‖MA.

O Small bust; monogram indistinct; inscribed KO[C‖M]A?

△ Monogram like those in the round stamps; inscribed ⲐⲰ‖MA.

DATE: This set of stamps resembles the stamps on nos. 1 and 2 and may, accordingly, be dated in the reign of Anastasius I, A.D. 491–518. The name IⲰANNOV may refer to John the Paphlagonian, *comes sacrarum largitionum* in A.D. 498 (see no. 2).

Principal References: Rosenberg, pp. 634–635; Matsulevich, *Byz. Ant.*, p. 76, note 1.

Source of Illustration: Museum of the History of the Latvian SSR, Riga.

No. 4. PLATE FROM SUTTON HOO

DESCRIPTION: Large platter with geometric designs on the rim, in a second interior border, and in the center (fig. a). In the second border are four medallions containing, alternately, the figure of a seated Tyche (Constantinople?) similar to the figure on fifth-century square stamps (see no. 82), and a running figure holding an unidentifiable object in her hands. The rim decoration also includes four medallions, each with a running figure.

Diam. 27″ (approx. 68.58 cm.); diam. of footring 11″ (approx. 27.94 cm.); ht. $2\frac{1}{2}$″ (approx. 6.35 cm.) (Kitzinger).

PLACE OF DISCOVERY: Found in 1939 as part of the treasure in an Anglo-Saxon ship-burial at Sutton Hoo, Suffolk.

CONTROL STAMPS: Four stamps on bottom of plate – two identical hexagonal, two identical long stamps (fig. b). No clear indication of when they were applied. The readings were taken from the object:

○ (fig. c) Monogram of Anastasius or Justinian, type a; inscribed ΘѠ‖MA; cross above and below monogram.

○ (fig. d) Same as above.

◠ (fig. e) Bust appears to be of type 1, although it is possible that the emperor is wearing a plumed helmet, in which case it would belong to an earlier type (p. 9); box-type monogram; inscribed DN ANASTA[S]‖IVS PP AV[G].

◠ (fig. f) Same as above.

DATE: Anastasius I, A.D. 491–518 (p. 6f).

Principal References: E. Kitzinger, "The Sutton Hoo Ship-Burial, V: The Silver," *Antiquity*, XIV (1940), pp. 40–50, pls. X, figs. D, E, XVI, XVII, XVIII; *The Sutton Hoo Ship-Burial, A Provisional Guide* (British Museum, London, 1952), pp. 28–30, 47, pls. 12, 14.

Source of Illustration: The British Museum, reproduction courtesy of the Trustees.

a. Plate from Sutton Hoo

b. Detail of Back

c. Hexagonal

d. Hexagonal

e. Long

f. Long

The Stamps

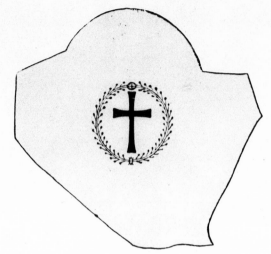

a. Drawing of Fragment of Plate with Niello Cross

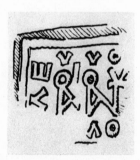

b. Hexagonal   c. Square   d. Long   e. Long

Drawings of the Stamps

No. 5. FRAGMENT OF PLATE WITH NIELLO CROSS

THE DISTRICT MUSEUM, RAZGRAD, BULGARIA; acc. no. 704

DESCRIPTION: Fragment of plate with niello cross in the center, surrounded by wreath (fig. a).

Diam. (originally) *ca.* 30 cm.; present diam. 17 cm.; diam. of footring 13 cm. (Gerasimov).

PLACE OF DISCOVERY: Found in 1925, in Svietlen, Aiazlar, Popovsko, Bulgaria.

CONTROL STAMPS: Four stamps – one hexagonal, one square, two identical long stamps. Gerasimov does not indicate whether they were applied before or after the decoration was finished. The readings of the stamps were taken from the drawings published by Gerasimov:

○ (fig. b) The relationship of the inscription and monogram to the sides of the hexagon differs from that usually found in Imperial stamps (see the corresponding stamps on nos. 2, 9, 72, 73). The box-type monogram reads ZENO; inscribed + ΘЄΟΔШΡΟV

□ (fig. c) Box-type monogram of Anastasius or Justinian, type a; inscribed ΛЄΟV....

◠ (fig. d) Bust, type 1; box-type monogram, undeciphered; inscribed [DN A]NA-STAS‖IVS [PP] AVG.

◠ (fig. e) Same as above; inscription is worn.

DATE: Anastasius I, A.D. 491–518 (p. 7). Although the monogram in the hexagon might denote Anastasius' predecessor Zeno, A.D. 474–491, and the object be thought, therefore, to precede the others of the reign of Anastasius, the substitution of a square stamp for a triangular one and the type of imperial bust suggest a position following nos. 1–4.

Principal Reference: T. Gerasimov, *Bulletin de l'Institut archéologique bulgare,* XIII (1939), pp. 335–337, figs. 367, 368 (drawings only) (in Bulgarian).

Source of Illustration: Gerasimov.

OBJECTS WITH IMPERIAL STAMPS FROM

THE REIGN OF JUSTINIAN I, A.D. 527–565

a. Dish with Ornamental Rosette

b. The Stamps

No. 6. DISH WITH ORNAMENTAL ROSETTE

THE STATE HISTORICAL MUSEUM, MOSCOW; acc. no. 10397

DESCRIPTION: Dish with delicate rosette ornament in central roundel and curved lines radiating to rim (fig. a).

Wt. 1600 gr.; diam. 38.7 cm.; diam. of central rosette 7.5 cm.; diam. of footring 16.3 cm. (Matsulevich).

PLACE OF DISCOVERY: District of Novobaiazet, former Government of Erivan, Russian Armenia (see nos. 96, 97).

CONTROL STAMPS: The five stamps – a round, a hexagonal, a square, a long, and a cruciform – disposed symmetrically on the base, were damaged when the ring around the rosette (fig. b) was worked. The readings were taken from the photograph:

O　Bust, type 1; inscribed ANΔ‖PЄOV.

○　Double strike; box-type monogram of either Anastasius or Justinian, type b; small, nimbed bust above the monogram; inscription barely legible.

□　Monogram not visible; inscription barely legible.

◠　Bust, type 1; box-type monogram; inscribed [Θ]ω‖MA.

✠　Square arms; monogram illegible; inscribed in vertical letters K‖V‖P‖V.

DATE: Although the imperial monogram, as well as the imperial bust, may belong to either Anastasius or Justinian, no cross stamps have been found among the stamps of Anastasius. This group, therefore, very probably belongs to the reign of Justinian I, A.D. 527–565 (see p. 7). The shape and lettering of the cross stamp, however, indicate an early date in Justinian's reign, as does the box-type monogram (see p. 15f.).

Principal References: Protasov, pp. 69–74, pl. IX, 3; Matsulevich, *Byz. Ant.*, p. 117f., figs. 29, 30.

Source of Illustration: The State Historical Museum.

No. 7. PLATE WITH RELIEF OF GRAZING HORSE

THE HERMITAGE, LENINGRAD; acc. no. W. 280

DESCRIPTION: Plate with relief, in central roundel, of a horse grazing in front of a tree (fig. a). A pattern of acanthus leaves and lotus flowers surrounds the roundel.

Wt. 1623 gr.; diam. 41 cm.; diam. of footring 16.7 cm. (Matsulevich).

PLACE OF DISCOVERY: Found in 1780 (?), near the village of Sludka, on the Kama River, Government of Perm (renamed Molotov in 1942).

CONTROL STAMPS: Five stamps – a round, a hexagonal, a square, a long, and a cruciform; disposed symmetrically on base of plate (fig. b). They appear to have been damaged during the beating of the relief (Matsulevich, p. 115). The readings were taken from casts and photographs:

O   The double strike has twisted the bust, type 1; inscribed ΔΙ..ΝΗ‖..VC.

O   The double strike has displaced the monogram and repeated the left-hand part of the inscription; monogram of Justinian or Anastasius, type b; inscription barely legible.

□   Monogram as above; inscribed ΙΤΑ‖ΛΟ[V].

Ω   Nimbed bust; the box-type monogram is similar to the monogram in the cross stamp, and may be the same as that in the long and cross stamps of nos. 8–13, where it reads ΠΕΤΡΟV; inscribed [ΕVΓ]ΕΝΙΟV (Matsulevich).

✠   Square arms; the monogram has been flattened out, but its right side, which is visible, suggests that it is similar to the monogram in the long stamp; inscribed in vertical letters ΚΟ‖ΝΩ‖..‖ΟC.

DATE: The secondary monogram may relate these stamps to those on nos. 8–13, which are assigned to the reign of Justinian I, A.D. 527–565 (see no. 11, and p. 13). This monogram probably belongs to Peter (? Barsymes), *comes sacrarum largitionum*. The early form of the Emperor's monogram suggests that this set of stamps, like those on nos. 8 and 9, may belong to the Petrus mentioned in 542 (see p. 28f., note 88 and Table V). The characteristics of the cross stamps also indicate an early date in the reign of Justinian (cf. no. 6).

Principal References: Rosenberg, pp. 702–703; Matsulevich, *Byz. Ant.*, p. 4, no. 5, pp. 79, 115–120, fig. 28, pl. 30.

Source of Illustration: The Hermitage.

a. Plate with Relief of Grazing Horse

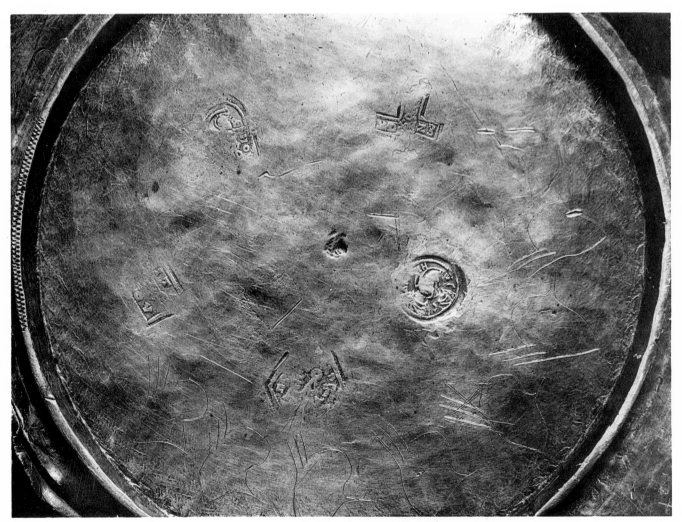

b. The Stamps

a. The Tyler Chalice

b. Round

c. Hexagonal

d. Hexagonal

f. Cruciform

e. Long

The Stamps

No. 8. THE TYLER CHALICE

The Dumbarton Oaks Collection, Washington, D. C.; acc. no. 55.18

DESCRIPTION: Chalice (fig. a) with gilded inscription around brim: + TA CA ЄK TⲰN CⲰN COI ΠPOCΦЄPOMЄN K(υρι)Є.

Wt. 527.7 gr.; diam. 16.8 cm.; ht. 17.4 cm.

PLACE OF DISCOVERY: Said to have been found with the Riha plate (no. 20) in a tomb supposed to be that of a bishop (Bréhier, p. 176). Riha is about 60 km. southeast of Antioch, on the way to Hama (see no. 20).

CONTROL STAMPS: The five stamps – a round, two hexagonal, a long, and a cruciform – were applied before the chalice was finished since they are inside the base where no stamping instrument could easily have reached (text p. 2). The readings of the stamps were taken from the object:

O (fig. b) Bust, type 1; inscribed BAX‖XOV.

O (fig. c) Monogram of Anastasius or Justinian, type b; inscribed ΠIЄN‖[TI]OV.

O (fig. d) Monogram barely visible; inscribed [ΠIЄN]‖TIOV?

O (fig. e) Bust, type 1; the box-type monogram reads ΠЄTPOV and is found again in the cross stamp and in the corresponding stamps of nos. 7, 9–13; inscribed CЄP‖[ΓIOV]? Identical with the corresponding stamp on no. 9.

☩ (fig. f) Square arms; monogram as in long stamp; inscribed in vertical letters Θ‖[Ⲱ]‖MA]‖C ✻; identical with the corresponding stamp on no. 9.

DATE: Justinian I, A.D. 527–565. The secondary monogram probably belongs to Peter (? Barsymes), *comes sacrarum largitionum* in 542 (see no. 7).

Principal References: Bréhier, p. 176 and *passim;* Rosenberg, pp. 700-701; H. Peirce and R. Tyler *Byzantine Art* (London, 1926), p. 26f., pl. xx; G. Downey, *AJA*, LV (1951), p. 351; *DOC*, no. 9.

Source of Illustration: Dumbarton Oaks.

No. 9. PLATE WITH RELIEF OF A SHEPHERD

THE HERMITAGE, LENINGRAD; acc. no. W. 277

DESCRIPTION: Plate with relief of a shepherd with two goats and a dog (fig. a). On the reverse, an ornamental leaf pattern with chalices.

Wt. 1381.1 gr.; diam. 24 cm.; diam. of footring 9.2 cm. (Matsulevich).

PLACE OF DISCOVERY: Klimova, district of Solikamsk, Government of Perm (renamed Molotov in 1942). Found, with nos. 36 and 100, in 1907.

CONTROL STAMPS: Five stamps, on the base – a round, a hexagonal, a square, a long, and a cruciform (fig. b). The hexagon appears to have been damaged during the soldering of the footring (Matsulevich, p. 113). The readings of the stamps were taken from casts and photographs:

O   Bust, type 1; inscription illegible.

O   Monogram of either Anastasius or Justinian, type b (see nos. 6, 7, 8), partially destroyed; there is a small, nimbed bust above the monogram; inscribed [AΘH]NOΓ‖ЄNOV (Matsulevich). The relative position of the inscription to the sides of the hexagon differs from that in the majority of instances in the Imperial series (see nos. 2, 5, 72, 73).

□   Monogram as above; inscription barely legible.

◖   Nimbed bust; monogram reads ΠЄTPOV, and is found again in the cross stamp and in the corresponding stamps of nos. 7, 8, 10–13. According to Matsulevich, the stamp is inscribed CЄP‖ΓIOV, but some of the letters cannot be determined from the reproduction. Identical with the corresponding stamp on no. 8.

✠   Square arms; stamp slipped badly in the striking so that the monogram is displaced; inscribed in vertical letters [ΘѠ)]‖MA‖C✳ (Matsulevich); identical with the corresponding stamp on no. 8.

DATE: The long and cruciform stamps date this piece in the same period as no. 8, Justinian I, A.D. 527–565. The secondary monogram probably belongs to Peter (? Barsymes), *comes sacrarum largitionum* in 542 (see no. 7).

Principal References: Rosenberg, pp. 698–699; Matsulevich, *Byz. Ant.*, p. 4, no. 4, p. 112f., pl. 31f.

Source of Illustration: The Hermitage.

a. Plate with Relief of a Shepherd

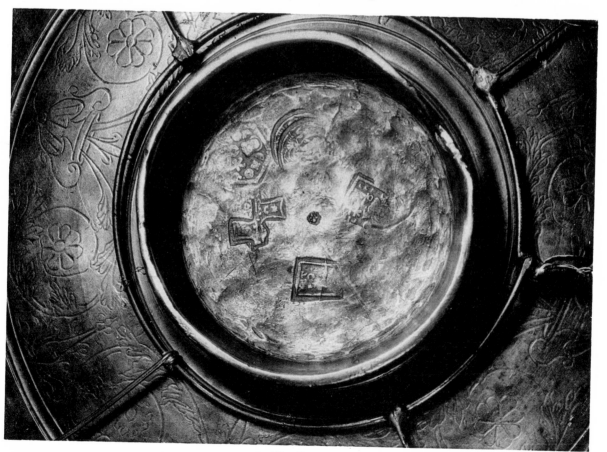

b. The Stamps

a. Fragment of Dish with Relief of Silenus

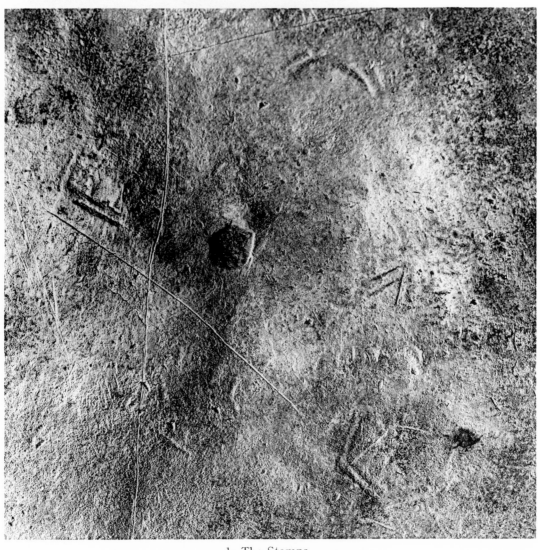

b. The Stamps

No. 10. FRAGMENT OF DISH WITH RELIEF OF SILENUS

THE DUMBARTON OAKS COLLECTION, WASHINGTON, D. C.; acc. no. 51.20

DESCRIPTION: Fragment of platter showing Silenus, reclining, and a dancing satyr playing on a pipe (fig. a).

Wt. 1652 gr.; diam. of plate (originally), *ca.* 55 cm.; diam. of footring, 22.3 cm.

PLACE OF DISCOVERY: This fragment has been traced by Mr. Marvin C. Ross to the collection of L. Pollak in Rome, but no further information is available.

CONTROL STAMPS: Five very indistinct stamps are discernible (fig. b); they are especially worn near the centering point which indicates that the plate was worked after the stamps had been applied. The object was examined in the original:

○   Illegible.

◌   Indistinct.

▢   Indistinct.

▢   (fig. b, upper left) A box-type monogram is clear, and it would appear to belong to the ΠЄΤΡΟV group (nos. 7–9, 11–13).

✠   The arms seem slightly flared; possibly a double strike.

DATE: Justinian I, A.D. 527–565: the box-type monogram in the long stamp dates these stamps not later than the reign of Justinian I, and the flared arms of the cross stamp indicate a date in the latter part of his reign (p. 15f). The ΠЄΤΡΟV monogram, as in nos. 7–9, 11–13, probably belongs to Peter (? Barsymes), *comes sacrarum largitionum*, and the stamps could be either of the period *ca.* 542 or 547–550 (see Table V and p. 28f., note 88).

Principal References: Matsulevich, "Prikam'e," p. 153f., pl. v:1; *idem, B-A,* p. 126, fig. 6; *DOH,* p. 56, no. 132, fig. on p. 63; *DOC,* no. 8.

Source of Illustration: Dumbarton Oaks.

No. 11. ORNAMENTED SALVER

The Hungarian National Museum, Budapest

DESCRIPTION: Fragment of salver with ornamental scroll, leaf motif, and decorative border (fig. a).

Wt. 721.97 gr.; length 24.6 cm.; length of foot 13 cm. (Thomas).

PLACE OF DISCOVERY: Tépe, Bihar, Hungary.

CONTROL STAMPS: On the broken edge of the salver the remains of five stamps are evident – a round, a hexagonal, a square, a long, and a cruciform (figs. b and c). It is not clear from the photograph whether these stamps were applied before or after the decoration was finished. The readings were taken from the photograph and cast:

○   Nimbed bust, type 1; inscribed IOVΛ‖[IANOV].

○   Monogram of Justinian I, type c (p. 13); small bust above monogram; inscribed XPIC[TO]‖ΦOPO[V].

□   Only bottom half remains; monogram of Justinian or Anastasius, type b; inscribed . . . . . . OV.

▯   Bottom half of nimbed bust is clear; monogram like that in the corresponding stamps on nos. 7–10, 12, 13, probably reads ΠETPOV; inscribed [Θ]ω‖M[A] ?

✠   One square arm is seen close to round stamp: part of one letter is visible and appears to be inscribed vertically.

DATE: The monogram in the hexagon belongs to Justinian I, A.D. 527–565. The secondary monogram belongs to Peter as in nos. 7–10, but in this case the later form of the Emperor's monogram suggests a later period. Possibly 547–550 (Table V).

Principal References: Rosenberg, pp. 714–715; Matsulevich, *Byz. Ant.,* p. 8, no. 16, pp. 110, 111, figs. 25, 26; G. Fehér, in the publication by G. László, *Études archéologiques sur l'histoire de la société des Avars = Archaeologia hungarica,* N.S., XXXIV (1955), pp. 255, 256, pls. LVII:1, LVIII; E. B.-Thomas, *Archäologische Funde in Ungarn* (Budapest, 1956), pp. 326, 327.

Source of Illustration: The Hungarian National Museum.

a. Ornamented Salver

b. Cast of Stamps

c. The Stamps

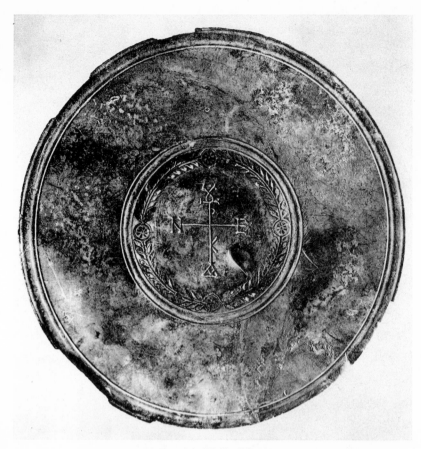

a. Plate with Niello Monogram

b. The Stamps

No. 12. PLATE WITH NIELLO MONOGRAM

EHEM. STAATLICHE MUSEEN, BERLIN-DAHLEM (formerly in the Kaiser-Friedrich Museum)

DESCRIPTION: Fragment of plate with cruciform monogram in center surrounded by wreath with four medallions (fig. a). There is a low footring.*

Diam. 18.5 cm. (Wulff).

PLACE OF DISCOVERY: Purchased in 1908. From Binbir-Kilisse, Asia Minor.

CONTROL STAMPS: Five stamps – a round, a hexagonal, a square, a long, and a cruciform; these were damaged when the niello design, which breaks into the stamps, was worked (fig. b). With the possible exception of the long stamp, all are identical with the stamps on no. 13. The readings were taken from the photograph and the interpretation of the inscriptions was derived from comparison with the stamps on no. 13:

○   Bust, type 1(?); inscribed ΔAN‖[NO]V.

○   Monogram of Justinian I, type c (p. 13); small, nimbed bust above monogram; inscribed [NI]‖ΛOV.

□   Monogram of Justinian I, as above, in reverse; inscribed ΛOV‖KA.

○   Bust, type 1; monogram barely discernible; inscribed EV[Γ‖ENIOV]? (see no. 7).

✚   Arms slightly flared; monogram, like that in the corresponding stamps of nos. 7–11, 13, reads ΠETPOV (the P seems to be missing); inscribed ✚ A‖[NΔ‖PE‖O]V.

DATE: Justinian I, A.D. 527–565. The secondary monogram may belong to Peter, 547–550 (see no. 11). A late date in Justinian's reign is suggested by the flared arms of the cross; the cruciform monogram on the face of the plate belongs to a period after *ca.* 536 (p. 16).

Principal References: O. Wulff, *Altchristliche Bildwerke,* I (Berlin, 1909), no. 1107 and pl. LVII; Rosenberg, pp. 718–719; Matsulevich, "Arg. byz.," p. 295; H. Schlunk, *Kunst der Spätantike im Mittelmeerraum* (Berlin, 1939), no. 110.

Source of Illustration: Ehem. Staatliche Museen, Berlin-Dahlem.

* Wulff, p. 227: "Schalenboden...Kreisrund mit niedrigem Ringfuss; ringsum gebrochen und die Ränder schadhaft, nahe der Mitte Eindruck eines scharfen Werkzeuges; die Niellomasse z.T. ausgefallen (aus dem Monogramm gänzlich); die Stempel der Rückseite z.T. von dem durchgedrückten Relief der niellierten Teile wieder weggepresst."

No. 13. THE CUP OF SYMEONIOS

DESCRIPTION: Chalice with gilded inscription around brim (fig. a): + VΠЄP ЄVXHC K(αι) CⲰTHPIAC CVMЄⲰNIOV MAΓICTP(ου) K(αι) TⲰN ΔIAФЄPONTⲰN AVTⲰ.

Diam. 12.3 cm.; ht. 13 cm. (*WAG*).

PLACE OF DISCOVERY: Found in 1910 in Hama, Syria, with nos. 34, 89, 98, and possibly nos. 18 and 80 (p. 20).

CONTROL STAMPS: Five stamps – a round, a hexagonal, a square, a long, and a cruciform; all, with the possible exception of the long, are identical with the stamps on no. 12. They are found in the base of the chalice where no stamping instrument could easily have reached and must have been applied, therefore, before the chalice was finally fashioned (see no. 8). The readings were taken from the object:

O   (fig. b) Nimbed bust, type 1(?); inscribed ΔAN‖NOV.

O   (fig. c) Monogram of Justinian I, as in the corresponding stamp of no. 12; small nimbed bust; inscribed NI‖ΛOV.

□   (fig. d) Reversed monogram of Emperor as on the square stamp of no. 12; inscribed ΛOV‖KA.

◻   (figs. b, e) Bust, type 1; box-type monogram belongs to the ΠЄTPOV group, as do the monograms in the cross stamp and the corresponding stamps of nos. 7–12; inscription in this stamp is barely legible.

✠   (figs. c, e) Arms very slightly flared as in cruciform stamp of no. 12; monogram as above; inscribed [+ A‖NΔ]‖PЄ‖OV.

DATE: Justinian I, A.D. 527–565. Secondary monogram belongs to Peter, possibly 547–550 (see no. 11).

Principal References: Diehl, p. 106, no. 2, pl. XIX:1; Rosenberg, pp. 728–729 (no stamps published); *WAG*, no. 395; Downey, *AJA*, LV (1951), p. 350.

Source of Illustration: The Walters Art Gallery.

a. The Cup of Symeonios

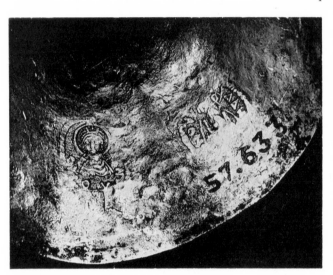

b. Long and Round

c. Hexagonal and Cruciform

d. Square

e. Cruciform and Long

The Stamps

a. *Trulla* from Cherchel

b. Stamps on the Base

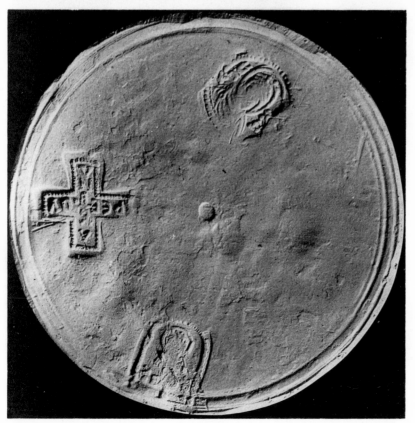

d. Hexagonal Stamp on Handle

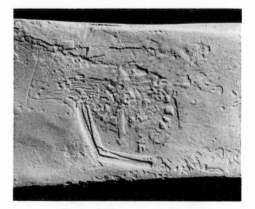

c. Cast of Stamps

e. Cast of Hexagonal Stamp

No. 14. *TRULLA* FROM CHERCHEL

THE LOUVRE, PARIS

DESCRIPTION: *Trulla* with gilded relief of fishermen and sea creatures on the outside of the bowl. Figure of Poseidon, standing on the back of a dolphin and holding a trident, decorates the handle (fig. a).

Wt. 1670 gr.; diam. 15 cm.; length of handle 15 cm. (Matsulevich).

PLACE OF DISCOVERY: Cherchel, Algeria.

CONTROL STAMPS: Five stamps – four on bottom of bowl (fig. b) include one round, slight remains of a square—barely visible on the cast (fig. c)—one long, and one cruciform; the fifth, a hexagon, is on the handle (figs. d and e). The stamps must have been applied before the bowl was finished, since the long stamp is cut by the incised circles on the bottom of the bowl. The readings were taken from the object:

O   Bust, type 1; inscribed KOC∥MA.

O   Monogram of Anastasius or Justinian, type a(?); small, nimbed bust above mono- gram; inscription illegible.

□   Not clear.

O   Bust, type 1; cruciform monogram; inscribed IOV∥[ΛI]O[V].

✠   Square arms; cruciform monogram as above, EVCEBIOV(?); inscribed A∥NΔ∥PE∥ OV (see the corresponding stamps on nos. 12 and 13. There is, however, no cross before the inscription as in the stamps on no. 12 and, perhaps, on no. 13).

DATE: Since the cruciform monogram in the long and cross stamps precludes a date in the reign of Anastasius, the imperial monogram in the hexagon may be assigned to Justinian I, A.D. 527–565 (p. 16). Moreover, the cruciform monogram, and the relationship between the cross stamp on the *trulla* and the corresponding stamps on nos. 12 and 13 suggest a date close to that of the ΠETPOV group (nos. 7–13). The square arms of the cruciform stamp suggests that these stamps could be earlier than those on nos. 10, 12, 13, that is, before *ca.* 547 (p. 15).

Principal References: Rosenberg, pp. 617, 680–681; Matsulevich, *Byz. Ant.*, p. 8, no. 15, pp. 71–75, figs. 7, 8; Peirce and Tyler, *L'art byz.*, II, p. 120, pl. 156.

Source of Illustration: The Louvre.

No. 15. PLATE FROM UST'-KISHERT'

THE HERMITAGE, LENINGRAD; acc. no. W. 351

DESCRIPTION: A simple plate with stylized rosette ornament in center surrounded by foliate design (fig. a).

Wt. 240 gr.; diam. 19.8 cm.; diam. of footring, 8.8 cm.; ht. of footring, 0.7 cm. (Matsulevich).

PLACE OF DISCOVERY: Found in 1916, in Ust'-Kishert', near Kungur, Government of Perm (renamed Molotov in 1942). Formerly in the Letunov Collection and the Museum of Kungur. Acquired in 1926.

CONTROL STAMPS: Five stamps – a round, a hexagonal, a square, a long, and a cruciform (figs. b and c). Matsulevich indicates that they were applied before the decoration was finished (p. 114). The readings are based on the photographs and cast:

O   Nimbed bust, type 1; inscribed ANT[O‖NIOV].

O   Monogram of Justinian I; type c (see nos. 12–13); small, nimbed bust above the monogram; inscribed ΛO[V]‖KA.

☐   As the result of a double strike the right-hand bar of the monogram appears twice. It is possible, however, to distinguish a monogram of the Anastasius-Justinian type; inscription illegible.

O   Bust, type 1(?); the cruciform monogram reads IOVΛIANOV and is found again in the cross stamp and in the corresponding stamps of no. 16; inscribed ....‖ AKTOV?

✠   Flared arms; monogram as above; inscribed IW‖[AN]‖N‖OV.

DATE: The flared arms of the cross and the cruciform secondary monogram place these stamps late in the reign of Justinian I, A.D. 527–565 (p. 15f., and nos. 12–14); this conclusion is supported by the relationship between these stamps and the stamps of no. 16. The secondary monogram may belong to Julian, *comes sacrarum largitionum*, whose period of office is not known (Table V).

Principal References: Rosenberg, pp. 716–717; Matsulevich, *Byz. Ant.*, p. 5, no. 7, pp. 76, 114, fig. 27, pl. 29.

Source of Illustration: The Hermitage.

82

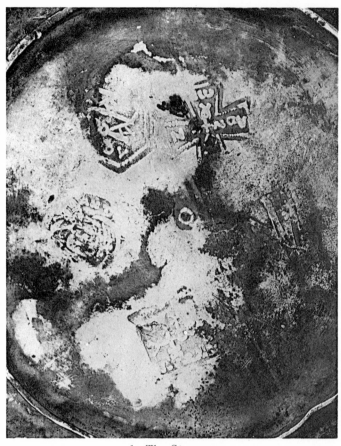

b. The Stamps

a. Plate from Ust'-Kishert'

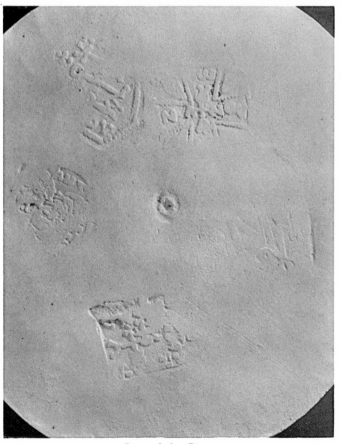

c. Cast of the Stamps

a. Plate with Relief of Venus in the Tent of Anchises

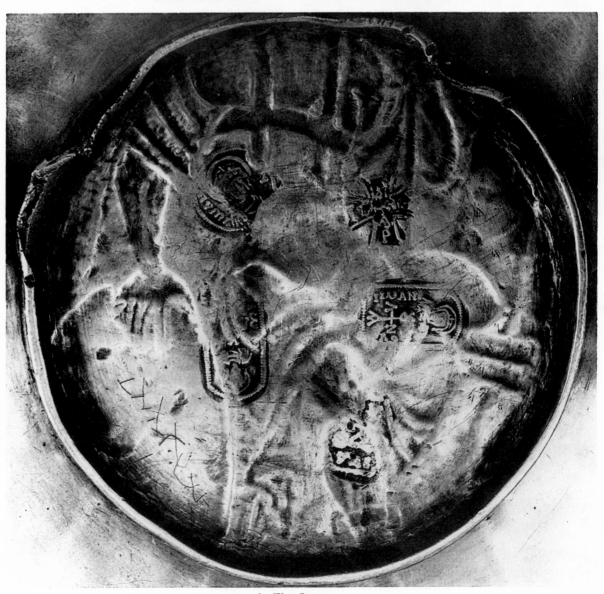

b. The Stamps

No. 16. PLATE WITH RELIEF OF VENUS IN THE TENT OF ANCHISES

THE HERMITAGE, LENINGRAD; acc. no. W. 350

DESCRIPTION: Plate with relief depicting Venus in the tent of Anchises (fig. a).

Wt. 837 gr.; diam. 26.5 cm.; diam. of footring 11 cm. (Matsulevich).

PLACE OF DISCOVERY: Found in 1925 in Kopchiki, near Kungur, Government of Perm (renamed Molotov in 1942).

CONTROL STAMPS: Five stamps – a round, a hexagonal, two long, and a cruciform (fig. b) which appear to be damaged by subsequent working of the relief on the front of the plate; for example, the line of the shield cuts into one of the long stamps. The readings were taken from the cast and photograph:

O   Bust, type 1; inscribed IѠAN‖[N]OV; identical with the corresponding stamps on nos. 17 and, possibly, 20, 21, and 22.

◯   Monogram of Anastasius or Justinian, type b; inscribed ITA‖[Λ]OV. This name is also found in the square stamps of no. 7, no. 17*A*, *B*, and no. 25.

◻   Bust, type 1; monogram IOVΛIANOV as in the cross stamp, and also in the corresponding stamps of no. 15; inscribed IѠAN‖NOV.

◻   Same as above, less clear.

✠   Flared arms; monogram as above; inscribed in vertical letters [CЄ]‖P‖ΓI‖OV (see the corresponding stamps on no. 17).

DATE: The relationship between these stamps and those on no. 15 dates them in the same period, late in the reign of Justinian I, A.D. 527–565. The relationships with succeeding numbers support their assignment to the latter part of the reign, that is, after *ca.* A.D. 550. The secondary monogram may belong to Julian, *comes sacrarum largitionum*, whose period of office is not known (Table V).

Principal References: Rosenberg, pp. 688–689; Matsulevich, *Byz. Ant.*, p. 3f., no. 3, pp. 25–31, pl. 3f.

Source of Illustration: The Hermitage.

No. 17 *A* and *B*. THE HERMITAGE RELIQUARY

THE HERMITAGE, LENINGRAD

DESCRIPTION: Reliquary with high lid decorated with two crosses (fig. a). It once contained a second reliquary in gold. On the sides, roundels with busts: Christ between Saints Peter and Paul, and the Virgin between two archangels; at each end, one saint in roundel, possibly Saints George and Demetrius. All figures are nimbed.

Ht. of box 6.5 cm.; ht. of box with lid 10 cm.; length 12 cm.; width 8 cm. (Rosenberg).

PLACE OF DISCOVERY: Found in 1897 in the excavations of a cruciform church in the ancient city of Chersonesus, Crimea.

CONTROL STAMPS: Two identical sets of four stamps – one group on bottom of box (fig. b) and one inside the lid (figs. c and d). In both the hexagonal is missing and in each group there is one round, one square, one long, and one cruciform. The cross in relief on the lid of the box breaks into the lines of one of the cross stamps which makes it evident that the reliquary was stamped before it was decorated, for the lines of the cross stamp are clearest in the hollow of the relief. The readings were taken from the photographs and one cast:

O   17 *A, bottom of reliquary:*
Nimbed bust; inscribed IѠA[N‖NOV] (see the corresponding stamps on nos. 16, 20, 21, 22).

□   Monogram of Justinian, type c; inscribed ITA‖[ΛOV] (see 17 *B*, and nos. 7, 16, 25).

◠   Nimbed bust; illegible cruciform monogram; inscribed ΠAV‖[ΛOV].

✠   Flared arms; cruciform monogram like the monogram in the long and cross stamps of 17 *B*, 18; inscribed C‖[EP]‖ΓI‖OV.

O   17 *B, top of reliquary:*
Nimbed bust; inscription illegible.

□   Monogram of Justinian, type c; inscribed [ITA]‖ΛOV (see above).

◠   Nimbed bust; cruciform monogram like that in the cross stamp, also found in the corresponding stamps of 17 *A*, 18; inscribed [Π]AV‖ΛO[V] (see above).

✠   Same as in 17 *A*.

DATE: Justinian I, A.D. 527–565. The relationship of the round stamps to the corresponding stamps on nos. 16, 20, 21, 22, and the fact that the inscribed name in the square is the same as that in the hexagon of no. 16, place the stamps in the latter part of Justinian's reign, after *ca.* A.D. 550.

Principal References: Rosenberg, pp. 704–705; N. Bêlaev, "Le reliquaire de Chersonèse," *Seminarium Kondakovianum,* III (Prague, 1929), pp. 115–131, pls. XVIII, XIX; résumé in French, pp. 131–132.

Source of Illustration: The Hermitage.

a. The Hermitage Reliquary

b. Stamps on Bottom of Reliquary

c. Square and Round

d. Cruciform and Long

Stamps on inside of Lid of Reliquary

a. The Chalice of St. Anne

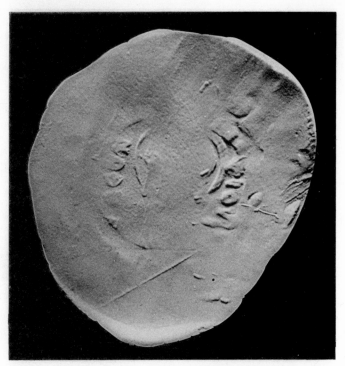

b. Cast of Round Stamp

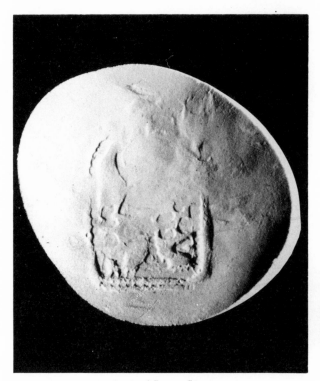

c. Cast of Long Stamp

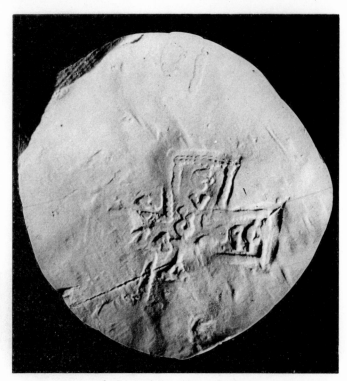

d. Cast of Cruciform Stamp

No. 18. THE CHALICE OF ST. ANNE

THE CONVENT OF ST. ANNE, JERUSALEM

DESCRIPTION: Chalice (fig. a) with gilded inscription around the brim: + VΠЄP ЄVXHC HΛIѠΔѠPOV K(αι) AKAKIOV TЄKNON ѲѠMA AMA TѠN ΔIAΦЄPONT[Ѡ]N AVTOIC (Skehan).

Ht. 19 cm. (Skehan).

PLACE OF DISCOVERY: Said to be from Kara, between Hama and Aleppo. This is almost certainly the actual find-spot of the famous "Antioch" and "Hama" treasures (see nos. 13, 34, 89, 98, and possibly no. 80), but there is no record of this chalice among the descriptions of these two treasures (see p. 20).

CONTROL STAMPS: "Inside the base are four stamps..." (letter of March 23, 1956, to Prof. G. Downey from Father Skehan, who was then at the American School of Oriental Research in Jerusalem). Casts of three stamps—a round, a long, and a cruciform—were taken by Prof. Henri Seyrig. The stamps are inside the foot of the chalice, as in the Tyler Chalice, no. 8, and, as in the case of the Tyler Chalice and of nos. 13 and 34, they were surely applied before the object was finished. The readings of the stamps were taken from the casts:

○   (fig. b) Nimbed bust; inscribed + ΛЄON‖TIOV.

◠   (fig. c) Nimbed bust; cruciform monogram like that in the cross stamp and like the monograms in the corresponding stamps on nos. 17A and B; inscription barely legible.

⊕   (fig. d) Flared arms; monogram as above; vertical lettering ЄV‖ΦPO‖N [I‖OV?].

DATE: The flared arms of the cross, the vertical lettering, the cruciform monograms, and the relationship between these monograms and the monograms in the corresponding stamps of no. 17 place these stamps in Justinian's reign, A.D. 527–565, and probably in the latter part, after ca. A.D. 550.

Principal References: J. Braun, *Das christliche Altargerät* (Munich, 1932), p. 78, pl. 11: 32.

Source of Illustration: Braun, *op. cit.* (fig. a); Dumbarton Oaks Photographic Collection (figs. b–d).

No. 19. CANDLESTICK

THE BRITISH MUSEUM, LONDON

DESCRIPTION: Slender candlestick or lampstand with no ornament (fig. a).

Wt. 333 gr.; ht. 20.8 cm.

PLACE OF DISCOVERY: Lampsacus, Hellespont. Found with nos. 24, 52, and 53. Acquired in 1848.

CONTROL STAMPS: Five stamps – a hexagonal, a square, a long, and two cruciform. They were applied before the base of the candlestick was finally fashioned, since they are stamped on the inside of the hollowed lobes of the base where no stamping instrument could have been applied without flattening out the lobe (see no. 90). The readings were taken from the object:

⬠   Overlapping one of the cross stamps (fig. b): the monogram is just discernible near the initial letters CЄ of the cross stamp inscribed CЄ[BA]CTOC. This stamp is clear enough to permit recognition of the Anastasius-Justinian type of monogram. There may possibly be an additional stroke in the A, which would make it a monogram belonging to Justinian alone, type c (cf. p. 13); the inscription in this stamp is not clear.

▢   In one of the lobes of the candlestick base near the long stamp (fig. d): barely legible.

⌂   Distinguishable by the remains of a small bust, a slightly arched rim, and part of the right-hand inscription (fig. d). Illegible.

✠   (fig. b) Flared arms; monogram not clear; inscribed in vertical letters CЄ‖[BA]‖ CT‖OC; see the inscription in the corresponding stamp of no.27, and in the long stamp of no. 25.

✠   (fig. c) Similar to above; less clear.

DATE: The monogram in the hexagon belongs to Anastasius I or Justinian I. The flared arms of the cross and the vertical letters date this group of stamps not earlier than the last half of the reign of Justinian I, A.D. 527–565. The relationship between the cross stamps and the corresponding stamp on no. 27 from the reign of Justin II support a late date in Justinian's reign.

Principal References: Dalton, *Catalogue,* p. 81, no. 376, pl. XXII; Rosenberg, pp. 712–713.

Source of Illustration: The British Museum, reproduction courtesy of the Trustees.

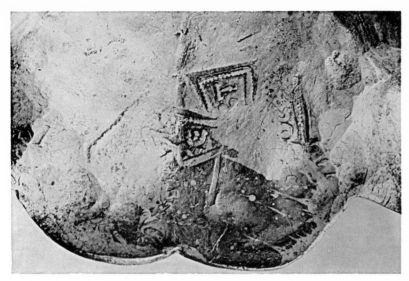

b. Hexagonal and Cruciform Stamps

a. Candlestick

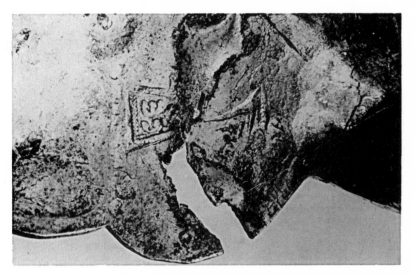

c. Cruciform Stamp

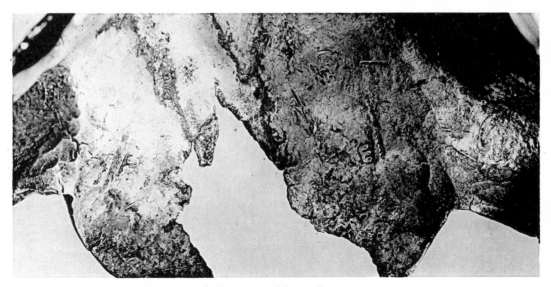

d. Square and Long Stamps

OBJECTS WITH IMPERIAL STAMPS FROM THE REIGN OF JUSTIN II, A.D. 565–578

a. The Riha Paten

b. The Stamps

No. 20. THE RIHA PATEN

THE DUMBARTON OAKS COLLECTION, WASHINGTON, D. C.; acc. no. 24.5

DESCRIPTION: Silver gilded paten with relief representing the Communion of the Apostles (fig. a). Inscribed around the rim: + VΠEP ΑΝΑΠΑVϹEⲰϹ ϹEΡΓΙΑϹ ΙⲰΑΝΝΟV Κ(αι) ΘEΟΔΟϹΙΟV Κ(αι) ϹⲰΤΗΡΙΑϹ ΜEΓΑΛΟV Κ(αι) ΝΟΝΝΟV Κ(αι) ΤⲰΝ ΑVΤⲰΝ ΤEΚΝⲰΝ.

Wt. 904 gr.; diam. 35 cm.

PLACE OF DISCOVERY: The village of Riha, 60 km. southeast of Antioch. Found with no. 21; also with no. 8? and probably with nos. 22, 27, and 29.*

CONTROL STAMPS: Four, possibly five stamps – a round, a square, a long, and a cruciform, clearly visible, and perhaps the remains of a hexagonal (fig. b). The stamps were applied before the relief was finished since they are clearest were the relief is deepest. The readings were taken from the object and were compared with the identical stamps on nos. 21 and 22:

○ On the altar cloth, at the right-hand front edge of the altar; the double strike displaces the left-hand side of the inscription: nimbed bust; inscribed ΙⲰΑΝ‖ΝΟV.

◖ Only a beaded corner remains, just below the outstretched arm of the Christ on the left.

□ On the front of the altar cloth; double strike: monogram of Justin II, type a (p. 13 f.); inscribed ΔⲰΡΟ‖[ΘEΟV].

⬠ On the altar cloth, just below the left-hand Christ; double strike: nimbed bust, type 1; cruciform monogram may be read ΘEΟΔⲰΡΟV and is identical with the monogram in the cross stamp and with the monogram in the corresponding stamps on nos. 21–26; inscribed [ΙⲰΑΝ‖Ν]ΟV (see nos. 21, 22).

✠ On the lower part of the right-hand Christ: flared arms; monogram as above; inscribed ΔΙ‖ΟΜ‖Ι [Δ]‖ΟV.

DATE: Justin II, A. D. 565–578. The secondary monogram on nos. 20–26 may belong to Theodorus Petri, *comes sacrarum largitionum* in A. D. 577 (p. 29; Table V).

Principal References: Bréhier, p. 176 and *passim;* Rosenberg, pp. 686–687; *DOH,* p. 55, no. 129, fig. on p. 68.; *DOC,* no. 10.

Source of Illustration: Dumbarton Oaks.

* The evidence suggesting that the objects said to have been found at Riha and Stuma respectively are parts of a single treasure will be discussed by M. C. Ross in vol. I of the Catalogue of the Byzantine and Early Mediaeval Antiquities in the Dumbarton Oaks Collection, which is forthcoming.

No. 21. THE RIHA FLABELLUM

THE DUMBARTON OAKS COLLECTION, WASHINGTON, D. C.; acc. no. 36.23

DESCRIPTION: Flabellum with peacock-feathered border (figs. a and b); in the center, a tetramorph having four wings (with eyes), hands, feet, and wheels of fire (cf. Ezek. 1:5ff.).

Wt. 485 gr.; ht. 30.9 cm.; width 25.5 cm.

PLACE OF DISCOVERY: Found in Riha, Syria, with no. 20, and probably with no. 8, and nos. 22, 27, and 29 (see no. 20).

CONTROL STAMPS: Four stamps, clearly visible – a round, a square, a long, and a cruciform, and possibly the remains of a hexagonal obscured by the square on the right-hand side of the handle (fig. c). The decoration of the peacock-feathered border cuts into the cross stamp at the top, indicating that the silver was stamped before it was decorated. The stamps are identical with those on nos. 20, 22. The readings were taken from the object:

O   Nimbed bust, type 1; inscribed IѠAN‖NOV.

O   ?

□   Monogram of Justin II, type a; inscribed ΔѠPO‖[ΘЄ]OV.

◻   Nimbed bust; cruciform monogram as in the cross stamp, ΘЄOΔѠPOV, and found again in the corresponding stamps on nos. 20, 22–26; inscribed IѠAN‖[N]OV.

✠   A double strike has disfigured the monogram which is the same as that above; flared arms; inscribed in vertical letters ΔI‖OM‖IΔ‖OV.

DATE: Justin II, A.D. 565–578. Theodorus Petri was *comes sacrarum largitionum* in A.D. 577 (see no. 20).

Principal References: Rosenberg, pp. 684–685; *DOH*, p. 54, no. 128, fig. on p. 67; *DOC*, no. 11.

Source of Illustration: Dumbarton Oaks.

a. Front

b. Back

The Riha Flabellum

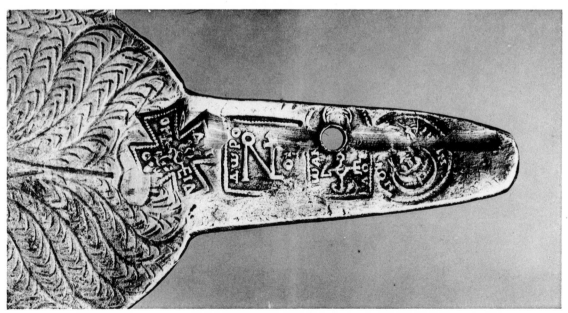

c. The Stamps

a. The Stuma Flabellum

b. Cast of Stamps

No. 22. THE STUMA FLABELLUM

THE ARCHAEOLOGICAL MUSEUM, ISTANBUL; acc. no. 3758

DESCRIPTION: Flabellum with peacock-feathered border (fig. a); in the center, cherubim, or seraphim, with six wings (eyeless), hands and feet, and wheels of fire.

Diam. 25 cm. (Rosenberg).

PLACE OF DISCOVERY: Allegedly from the village of Stuma, near Riha, Syria. Found with nos. 27, 29, and also, probably, with nos. 8, 20, 21 (see no. 20).

CONTROL STAMPS: Four stamps are visible on the front of the object – a round, a square, a long, and a cruciform (fig. b); identical with the corresponding stamps on nos. 20, 21. There may be the remains of a hexagonal between the cross and the long. The decoration was incised after the stamps were applied, since the feather at the base of the fan is not finished around the cross stamp. The readings were taken from the cast and photograph:

O   Nimbed bust, type 1; inscribed IѠAN‖N[OV].

□   Incomplete monogram of Justin II, type a (see nos. 20, 21); inscribed [ΔѠPO]‖ ΘЄOV.

◠   Nimbed bust; monogram ΘЄOΔѠPOV as in the cross stamp, and also in the corresponding stamps of nos. 20, 21, 23–26; inscribed [IѠAN‖N]OV.

✠   Flared arms; monogram as above; inscribed in vertical letters ΔI‖[OM]‖IΔ‖OV.

DATE: Justin II, A.D. 565–578; Theodorus Petri was *comes sacrarum largitionum* in A.D. 577 (see no. 20).

Principal References: Ebersolt (see no. 27); Rosenberg, pp. 682–683.

Source of Illustration: Giraudon (fig. a); Dumbarton Oaks Photographic Collection (fig. b; from cast taken by the Byzantine Institute, by permission of Dr. Rüstem Duyuran, Archaeological Museum, Istanbul).

No. 23. PLAIN BOWL

DESCRIPTION: Plain, deep bowl with no decorative relief (fig. a).

Diam. 8.4 cm.; ht. 4.4 cm.; diam. of base 5.6 cm. (Matsulevich).

PLACE OF DISCOVERY: Found at Martynovtsy, near Kiev.

CONTROL STAMPS: There are at least five stamps, but the individual shapes are not easily distinguishable (fig. b). The long stamp has been struck twice. There appear to be, in addition, a hexagonal, a square, and a cross. It is difficult to say whether they were applied before or after the vessel was finished, but they seem to have been damaged in the process of beating the bottom of the bowl (see the cross stamp). The readings of the stamps are based on what is visible in the photograph, and on the interpretations of Matsulevich given below:

○   Beneath the left-hand long stamp. Illegible.

□   Monogram partially visible, probably that of Justin II, type a; inscribed [CV]ME‖ωN[IC] (Matsulevich) or [CVM]Є‖ωN[HC]? (see the long stamp, no. 24).

○   Nimbed bust; monogram ΘЄ[OΔ]ω[POV] (Matsulevich*), as in the cross stamp, and found again in the corresponding stamps of nos. 20–22, 24–26; inscribed [CVMЄω]NIC (Matsulevich*).

○   Same as above (Matsulevich).

⌖   Flared arms; monogram as above; inscribed Iω‖[AN]‖N‖OV (Matsulevich).

DATE: Justin II, A.D. 565–578; Theodorus Petri was *comes sacrarum largitionum* in A.D. 577 (see no. 20).

Principal References: N. Fettich, "Die Metallkunst der landnehmenden Ungarn," *Archaeologia hungarica*, XXI (1937), p. 283, pl. CXXIV, 2; Matsulevich, "Prikam'e," p. 152 f., pl. V, fig. 2; idem, *B-A*, p. 125 f., fig. 5; N. Fettich, *Archäologische Studien zur Geschichte der späthunnischen Metallkunst = Archaeologia hungarica*, XXXI (1951), p. 134.

Source of Illustration: The Hermitage.

* Matsulevich considers the fragment containing the monogram and the inscribed name as part of a separate (square) stamp.

a. Plain Bowl

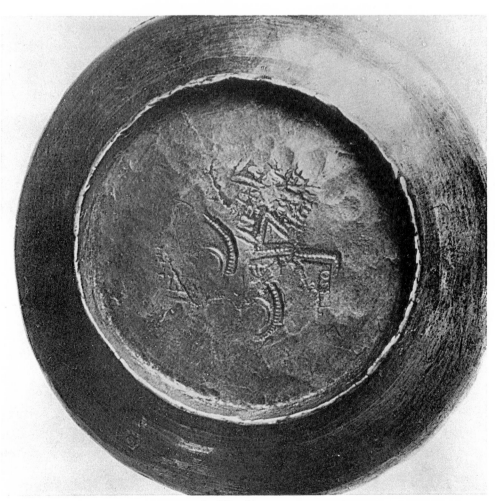

b. The Stamps

a. Pendant Lamp Dish

b. The Stamps

No. 24. PENDANT LAMP DISH

DESCRIPTION: Low dish in fragmentary condition with pierced decoration consisting of monogram of Christ (?) in the center, and crosses alternating with palmette design around the rim (fig. a). Lamp is suspended on three chains.

Diam. 24.8 cm.; diam. of inside depression 16.9 cm.; diam. of base 14.4 cm.

PLACE OF DISCOVERY: Lampsacus, Hellespont. Found with nos. 19, 52, and 53. Acquired in 1848.

CONTROL STAMPS: Since most of the central part of the base is lost, only two stamps remain – a round and a long (fig. b). Circular marks of the lathe cut into the stamps, indicating that they were worn when the dish was being polished before it was finished; the readings were taken from the object:

O   Nimbed bust, type 1; inscribed ΔOV......

◯   Nimbed bust; monogram ΘЄOΔѠPOV, as in the corresponding stamps on nos. 20–23, 25; inscribed CV[MЄ]‖ѠNHC. The right-hand side of the inscription has slipped in the striking. See the square and long stamps of no. 23.

DATE: The relationship between the secondary monogram and the corresponding monograms on nos. 20–23, 25, 26 places these stamps also in the reign of Justin II, A.D. 565–578; Theodorus Petri was *comes sacrarum largitionum* in A.D. 577 (see no. 20).

Principal References: Dalton, *Catalogue*, no. 393.

Source of Illustration: The British Museum, reproduction courtesy of the Trustees.

No. 25. INSCRIBED PLATE WITH CROSS

COLLECTION OF MR. AND MRS. PAUL MALLON, NEW YORK

DESCRIPTION: Plate with cross in center (fig. a). Inscribed around the cross: + ΥΠΕΡ ΕΥΧΗС ΚΑΙ СωΤΗΡΙΑС ΑΓΑΘΑΓΓΕΛΟΥ ΚΑΙ ΘΕΟΔωΡΟΥ ΕΞΚΟΥΒΙΤΟΡΟС.

Diam. 37–37.8 cm.; diam. of base 26.4 cm.

PLACE OF DISCOVERY: Said to have been found near Latakia, Syria.

CONTROL STAMPS: Five stamps – a round, a hexagonal, a square, a long, and a cruciform. It is not easy to determine whether the stamps were applied before or after the decoration of the plate, but they appear to have been damaged during a subsequent beating of the silver. The readings were taken from the object:

O (fig. b) Bust, type 1; inscribed ΕΘΕ‖ΡΙ[ΟΥ].

⬡ (fig. c) Monogram of Justin II, type a; small, nimbed bust above the monogram; inscribed ΙωΑΝ‖ΝΟΥ.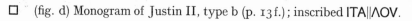

□ (fig. d) Monogram of Justin II, type b (p. 13 f.); inscribed ΙΤΑ‖ΛΟΥ.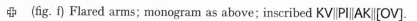

⬭ (fig. e) Nimbed bust; monogram ΘΕΟΔωΡΟΥ like the monogram in the cross stamp, and found again in the corresponding stamps of nos. 20–24, 26; inscribed [СΕ]Β[Α]‖СΤΟΥ? (see the inscribed names in the cross stamps of nos. 19 and 27).

⬤ (fig. f) Flared arms; monogram as above; inscribed ΚΥ‖ΡΙ‖ΑΚ‖[ΟΥ].

DATE: Justin II, A.D. 565–578; Theodorus Petri was *comes sacrarum largitio num* in A.D. 577 (see no. 20).

Unpublished.

Source of Illustration: Dumbarton Oaks Photographic Collection.

a. Inscribed Plate with Cross

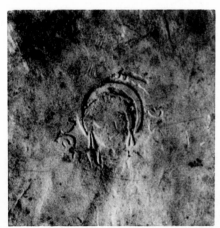

b. Round   c. Hexagonal   d. Square

e. Long   f. Cruciform

The Stamps

a. Dish with Relief of "Euthenia"

b. The Stamps

No. 26. DISH WITH RELIEF OF "EUTHENIA"

PRESENT LOCATION UNKNOWN

DESCRIPTION: Fragment of deep plate with relief in repoussé representing personification of "Abundance" (fig. a).

PLACE OF DISCOVERY: Kama River region, Russia. Formerly in the Alin Collection (Matsulevich).

CONTROL STAMPS: Five stamps are visible on the photograph reproduced by Matsulevich – a round, a hexagonal, two long, and a cruciform (fig. b). From their positions in the hollows of the relief it is evident, as in the case of the Riha paten, no. 20, that they were applied before the relief was beaten out. The readings were taken from the published illustration and from Matsulevich's text:

○   On the right-hand shoulder of the bust. Almost obliterated.

◌   On the right-hand shoulder, below the round stamp: monogram of Justin II, type a; inscription not clear.

◠   Above the line of fruit, below and to the left of the hexagon: nimbed bust just distinguishable with three-pronged diadem, type 1.

◠   A little lower, to the left: same as the above, less clear.

✠   On the left-hand shoulder of the figure near the neck: monogram ΘΕΟΔѠΡΟV is discernible, corresponding to monograms on nos. 21–25; inscribed ΕV‖[ΓΕ]‖ΝΙ‖ OV, according to Matsulevich; all of the letters cannot be made out in the reproduction and it is not clear whether they are inscribed vertically or in a clockwise direction around the arms of the cross.

DATE: Justin II, A.D. 565–578; Theodorus Petri was *comes sacrarum largitionum* in A.D. 577 (see no. 20).

Principal References: Matsulevich, "Prikam'e," p. 151 ff., pl. IV: 1, 2; *idem, B-A*, pp. 123–126, fig. 4; Kitzinger (1958), p. 4.

Source of Illustration: Matsulevich, "Prikam'e."

No. 27. THE STUMA PATEN

THE ARCHAEOLOGICAL MUSEUM, ISTANBUL; acc. no. 3759

DESCRIPTION: Gilded silver paten with relief representing the Communion of the Apostles (fig. a); inscribed around the rim: + VΠEP EVXHC K(αι) C[ωTHPIA]C CEPΓIOV T[OV] APΓVPOΠPATOV K(αι) ANAΠAVCEωC MAPIAC THC AVTOV CVMBIOV K(αι) TωN AVTωN ΓωNEωN.

Diam. 37 cm. (Ebersolt).

PLACE OF DISCOVERY: From the village of Stuma, near Riha, Syria. Found with nos. 22 and 29, and also, probably, with nos. 8, 20, 21 (see no. 20).

CONTROL STAMPS: Five stamps on back of paten – a round, a hexagonal, a square, a long, and a cruciform (fig. b). As in the case of the Riha paten (no. 20), the stamps must have been applied before the relief was formed, since, for example, the hexagon on the back of the apostle bending over at the left is clearest where the relief is deepest, which could not have been so had the stamp been struck after the relief was hollowed out. The readings were taken from the photograph and from casts:

O (fig. c) On the draped arm and back of the left-hand Christ: nimbed bust with circular ornament on the crown, type 2; inscribed CTEΦ‖ANOV.

O (fig. d) On the back of the bending apostle on the left: monogram of Justin II, type a; inscribed MEΓA‖ΛOV. See also no. 29. There is a small bust above the monogram.

□ (fig. e) On the draped arm and back of the right-hand Christ: monogram as above; inscription damaged.

⊓ (fig. f.) On the hands and chin of the apostle, on the left, bending over: monogram ΠETPOV, as in the cross stamp, and found again in the corresponding stamps of no. 28; inscribed Iω[A]‖NN[IC]. This stamp is similar to the long stamp on no. 28, but the placement of the letters is slightly different.

⊹ (fig. g) On the altar cloth to the right of the long stamp: flared arms; the double strike has disfigured the monogram ΠETPOV; inscribed in a circular direction +CE‖[BA]‖CT‖[OV] (see no. 19).

DATE: Justin II, A.D. 565–578. The diadem of the imperial bust and the inscription in the cross stamp date these stamps after the ΘEOΔωPOV group, nos. 20–26. This date is supported by the relationship between the long stamp in this group and the corresponding stamp on no. 28: thus, A.D. 577–578 (p. 30).

Principal References: Ebersolt, "Le trésor de Stuma," *Revue archéologique*, XVII (1911), pp. 407–419; Bréhier, p. 174 and *passim.*; Peirce and Tyler, *L'art byz.*, II, pl. 140; Kitzinger (1958), pp. 18–19, fig. 19.

Source of Illustration: Archaeological Museum (fig. a); Giraudon (fig. b); Dumbarton Oaks Photographic Collection (figs. c–g; from casts taken by the Byzantine Institute, by permission of Dr. Rüstem Duyuran, Archaeological Museum, Istanbul).

a. The Stuma Paten

b. The Stamps

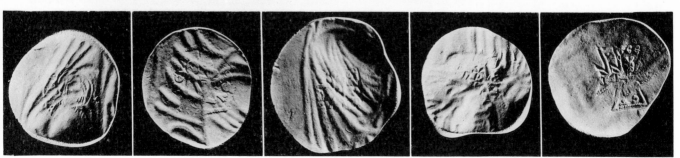

c. Round   d. Hexagonal   e. Square   f. Long   g. Cruciform

Casts of Stamps

OBJECTS WITH IMPERIAL STAMPS FROM THE REIGN OF TIBERIUS II CONSTANTINE, A.D. 578–582

a. Plate with Niello Cross

b. The Stamps

No. 28. PLATE WITH NIELLO CROSS

The British Museum, London

DESCRIPTION: Flat plate decorated in niello with cross in center, surrounded by ivy wreath (fig. a). Traces of gilding.

Wt. 1169 gr.; diam. 26.9 cm.; diam. of footring 11.8 cm.

PLACE OF DISCOVERY: Found near the monastery of Acheiropoietos, six miles west of Kyrenia, Cyprus, with nos. 35 and 78; from the "First Cyprus Treasure" Acquired in 1899.

CONTROL STAMPS: Five stamps – a round, a hexagonal, a square, a long, and a cruciform (fig. b). It is difficult to determine whether they were applied before or after the decoration was finished. The readings were taken from the object:

O   Nimbed bust, type 2; inscribed +Θ[ω]‖M[A].

O   Monogram reads KωNCTANTINOV; inscribed [I]ωA[N]‖NOV. There is a small bust above the monogram. This is the first instance in the regular Imperial series where the monogram in the hexagon does not resemble that in the square (see nos. 36, 41, and p. 11 f.).

□   Damaged monogram; it may belong to the Emperor Tiberius II (p. 12); inscribed TPV[Φ]‖ωN?

O   Bust, type 2; monogram ΠΕTPOV, as in the cross, and also found in the corresponding stamps on no. 27; inscribed IωA‖NNIC.

✠   Double strike; flared arms; monogram as above; inscribed in a circular direction [CI]‖CI‖NN‖IC (see no. 36).

DATE: The portrait type in the round stamp of no. 28 (type 2) could belong to Justin II, Tiberius Constantine, or Mauricius Tiberius. The monograms in the square and hexagon are not like those of either Justin II or Mauricius. The long and the cross stamps, however, are related to the corresponding stamps on no. 27, and thus indicate a date close to the reign of Justin II. These factors point to the reign of Tiberius II Constantine, A.D. 578–582.

Principal References: Dalton, *Arch.* 57, pp. 159, 165–168, pl. XVI: 2 (the stamps are also reproduced in a drawing in the text); *idem, Catalogue,* no. 397, pl. XXIV: Rosenberg, pp. 676–677; Matsulevich, "Arg. byz.," pp. 295, 299.

Source of Illustration: The British Museum, reproduction courtesy of the Trustees.

No. 29. INSCRIBED PLATE WITH CROSS

The Archaeological Museum, Istanbul; acc. no. 3761

DESCRIPTION: Plate with cross in center (fig. a); inscribed around the rim: + VΠЄΡ ЄVXHC K(αι) CѠTHPIAC CЄΡΓIOV K(αι) ANNAC K(αι) ANAΠAVCЄѠC ΔOMЄTIOV [K(αι)] IѠANNOV (Ébersolt).

Diam. 35 cm. (Ébersolt).

PLACE OF DISCOVERY: The village of Stuma, near Riha, Syria. Found with nos. 22 and 27, and probably also with nos. 8, 20, 21 (see no. 20).

CONTROL STAMPS: Five stamps on back of paten (fig. b) – a round, a hexagonal, a square, a long, and a cruciform. It is difficult to determine whether they were applied before or after the paten was decorated. The readings were taken from casts and photographs:

O (fig. c) Imperial bust without nimbus, beardless, wearing crown with pendants and circular ornament with cross, type 3; inscribed .IѠN‖....

O (fig. d) The identification of the monogram is not clear, but the stamp seems to be identical with the corresponding stamp on no. 27, in which case the monogram is that of Justin II, type a; inscribed MЄΓA‖Λ[OV]; there is a small bust above the monogram.

□ (fig. e) The monogram is distorted, but it is different from the monogram in the hexagon and clearly does not belong to Justin II. It is possible that it reads KѠN-CTANTINOV (see the hexagon on no. 28) but the Ѡ is not visible. The inscription is not clear.

◌ (fig. f) The imperial bust is like that in the round stamp; cruciform monogram; inscription not clear; the stamp has slipped in the striking, as shown especially by the lower part of the imperial bust. In this slip it is possible that the Λ to the left of the monogram was struck twice.

✠ (fig. g) Only part of the monogram is visible and it is difficult to determine whether it is the same as or different from the monogram in the long stamp; inscribed around the arms in vertical letters: Θ‖Ѡ‖M‖A (see nos. 30, 31).

DATE: The imperial bust type belongs to Mauricius or Tiberius. The monogram in the hexagon appears to be that of Justin II, whereas the monogram in the square resembles that in the hexagon of no. 28 attributed to Tiberius. The name in the cross occurs in corresponding stamps from the reign of Mauricius. These factors suggest the brief reign of Tiberius II, A.D. 578–582, rather than that of Justin II or Mauricius (see p. 12).

Principal References: J. Ébersolt, "Le trésor de Stuma," *Revue archéologique*, XVII (1911), pp. 407–419.

Source of Illustration: Dumbarton Oaks Photographic Collection (courtesy of Dr. Rüstem Duyuran, Archaeological Museum, Istanbul).

a. Inscribed Plate with Cross

b. The Stamps

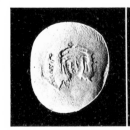    

c. Round   d. Hexagonal   e. Square   f. Long   g. Cruciform

Casts of Stamps

OBJECTS WITH IMPERIAL STAMPS FROM THE REIGN OF MAURICIUS TIBERIUS, A.D. 582–602

a. *Trulla* from Malaia Pereshchepina

b. Hexagonal Stamp

c. Stamps on the Bowl

No. 30. *TRULLA* FROM MALAIA PERESHCHEPINA

THE HERMITAGE, LENINGRAD; acc. no. W. 825

DESCRIPTION: Ten-sided *trulla* with ornamental rosette in center surrounded by scroll of leaves (fig. a). Evidently part of a two-piece set, with no. 31.

Wt. 1265.2 gr.; diam. 22.7 cm.; length of handle 13.5 cm.; ht. 7.2 cm.; diam. of footring 11.5 cm.; ht. of footring 2 cm. (Matsulevich).

PLACE OF DISCOVERY: Found in 1912, in Malaia Pereshchepina, Government of Poltava, with nos. 2, 31, 73, 79.

CONTROL STAMPS: Five stamps – a hexagonal (on the handle, fig. b), a round, a square, a long, and a cruciform (fig. c). The relief on the inside of the bowl cuts into the stamps indicating that they were applied before the bowl was decorated (Matsulevich, p. 82). All of the stamps are identical with those on no. 31. The readings were taken from the photographs and casts and were compared with the stamps on no. 31:

O   Nimbed bust, type 2; inscribed +ΠΑΤ[P]‖ΙΚΙϹ.

⬠   Monogram of Mauricius, somewhat damaged (p. 14); inscribed [ΠΑΤPΙ‖ΚΙ]Ϲ (see no. 31). There is a small bust above the monogram.

◻   Monogram as above, damaged by a double strike; inscribed ΜΑΞΙ‖ΜΟϹ.

◻   Nimbed bust, type 2; the monogram resembles the imperial monogram in the square and hexagonal stamps and is not the same as the monogram in the cross. It is, with no. 31, the only such case in the Imperial series (Table III, p. 15); inscribed [+] ΠΑΤ‖PΙΚ[ΙϹ].

✠   Double strike; flared arms; cruciform monogram; inscribed in vertical letters Θ‖Ѡ‖Μ‖Α.

DATE: Mauricius Tiberius, A.D. 582–602. The relationship between the inscribed name in the cross and the name in the round stamp of no. 28 suggests that these stamps belong to the earlier part of the reign of Mauricius.

Principal References: Rosenberg, pp. 690–691; Matsulevich, *Byz. Ant.*, p. 7, no. 12, pp. 80–83, figs. 13, 14, pl. 17.

Source of Illustration: The Hermitage.

No. 31. EWER FROM MALAIA PERESHCHEPINA

The Hermitage, Leningrad, acc. no. W. 826

DESCRIPTION: Eight-sided jug with handle (fig. a). Evidently part of a two-piece set, with no. 30.

Wt. 1335.3 gr.; ht. 25 cm.; diam. of neck 7.5 cm.; diam. of body 7.8–10 cm. (Matsulevich).

PLACE OF DISCOVERY: Found in 1912, in Malaia Pereshchepina, Government of Poltava, with nos. 2, 30, 73, 79.

CONTROL STAMPS: Five stamps – a round, a hexagonal, a square, a long, and a cruciform (fig. b), identical with those on no. 30. Since this ewer is a companion piece to no. 30 and since the stamps are identical with those of no. 30, it is likely that they, too, were applied before the object was finished (Matsulevich, p. 85). The readings were taken from the photograph and were compared with the stamps on no. 30:

O   Nimbed bust, type 2; inscribed [+ ΠΑΤΡ‖I]ΚΙC.

O   Monogram of Mauricius as in the square and the long, and the corresponding stamps on no. 30 (see no. 30); inscribed [Π]ΑΤΡΙ‖ΚΙC.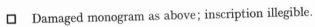

□   Damaged monogram as above; inscription illegible.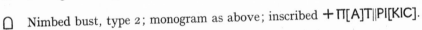

O   Nimbed bust, type 2; monogram as above; inscribed + Π[Α]Τ‖ΡΙ[ΚΙC].

✠   Flared arms; cruciform monogram, like the corresponding monogram on no. 30; inscribed in vertical letters Θ‖ω‖Μ‖Α.

DATE: Mauricius Tiberius, A.D. 582–602 (see no. 30).

Principal References: Rosenberg, pp. 692–693; Matsulevich, *Byz. Ant.*, p. 6, no. 9; pp. 82–85, figs. 15–17, pl. 18.

Source of Illustration: The Hermitage.

a. Ewer from Malaia Pereshchepina

b. The Stamps

OBJECTS WITH IMPERIAL STAMPS FROM THE
REIGN OF PHOCAS, A.D. 602–610

a. Plate "A" with Niello Cross from Mytilene (Lesbos). View of Back

b. The Stamps

No. 32. PLATE "A" WITH NIELLO CROSS FROM MYTILENE (LESBOS)

THE ARCHAEOLOGICAL MUSEUM, MYTILENE

DESCRIPTION: Simple plate, rather crudely decorated with concentric circles around rim and around niello cross in center (*Prakt.* [1954], p. 319, fig. 3, no. 4). Identical in design and execution with Plate "B" from Lesbos, no. 40 (p. 33f).

PLACE OF DISCOVERY: Found in 1951, on the Island of Mytilene (Lesbos), with nos. 40–43, 48–50, and with coins from the reigns of Phocas and Heraclius.

CONTROL STAMPS: Five badly damaged stamps on base of plate – one round, one hexagonal, two square, and a cruciform (figs. a and b). They were applied before the plate was decorated since they have been cut off by the incised circles inside the footring and shattered by the centering point. The readings were taken from the photograph:

O   Nimbed bust with pointed beard, type 4a; inscription illegible.

O   Only the top part is visible under the incised circles, below and to the left of the round stamp; it has been struck twice so that some of the monogram is repeated. Those parts of the monogram that are visible are portions of the Φ, the K, and the ω, and these could belong only to the Emperor Phocas.

☐   Above the round stamp, also cut by the incised lines: the monogram of Phocas; inscribed [ΘЄOΔ]‖ω[POC]; similar to the corresponding stamps on nos. 33, 34.

☐   Beside the first square, also cut by the incised lines: same as the above; though the monogram is less clear, its inscription is more legible: [ΘЄOΔ]‖ ωPOC.

✠   In the center of the plate, seriously damaged and struck at least twice so that the reading is confused.

DATE: The bust and monogram belong to the Emperor Phocas, A. D. 602–610; the nimbus on the bust suggests an early date in the Emperor's reign, and this supposition is supported by the relationship between these stamps and the stamps on no. 33, provisionally dated in A.D. 605.

Principal References: BCH, LXXIX, 1 (1955), p. 285; M. S. F. Hood, in *Journal of Hellenic Studies*, LXXV (1955), suppl., p. 16; A. K. Vavritsas, "Anaskaphe Krategou Mytilenes," *Prakt.* (1954, published in 1957), pp. 317–329.

Source of Illustration: Dumbarton Oaks Photographic Collection.

No. 33. PLATE WITH NIELLO MONOGRAM

THE MUSEUM OF ANTIQUITIES, NICOSIA, CYPRUS; acc. no. J. 455

DESCRIPTION: Plain plate with central wreath of leaves and monogram in niello, framed by two gilded bands (figs. a and b).

Diam. 44 cm.; diam. of footring 19.4 cm.

PLACE OF DISCOVERY: Found in 1902 in Karavas (near ancient Lapithos), six miles west of Kyrenia, not far from the monastery of Acheiropoietos, Cyprus, with nos. 54, 58–66; from the "Second Cyprus Treasure."

CONTROL STAMPS: Five stamps – a round, a hexagonal, a square, a long, and a cruciform, applied before the relief was finished, since the decoration on the obverse cuts into the square stamp and the heavy strokes beaten near the cross stamp have obliterated part of the arms (fig. c). The readings were taken from the object:

○ Bust with pointed beard and without a nimbus, type 4b; inscribed ✛ AI[Θ]‖ЄPIC (see nos. 44, 45).

⬭ Monogram of Phocas; small, nimbed bust above the monogram; inscribed ✛ KOC‖ [MAC].

☐ Double strike disfigures the monogram and the inscription; monogram as above; inscribed ✛ ΘЄOΔ‖ѠPOC✛ (see the corresponding stamps on nos. 32, 34).

⬭ Bust disfigured; cruciform monogram reads AΘANACIOV and is similar to, but not identical with, the monogram in the cross stamp; inscribed ✛ IѠ[A‖NNIC].

✥ Flared arms; the cruciform monogram contains the same letters as the monogram in the long stamp but they are arranged differently; inscribed CI‖[CI]‖NN‖IC (see no. 37).

DATE: Phocas, A.D. 602–610. Athanasius was *comes sacrarum largitionum*, killed by Phocas in 605 (Table V).

Principal References: Dalton, *Arch.* 60, p. 3, pl. 1 : 1, stamps on p. 14; Rosenberg, pp. 672–673; Matsulevich, "Arg. byz.," pp. 295, 299; P. Dikaios, *A Guide to the Cyprus Museum* (Nicosia, 1947), p. 118; *Byz. Art, 1958*, no. 38.

Source of Illustration: The Department of Antiquities, Cyprus.

a. Plate with Niello Monogram

b. Detail of Center Medallion

c. The Stamps

a. The Cup of Theophilos

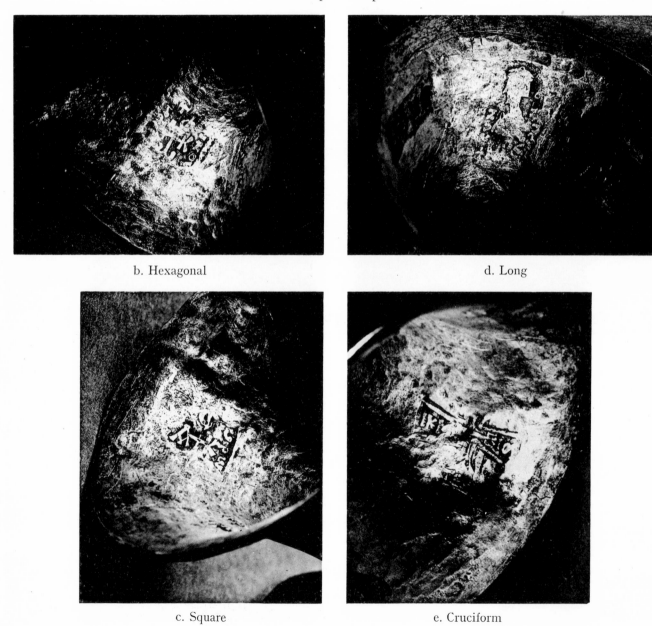

b. Hexagonal

d. Long

c. Square

e. Cruciform

The Stamps

No. 34: THE CUP OF THEOPHILOS

THE WALTERS ART GALLERY, BALTIMORE; acc. no. 57.642

DESCRIPTION: Chalice with a gilded inscription around rim (fig. a): + VΠЄP ЄVXHC KAI CⲰTHPIAC IⲰANNOV KAI ⲐⲰMA KAI MANNOV TⲰN ⲐЄOΦIΛOV.

Diam. 14 cm.; ht. 15.5 cm. (*WAG*).

PLACE OF DISCOVERY: Found in 1910, in Hama, Syria, with nos. 13, 89. 98, and possibly nos. 18 and 80 (p. 20).

CONTROL STAMPS: Only four stamps are distinguishable – a hexagonal, a square, a long, and a cruciform. They were applied inside the base where a stamping instrument could not easily have reached once the chalice was fashioned (see no. 8). The readings were taken from the object:

○ (fig. b) Disfigured monogram of Phocas; inscribed [IⲰA]‖NNOV; two crosses above the monogram.

▢ (fig. c) Monogram as above; inscribed [ⲐЄOΔ]‖ⲰP[O]V (see the corresponding stamps on nos. 32, 33; in this case the last two letters have been distorted so as to resemble an Ⲱ).

◻ (fig. d) Bust of Phocas, type 4b; the instrument slipped in the striking and thereby so elongated the bust as to make it seem to be in profile. An examination of the inscription on the right and of the diadem with circular ornament in the center indicates that this is not, however, a profile bust. Cruciform monogram like that in the cross stamp, also found in the corresponding stamps of nos. 35, 36. This monogram contains all the letters of the name KOCMAC, but it is unusual to find the initial letter K in such an obscure place, that is, within the arms of the C on the right (cf. nos. 35, 36, where the K is clearer). Inscribed CVMЄ‖[Ⲱ]NIC.

✠ (fig. e) Flared arms; monogram as above; inscribed in vertical letters [ΠA]‖TP-IK‖IOV.

DATE: Phocas, A.D. 602–610. The relationships between the square stamp and the corresponding stamp on no. 33, on the one hand, and between the secondary monogram and the secondary monograms on nos. 35 and 36, on the other, suggest that this group of stamps follows after *ca.* A.D. 605 (see no. 33).

Principal References: Diehl, p. 106, no. 1, pl. XIX: 2; Rosenberg, pp. 726–727; *WAG*, no. 396.

Source of Illustration: The Walters Art Gallery.

No. 35. CENSER

DESCRIPTION: Six-sided vessel (fig. a); on each side a roundel containing a nimbed bust (Christ, the Virgin, Saints Peter, Paul, John the Evangelist, and James). The roundels are separated by foliate motifs with central discs containing a cross.

Wt. 255.5 gr.; diam. 10.9 cm. (corner to corner); diam. of footring 6.1 cm.

PLACE OF DISCOVERY: Found near the monastery of Acheiropoietos, six miles west of Kyrenia, Cyprus, with nos. 28 and 78; from the "First Cyprus Treasure." Acquired in 1899.

CONTROL STAMPS: Five stamps visible – a round, a square, a long, and two cruciform (fig. b). They are cut off by the rings inscribed on the base and were, therefore, applied before the object was finally decorated. The readings were taken from the object:

○ (fig. b, upper left) Cut off by the rings of the base: barely visible, but a bust without nimbus and with pointed beard can be distinguished, type 4b.

☐ Double strike; near the round stamp, also cut off by the rings of the base: part of the monogram of Phocas can be seen and the inscription [IѠA]‖NNOV.

⌂ Below the square, also cut by the rings of the base: a bearded bust is discernible, type 4b, and part of a cruciform monogram like that in the cross stamps and in the corresponding stamps of nos. 34 and 36; inscribed +IѠA‖NNIC (identical with the long stamp on no. 36).

✠ Close to the center of the base: flared arms; monogram as above; inscribed in a circular direction CI‖CI‖NN‖IC (see no. 37; identical with the cross stamp on no. 36).

✠ As above; incomplete and cut off by the rings of the base.

DATE: Phocas, A.D. 602–610. The relationship between the secondary monograms on this object and on no. 34 dates it in the same period, after ca. A.D. 605.

Principal References: Dalton, *Catalogue,* no. 399; *idem, Arch.* 57, p. 168f., pl. XVII; Rosenberg, pp. 670–671; Matsulevich, "Arg. byz.," p. 297.

Source of Illustration: The British Museum, reproduction courtesy of the Trustees.

a. Censer

b. The Stamps

a. Plate "A" with Niello Cross from Klimova

b. The Stamps

No. 36. PLATE "A" WITH NIELLO CROSS FROM KLIMOVA

THE HERMITAGE, LENINGRAD; acc. no. W. 192

DESCRIPTION: Plain plate with niello cross in center, surrounded by floral wreath (fig. a).

Wt. 2294 gr.; diam. 45 cm. (Matsulevich).

PLACE OF DISCOVERY: Klimova, district of Solikamsk, Government of Perm (renamed Molotov in 1942). Found, with nos. 9 and 100, in 1907.

CONTROL STAMPS: Five stamps – a round, a hexagonal, a square, a long, and a cruciform (fig. b). The decoration of the floral wreath cuts into the stamps, indicating that they must have been applied before the decoration was finished (Matsulevich, "Arg. byz.," p. 296). The readings were taken from the photograph and cast:

O Bearded bust of Phocas without nimbus, type 4b; inscribed Θ.. ΠΕ‖.ΠΤΟC.

O Monogram KⲰNCTANTINOV (p. 12, and nos. 28 and 41); nimbed bust above the monogram; inscribed CVME‖ⲰNIC.

□ Monogram of Phocas; inscribed +Λ...‖ⲱ.ΓIC.

◠ Bearded bust, type 4b; cruciform monogram like that in the cross stamp and in the corresponding stamps of nos. 34, 35; inscribed +IⲰA‖NNIC (identical with the corresponding stamp on no. 35).

⳨ Flared arms; monogram as above; inscribed in a circular direction [CI]‖CI‖NN‖IC (see no. 37; identical with the cross stamps on no. 35).

DATE: Phocas, A.D. 602–610. The relationship between the long and cross stamps on this object and the corresponding stamps on no. 35 place it in the same period, after ca. A.D. 605 (see no. 35).

Principal References: Rosenberg, pp. 674–675; Matsulevich, "Arg. byz.," p. 293, no. 5, pl. XLV: 4.

Source of Illustration: The Hermitage.

OBJECTS WITH IMPERIAL STAMPS FROM THE REIGN OF HERACLIUS, A.D. 610–641

a. Plate with Niello Monogram

b. The Stamps

No. 37. PLATE WITH NIELLO MONOGRAM

THE METROPOLITAN MUSEUM OF ART, NEW YORK, Fletcher Fund; acc. no. 52.25.2

DESCRIPTION: Plain, flat plate with niello monogram in center surrounded by ivy wreath (fig. a). Identical in design with nos. 38 and 39.

Diam. 13.4 cm.; diam. of footring 5.4 cm.

PLACE OF DISCOVERY: Cyprus? (see nos. 38 and 39).

CONTROL STAMPS: Five stamps – a round, a hexagonal, a square, a long, and a cruciform (fig. b). The bottom of the plate is greatly deteriorated; while it is difficult to determine with certainty whether the stamps were applied before or after the decoration was finished, the centering point breaks into a cross stamp, and concentric lines on the bottom of the plate, produced by work in the lathe, break into the stamps, particularly the square and the round. The stamps are all identical with the stamps on the other two plates of the set, nos. 38 and 39. The readings were taken from the object:

O Barely visible near the footring: nimbed bust.

O (fig. b, upper left) Monogram of Heraclius partially destroyed, type a; inscribed [IѠA]‖NNI[C] or [CICI]‖NNI[C]. Small crosses between the arms of the monogram.

□ (fig. b, upper right) Monogram of Heraclius, type b; inscribed MA[Г‖NЄ]C[✱].

⬠ (fig. b, lower left) Nimbed bust, type 5; cruciform monogram barely visible; inscribed [KOC]‖M[AC] (see the corresponding stamps on nos. 39, 41–47, 51).

✠ Struck twice; flared arms; cruciform monogram identical with the secondary monograms on nos. 38–40; inscribed [CI‖CI]‖NN‖[IC] (this name is found in the corresponding stamps on nos. 28, 33, 35, 36, 38–40, 44–46; notice also the variant spelling in the cross stamps on nos. 50–53).

DATE: Heraclius, A.D. 610–613. The imperial bust (p. 10), the early form of Heraclius' monogram in the square, and the inscribed name in the cross stamp, which is like that in corresponding stamps from the reign of Phocas, suggest that these stamps, like the stamps on nos. 38 and 39, belong to the early part of the reign of Heraclius. These stamps begin a long and closely interrelated series from the reign of Heraclius (for these relationships, all of which cannot be mentioned in the Catalogue, see Tables I–IV). Although occasionally a group of related objects might be placed, on the evidence of their stamps, in a slightly different position in the series, the objects must have been stamped approximately in the order given. It is not possible to date them more closely at this juncture, since not a single *comes sacrarum largitionum* from this period is known (p. 29).

Unpublished.

Source of Illustration: The Metropolitan Museum of Art.

No. 38. PLATE WITH NIELLO MONOGRAM

THE WALTERS ART GALLERY, BALTIMORE; acc. no. 57.652

DESCRIPTION: Plain, flat plate with niello monogram in center surrounded by ivy wreath (fig. a). Identical in design with nos. 37 and 39. This plate is the largest of the set of three.

Diam. 25.5 cm. (*WAG*).

PLACE OF DISCOVERY: Said to be from Cyprus.

CONTROL STAMPS: Five stamps – identical with those on nos. 37 and 39 and rather better preserved (fig. b). The round stamp was worn when work was done around the centering point. The readings were taken from the object:

O Nimbed bust, type 5; inscribed [ANΔ]∥PEIC (see the corresponding stamp on no. 40).

O Monogram of Heraclius partially visible, type a; inscribed [IѠA]∥NNI[C] or [CICI]∥ NNI[C].

□ Monogram of Heraclius, type b; inscribed MAΓ∥NEC✶.

Ω Nimbed bust, type 5; cruciform monogram like the monogram in the cross stamp and like the corresponding monograms on nos. 37, 39, 40; inscription not clear.

✠ Flared arms; monogram as above; inscribed CI∥CI∥[NN∥IC]; identical with the corresponding stamps on nos. 37, 39, 40 (see no. 37).

DATE: Heraclius, A.D. 610–613 (see no. 37).

Principal Reference: WAG, no. 378.

Source of Illustration: The Walters Art Gallery.

a. Plate with Niello Monogram

b. The Stamps

a. Plate with Niello Monogram

b. The Stamps

No. 39. PLATE WITH NIELLO MONOGRAM

THE DUMBARTON OAKS COLLECTION, WASHINGTON, D. C.; acc. no. 60.60

DESCRIPTION: Plain, flat plate with niello monogram in center surrounded by ivy wreath (fig. a). Identical in design with nos. 36 and 37.

Wt. 313 gr.; diam. 13.5 cm.; diam. of footring, 6 cm.; ht. of footring 1 cm.

PLACE OF DISCOVERY: "It is practically certain that both [this plate and the plate in the British Museum with a cross in the center, no. 28] were found in the same place [i. e., in Cyprus], though not necessarily at the same time (Dalton, *BZ*, p. 615).

CONTROL STAMPS: Five stamps – identical with those on nos. 37 and 38 (fig. b). They are most damaged around the centering point and near the solder of the footring, which indicates that they were applied before the object was finished. The readings were taken from the plate itself:

O   Nimbed bust of Heraclius, type 5; inscription illegible.

O   Monogram of Heraclius, partially destroyed, type a; two crosses within the arms of the monogram; inscription illegible.

□   Monogram of Heraclius, type b; inscribed [M]A[Γ‖N]ЄC[✱].

∩   Imperial bust, type 5; cruciform monogram as in the cross stamp and in the corresponding stamps of nos. 37, 38, 40; inscribed [KOC‖MA]C (see no. 37).

✠   Flared arms; monogram as above; inscribed in a circular direction [CI‖C]I‖[NN‖IC] (see no. 37; also nos. 38, 40).

DATE: Heraclius, A.D. 610–613 (see no. 37).

Principal References: Dalton, *BZ*, pp. 615–617 (no stamps published); Rosenberg, pp. 678–679 (no stamps published); *DOC*, no. 17.

Source of Illustration: Dumbarton Oaks.

No. 40. PLATE "B" WITH NIELLO CROSS FROM MYTILENE (LESBOS)

THE ARCHAEOLOGICAL MUSEUM, MYTILENE

DESCRIPTION: Plate crudely decorated with concentric circles around rim and around niello cross in center (*Prakt.* [1954], p. 319, fig. 3, no. 4). Identical in design and execution with Plate "A" from Lesbos, no. 32 (p. 33f.).

PLACE OF DISCOVERY: Found in 1951, on the Island of Mytilene (Lesbos), about 8 km. from the town of Mytilene, with nos. 32, 41–43, 48–50, and with coins from the reigns of Phocas and Heraclius.

CONTROL STAMPS: Five stamps on bottom of plate – a round, a hexagonal, a square, a long, and a cruciform (figs. a and b). Since they are cut off by the concentric circles incised on the base, they were applied before the decoration was finished (see no. 32). The readings were taken from the photograph:

○   Bust of Heraclius, type 5; inscribed +AN[Δ‖PЄ]IC. This stamp is probably identical with the corresponding stamps on nos. 37–39 (see no. 38).

⬡   This stamp is not clear, but the edge can be discerned between the square and long stamps.

▢   Beneath the cross stamp and cut off by the incised circles on the base: monogram of Heraclius partially destroyed, type a or b; inscribed [ANΔ]‖P[ЄA]C. This stamp appears to be identical with the corresponding stamps on nos. 41–43.

⬭   Imperial bust, type 5; cruciform monogram like that in the cross stamp, also found in the corresponding stamps of nos. 37–39; inscription not clear.

⊹   Flared arms; cruciform monogram as above; inscribed [CI‖CI]‖NN‖[IC]; appears to be identical with the corresponding stamps on nos. 37–39 (see no. 37).

DATE: Heraclius, A.D. 610–613. The relationship of the round and cross stamps to the corresponding stamps on nos. 37–39, and of the square stamp to the square stamps on nos. 41–43 suggest that this object is dated between the two groups. There are seven stamped silver objects from Lesbos dated in the reign of Heraclius, nos. 40–43, 48–50, and one dated in the reign of Phocas, no. 32. Nos. 40 and 32 are identical in workmanship and decoration; it is, therefore, interesting that the analysis of the stamps also results in no. 40 being assigned a position relatively close to no. 32.

Principal References: Same as for no. 32.

Source of Illustration: Dumbarton Oaks Photographic Collection.

a. Plate "B" with Niello Cross from Mytilene (Lesbos). View of Back

b. The Stamps

a. Plate "C" with Niello Cross from Mytilene (Lesbos). Detail of Back

b. The Stamps

No. 41. PLATE "C" WITH NIELLO CROSS FROM MYTILENE (LESBOS)

THE ARCHAEOLOGICAL MUSEUM, MYTILENE

DESCRIPTION: Large plate with niello cross in center surrounded by stylized wreath of leaves (*Prakt.* [1954], p. 319, fig. 3, no. 6).

PLACE OF DISCOVERY: Found in 1951, on the Island of Mytilene (Lesbos), with nos. 32, 40, 42, 43, 48–50 (see no. 32).

CONTROL STAMPS: Five stamps – a round, a hexagonal, a square, a long, and a cruciform (figs. a and b); they appear to have been damaged by the wreath on the obverse, which indicates that they were applied before the plate was decorated. The stamps are identical with those on nos. 42, 43. The readings were taken from the photograph:

O   Bust of Heraclius, type 6a; inscribed +ΓΕΟ‖ΡΓΙC.

O   Just visible between the square and round stamps: monogram ΚωΝCΤΑΝΤΙΝΟV, see nos. 28, 36 (p. 12).

□   Monogram of Heraclius, badly battered, type b; inscribed +ΑΝΔ‖[Ρ]ΕΑC (the N is reversed, see also no. 43); this stamp is identical with the corresponding stamp on no. 43, and at least very similar to those on nos. 40, 42.

⬭   Bust of Heraclius, type 6a; cruciform monogram reads CΕΡΓΙΟV and is found again in the cross stamp and in the corresponding stamps of nos. 42–50; inscribed +ΚΟC‖ MAC.

✠   Double strike displaces part of the monogram and inscription; flared arms; monogram as above; inscribed [CV‖ΜΕ‖ΟΝ]‖ΗC (see the corresponding stamps on nos. 42, 43).

DATE: Heraclius, A.D. 613–629/30. The relationship between the square stamp and the corresponding stamp on no. 40, and the relationship of the secondary monograms to the monograms on nos. 42–50 determine the placing of this group of objects, nos. 41–43, in the sequence.

Principal References: Same as for no. 32.

Source of Illustration: Dumbarton Oaks Photographic Collection.

No. 42. PLATE "D" WITH NIELLO CROSS FROM MYTILENE (LESBOS)

THE ARCHAEOLOGICAL MUSEUM, MYTILENE

DESCRIPTION: Plate with niello cross in the center surrounded by ivy wreath (*Prakt.* [1954], p. 319, fig. 3, no. 5).

PLACE OF DISCOVERY: Found in 1951, on the Island of Mytilene (Lesbos), with nos. 32, 40, 41, 43, 48–50 (see no. 32).

CONTROL STAMPS: Four (possibly five) stamps – identical with the corresponding stamps on nos. 41 and 43 (figs. a and b). The niello wreath cuts into the stamps, indicating that the plate was decorated after it was stamped. The readings were taken from the photograph:

O   Bust of Heraclius, type 6a; inscribed +ΓЄO‖ΡΓIC.

◯   Slight remains can be discerned just below the cross stamp, near the long arm of the niello cross.

☐   Greatly damaged; part of the monogram of Heraclius is seen, type b(?); inscribed +[AN]Δ‖[PEΛC] (see nos. 40, 41 ,43).

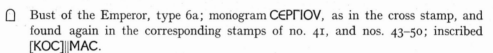

◻   Bust of the Emperor, type 6a; monogram CЄΡΓIOV, as in the cross stamp, and found again in the corresponding stamps of no. 41, and nos. 43–50; inscribed [KOC]‖MAC.

✠   Flared arms; monogram as above; inscribed C[V‖M]Є‖[ON]‖HC (see nos. 41, 43).

DATE: Heraclius, A.D. 613–629/30 (see no. 41).

Principal References: Same as for no. 32.

Source of Illustration: Dumbarton Oaks Photographic Collection.

a. Plate "D" with Niello Cross from Mytilene (Lesbos).
Detail of Back

b. The Stamps

Stamps on Lamp from Mytilene (Lesbos)

No. 43. LAMP FROM MYTILENE (LESBOS)

The Archaeological Museum, Mytilene

DESCRIPTION: Plain hanging lamp on low foot (*Prakt.* [1954], p. 319, fig. 3, no. 8).

PLACE OF DISCOVERY: Found in 1951, on the Island of Mytilene (Lesbos), with nos. 32, 40–42, 48–50 (see no. 32).

CONTROL STAMPS: Four stamps (possibly five) – identical with the corresponding stamps on nos. 41, 42 (see fig.). Since they appear to have been damaged in the area of the centering point while the bottom of the lamp was being worked, they must have been applied before the lamp was finished. The readings were taken from the photograph:

O   Bust of Heraclius, type 6a; inscribed [+]Γ[ΕΟ‖ΡΓΙ]C.

O   There may be slight remains between the cross and the long stamp.

□   Monogram of Heraclius, disfigured: the **A** has been pushed to the lower right-hand corner, and the **H**, only partly visible, is attached to the **K** (see the corresponding stamp on no. 58); inscribed +AN[Δ]‖PEAC (see nos. 40–42).

⌂   Bust of the Emperor, type 6a; monogram **CEPΓΙΟV**, as in the cross stamp and also in the corresponding stamps of nos. 41–42, 44–50; inscribed KOC‖MA[C].

⊹   Flared arms; monogram as above; inscribed C[V‖M]E‖ON‖HC (see nos. 41, 42).

DATE: Heraclius, A.D. 613–629/30 (see no. 41).

Principal References: Same as for no. 32.

Source of Illustration: Dumbarton Oaks Photographic Collection.

No. 44. SMALL, PLAIN PLATE

DESCRIPTION: Small, flat plate without design (fig. a).

Wt. 194.2 gr., diam. 13.3 cm.

PLACE OF DISCOVERY: Said to have been found in or near Smyrna, with no 45 and possibly with no. 46. Acquired in 1951.

CONTROL STAMPS: Five stamps clearly visible – a round, a hexagonal, a square, a long, and a cruciform (fig. b). An additional stamp, very worn, perhaps hexagonal, can be discerned near one of the arms of the cross. It has been struck twice, possibly before the others were struck (see nos. 54, 55, 64, 65, p. 8), Circular marks of the lathe cut into the square and round stamps and the latter was disfigured when the plate was beaten near the footring. The centering point breaks into the cross stamp. Four of the stamps are identical with those on nos. 45, 46, but the clearly visible hexagon is different. The readings were taken from the object:

O   Nimbed bust of Heraclius, type 6a; inscribed [+AIⱭ]‖ЄPIC (see nos. 33 and 45).

O   Near the long stamp, greatly damaged: the monogram of the Emperor is distinguishable, type b; inscribed [+]A[NⱭ]‖PЄAC.

□   Monogram of the Emperor, type b; inscribed ΛAMΠP‖OTAT[OV] or ΛAMΠP‖OTAT-[OC] (see no. 52).

∩   Bust of the Emperor Heraclius, type 6a; monogram CЄPΓIOV, as in the cross stamp and also in the corresponding stamps on nos. 41–43, 45–50; inscribed +KO[C‖MAC] (see nos. 37–39, 41–43).

⊹   Flared arms; monogram as above; inscribed in a circular direction [CI‖CI]‖NN‖IC (see no. 37).

DATE: Heraclius, A.D. 613–629/30. The nimbed bust of the Emperor places this series, nos. 44, 45, 46, in the early part of his reign, with nos. 37–43; the long stamp is the same as on nos. 37–39, 41–43; the secondary monogram relates the stamps to nos. 41–43, 47–50; the square stamp is similar to corresponding stamps on nos. 51–54A. These factors combine to determine the placing of the three plates in the sequence.

Principal References: DOH, p. 56, no. 133; *DOC*, no. 16:3.

Source of Illustration: Dumbarton Oaks.

a. Small, Plain Plate

b. The Stamps (actual size)

a. Plate with Niello Cross, ΘΕΟΥ ΕΛΠΙC

b. The Stamps (twice actual size)

No. 45. PLATE WITH NIELLO CROSS, ΘΕΟV ЄΛΠIC

THE DUMBARTON OAKS COLLECTION, WASHINGTON, D. C.; acc. no. 51.23

DESCRIPTION: Small plate decorated in niello with cross in center surrounded by ivy wreath (fig. a). Inscribed between arms of cross: ΘΕΟV ЄΛΠIC.

Wt. 320.9 gr.; diam. 13.7 cm.

PLACE OF DISCOVERY: Said to have been found in or near Smyrna, with no. 44 and possibly with no. 46. Acquired in 1951.

CONTROL STAMPS: Five stamps clearly visible (fig. b), four of which are identical with those on nos. 44 and 46, while the hexagon is different. Circular marks made by the lathe when the bottom of the plate was being polished wore down the stamps, which suggests that the plate was worked on after the stamps had been applied. The readings were taken from the object:

O   Bust of Heraclius, type 6a; inscribed [+AIΘ‖Є]PIC (see no. 44).

O   Monogram of Heraclius, type b. A small bust of Christ with crossed nimbus is seen above the monogram (p. 11). The inscription is not clear, but it begins with a cross and probably resembles the inscription in the corresponding stamp of no. 46.

☐   Monogram of the Emperor, type b; inscribed [ΛA]MΠP‖OTATO[V?] (see no. 44).

O   Imperial bust, type 6a; monogram CЄPΓIOV, as in the cross stamp, and in the corresponding stamps of nos. 41–44, 46–50; inscribed [+]KOC‖[MAC].

✠   Flared arms; monogram as above; inscribed in a circular direction [CI‖CI]‖NN‖[IC] (see no. 37).

DATE: Heraclius, A.D. 613–629/30 (see no. 44).

Principal References: DOH, p. 56, no. 133; DOC, no. 16:2.

Source of Illustration: Dumbarton Oaks.

No. 46. PLATE WITH NIELLO CROSS, ΘΕΟV TIMH

DESCRIPTION: Small plate decorated in niello with cross in center surrounded by ivy wreath (fig. a). Inscribed between arms of cross: ΘΕΟV TIMH.

Wt. 320 gr.; diam. 13.7 cm.

PLACE OF DISCOVERY: The plate belongs to a set of three, along with nos. 44 and 45, and was probably found with the latter two, possibly in Smyrna. It was acquired by Dumbarton Oaks in 1951, having previously been in a Swiss collection.

CONTROL STAMPS: Five stamps, four of which are identical with those on nos. 44, 45, while the hexagon of no. 44 is different (fig. b). As on no. 44, the marks of the lathe appear to run across the stamps, indicating that work was done on the plate after it was stamped. The readings were taken from the object:

○   Bust of Heraclius, type 6a; inscription not clear.

○   Monogram of Heraclius, type b; small bust of Christ with crossed nimbus above the monogram; inscribed +TEI.....

□   Monogram as above; inscribed ΛΑ[M]ΠP‖[OTATOV?] (see no. 44).

◠   Bust of the Emperor, type 6a; monogram CEPΓIOV, as in the cross stamp and in the corresponding stamps of nos. 41–45, 47–50; inscribed [KOC]‖MAC.

✠   Double strike; flared arms; monogram as above; inscribed in a circular direction [CI‖CI‖NN‖I]C (see no. 37).

DATE: Heraclius, A.D. 613–629/30 (see no. 44).

Principal References: DOH, p. 56, no. 133; *DOC*, no. 16:1.

Source of Illustration: Dumbarton Oaks.

a. Plate with Nicello Cross, ΘΕΟΥ ΤΙΜΗ

b. The Stamps (actual size)

a. The Vatican Reliquary

b. The Stamps

No. 47. THE VATICAN RELIQUARY

Museo Sacro, Vatican

DESCRIPTION: Gilded silver reliquary with Christ and six saints in roundels on the sides (fig. a). On the lid are two angels between arms of a cross and, above, a hand and a dove. The figures are nimbed.

Ht. with lid 10.5 cm.; ht. of lid 5.5 cm.; ht. of box 5.8 cm.; length 19.5 cm.

PLACE OF DISCOVERY: Found in 1906 when the reliquary chest of Leo III, under the altar of the chapel of the Sancta Sanctorum in the Lateran, was opened.

CONTROL STAMPS: The remains of five badly deteriorated stamps can be seen. They appear to be (fig. b, from left to right): a hexagon (?), a square, a cross (?), a round, and a long (?). The outline of the round stamp sets the scale for the others. It is impossible to say whether they were applied before or after the object was decorated. The readings were taken from the object:

○ Not clear.

⬡ ?

▢ Monogram of Heraclius, type a; there seems to be an additional bar on the K which is unusual.

⌂ Although scarcely distinguishable, the monogram may be the same as in the corresponding stamps of 41–46, 48–50. The reading [KOC]‖MAC is suggested for the inscribed name.

✠ Indistinguishable.

DATE: Heraclius, A.D. 610–641. The object is placed tentatively in this position in the series on the evidence of the inscription in the long stamp (see nos. 37–39, 41–46), which is not certain.

Principal References: P. Lauer, "Le trésor du Sancta Sanctorum," *Mon. Piot*, XV (1906), p. 71f., pl. XII:3; O. M. Dalton, *Byzantine Art and Archaeology* (Oxford, 1911), p. 564; Rosenberg, pp. 706–707. Good reproductions of the reliquary may be found in H. Grisar, *Die römische Kapelle Sancta Sanctorum und ihr Schatz* (Freiburg, 1908), p. 109f.; C. Cecchelli, "Il tesoro del Laterano," *Dedalo*, VII (1926), p. 231, fig. on p. 233.

Source of Illustration: The Vatican Library.

No. 48. PLAIN *TRULLA* FROM MYTILENE (LESBOS)

THE ARCHAEOLOGICAL MUSEUM, MYTILENE

DESCRIPTION: Simple, undecorated *trulla* with rounded handle (*Prakt.* [1954], p. 319, fig. 3, no. 9).

PLACE OF DISCOVERY: Found in 1951, on the Island of Mytilene (Lesbos), with nos. 32, 40–43, 49, 50 (see no. 32).

CONTROL STAMPS: Five stamps – a round, a hexagonal, a square, a long, and a cruciform (see fig.). Three of the stamps at least—the round, the long, and the cross—are identical with the stamps on no. 49. It is difficult to determine whether they were applied before or after the object was decorated. The readings were taken from the photograph:

O Bust of Heraclius without nimbus, type 6b; inscribed ΦΙΛΙ‖ΠΠΟC.

⬡ Indistinct.

☐ Monogram of Heraclius, type a; inscribed .....‖NTAC.

⬭ Bust without nimbus; monogram CEPΓOV, but with larger letters than in the previous examples of this monogram in the long stamps of nos. 41–46 and similar to the corresponding monograms on nos. 49, 51, 58–70; inscribed ANΔ‖[PE]AC.

✣ Flared arms; monogram as above, but with smaller letters (cf. 41–46, 49, 50); inscribed +I‖ωA‖NN‖IC.

DATE: Heraclius, A.D. 613–629/30. The bust of the Emperor without nimbus suggests that the stamps belong to a later period than nos. 37–46. The secondary monogram relates the stamps to nos. 41–46, but the larger size of this monogram in the long stamp relates the stamps to numbers 49, 51, 58–70.

Principal References: Same as for no. 32.

Source of Illustration: Dumbarton Oaks Photographic Collection.

Stamps on Plain *Trulla* from Mytilene (Lesbos)

Stamps on Ewer from Mytilene (Lesbos)

No. 49. EWER FROM MYTILENE (LESBOS)

THE ARCHAEOLOGICAL MUSEUM, MYTILENE

DESCRIPTION: Simple ewer (*Prakt.* [1954], p. 319, fig. 3, no. 2).

PLACE OF DISCOVERY: Found in 1951, on the Island of Mytilene (Lesbos), with nos. 32, 40–43, 48, 50 (see no. 32).

CONTROL STAMPS: Five stamps distinguishable, three of which—the round, the long, and the cross—are identical with the corresponding stamps on no. 48 (see fig.). The hexagon and the square are too worn to be clearly distinguished. The stamps are most worn near the centering point, which has virtually destroyed the hexagon, indicating that work was done in the lathe after the stamps were applied. The readings were taken from the photograph:

O   Bust without nimbus, type 6b (see no. 48); inscribed Φ[IΛI]∥ΠΠOC.

⬡   ?

▢   Monogram of Heraclius, incomplete; inscription not clear.

⌂   The bust has been damaged; the monogram CEPΓIOV is visible though partially destroyed; inscription [ANΔ∥PEA]C (see no. 48).

⬚   Flared arms; the monogram is partially visible and is the same as in the cross stamp of no. 48: CEPΓIOV; inscribed [+I∥ωA]∥NN∥IC.

DATE: Heraclius, A.D. 613–629/30 (see no. 48).

Principal References: Same as for no. 32.

Source of Illustration: Dumbarton Oaks Photographic Collection.

No. 50. *TRULLA* WITH DECORATED HANDLE FROM MYTILENE (LESBOS)

DESCRIPTION: *Trulla* with crude decoration on handle depicting female figure on pedestal and face (of Poseidon) beneath. On either side of the face are three roundels, each of the first two containing a bust and the last a rosette. Concentric circles decorate the inside of the bowl and a wave-crest pattern ornaments the rim (*Prakt.* [1954], p. 328, fig. 15).

Diam. 16.5 cm.; diam. with handle 31.3 cm.; depth 7.3 cm.; diam. of footring 10.7 cm. (Vavritsas).

PLACE OF DISCOVERY: Found in 1951, on the Island of Mytilene (Lesbos), with nos. 32, 40–43, 48, 49 (see no. 32).

CONTROL STAMPS: Five stamps – a round, a hexagonal, a square, and two cruciform (see fig.). It is difficult to judge whether they were applied before or after the *trulla* was decorated. The readings were taken from the photograph:

O Nimbed bust of Heraclius, type 6a; inscribed CXOΛA‖CTIKIC; this name occurs frequently in the remaining stamps of the Imperial series (see Table IV, nos. 51–74).

⬡ Not clear.

▢ Monogram of Heraclius, type a; inscribed K[OC]‖M[A]C.

✠ Flared arms; monogram CEPΓIOV (see nos. 41–49); inscribed CI‖[CI‖NN]‖HC (see also no. 37, where the name is spelled slightly differently; the present spelling is also found in the cross stamps of nos. 51–53).

✠ Struck twice; same as above; inscribed [CI‖CI]‖NN‖HC.

DATE: Heraclius, A.D. 613–629/30. The nimbed bust of the Emperor suggests an earlier date than that of nos. 48 and 49, but the relationship between these stamps and stamps later in the series supports the position here assigned to the object.

Principal References: Same as for no. 32.

Source of Illustration: Dumbarton Oaks Photographic Collection.

Stamps on *Trulla* with Decorated Handle from Mytilene (Lesbos)

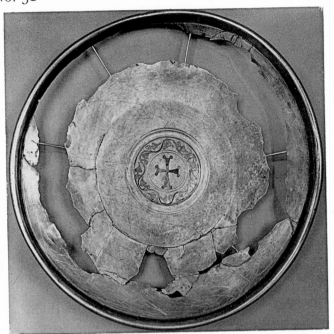

a. Front

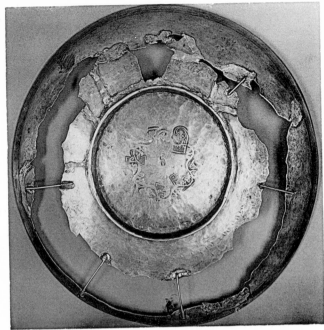

b. Back

Plate "A" with Niello Cross from Kalganovka

c. The Stamps

No. 51. PLATE "A" WITH NIELLO CROSS FROM KALGANOVKA

THE HERMITAGE, LENINGRAD; acc. no. W. 284

DESCRIPTION: Plain plate decorated with niello cross in center surrounded by ivy wreath (figs. a and b).

Diam. 24.5 cm. (Matsulevich).

PLACE OF DISCOVERY: Found in 1878, with nos. 55 and 70, at Kalganovka, district of Solikamsk, Government of Perm (renamed Moloto vin 1942). Formerly in the Stroganov Collection.

CONTROL STAMPS: Five stamps – a hexagonal, a square, a long, and two cruciform (fig. c). The square, the long, and the cross are found again on nos. 52 and 54A. The ivy wreath on the obverse cuts into the stamps, indicating that the plate was decorated after it was stamped (Matsulevich, "Arg. byz.," p. 296). The readings were taken from the photograph and cast:

○ Between the long and the cross: inscribed CXOΛ[A||CTIKIC] (see the round stamp on no. 50).

□ Monogram of Heraclius, type a; inscribed Λ[AM]Π[P]||OTA[TOC] (see nos. 44–46, 52, and 54A).

◠ Nimbed bust of Heraclius with three-pronged diadem, type 6d; cruciform monogram ΦωTINOV. The large format of the monogram resembles the later examples of the CEPΓIOV series, nos. 48, 49, and this type of lettering occurs again in later stamps, nos. 58–70; the same monogram, with smaller letters, is found in the cross stamp, and the same pair occurs in the stamps of no. 52. This stamp is inscribed KOC||MAC.

✠ Flared arms; monogram as above; inscribed [CI]||CI||NN||HC (see the corresponding stamps on nos. 50, 52, 53).

✠ Same as above; inscribed CI||[CI]||N[N]||HC.

DATE: Heraclius, A.D. 613–629/30. As in the case of no. 50, the nimbed bust suggests an early date for these stamps. On the other hand, the secondary monogram does not belong to the CEPΓIOV group (nos. 41–46, 48–50) and the relationship between these stamps and the stamps on no. 54A supports a later date.

Principal References: Rosenberg, pp. 708–709; Matsulevich, "Arg. byz.," p. 293, no. 3, pl. XLV: 2.
Source of Illustration: The Hermitage.

165

No. 52. BOWL "A" FROM LAMPSACUS

The British Museum, London

DESCRIPTION: Simple bowl with gilt cross in center. The arms of the cross extend to the rim, and in its center is a niello monogram of the proper name MHNA, or perhaps AMHN. The bowl is similar to, but slightly smaller than, no. 53, and was found in the same treasure (fig. a).

Wt. 191.5 gr.; diam. 16 cm.

PLACE OF DISCOVERY: Lampsacus, Hellespont. Found with nos. 19, 24, and 53. Acquired in 1848.

CONTROL STAMPS: Remains of five stamps – a square, a long, and three cruciform. Four of these, on the back of the plate, have been damaged by the decoration on the bowl, as is indicated by the concentric lines cutting into the stamps (fig. c). The fifth stamp, a cross, is found on the inside of the bowl, between the A and the N of the monogram, which also has damaged the stamp (fig. b). This bowl, and no. 53, are the only examples in the Imperial series on which the stamps are applied inside as well as outside the object. The stamps are the same as the corresponding ones on no. 51. The readings were taken from the object:

☐ Monogram of Heraclius, type a, incomplete; inscribed [ΛΑΜΠΡ]‖ΟΤΑ[ΤΟ]C (see no. 51).

⌂ Only the top is visible, beside the circles incised on the bottom of the bowl: a nimbed bust with trefoil ornament on crown, type 6d; cf. no. 51.

✠ Nearest the square: a cruciform monogram like that in the corresponding stamps on no. 51; inscribed CI‖[CI‖NN]‖HC.

✠ Nearest the long stamp: monogram as above(?); inscribed CI‖[CI‖N]N‖HC.

✠ On the inside of the bowl; inscribed [CI‖CI‖N]N‖HC.

DATE: Heraclius, A.D. 613–629/30 (see no. 51).

Principal References: Dalton, *Catalogue*, no. 379; Rosenberg, pp. 710–711.

Source of Illustration: The British Museum, reproduction courtesy of the Trustees.

a. Inside of Bowl

b. Detail of Center Monogram

Bowl "A" from Lampsacus

c. The Stamps

a. Inside of Bowl

b. Detail of Center Medallion

Bowl "B" from Lampsacus

c. The Stamps

No. 53. BOWL "B" FROM LAMPSACUS

DESCRIPTION: Bowl with gilt cross in center. The arms of the cross extend to the rim, and in its center is a monogram in niello. Identical with no. 52, but slightly larger (fig. a).

Wt. 260 gr.; diam. 18 cm.

PLACE OF DISCOVERY: Lampsacus, Hellespont. Found with nos. 19, 24, and 52. Acquired in 1886.

CONTROL STAMPS: Three cruciform stamps clearly visible, and traces of other stamps remain, but their shapes are not easily distinguishable (fig. c). The clearest stamp, a cross, is on the inside of the bowl (fig. b) (see no. 52). The stamps appear to be identical with the stamps on no. 52, except that the square on no. 52 is here replaced by a hexagon. Like the stamps on no. 52, these were damaged by the decoration of the niello monogram. The readings were taken from the object:

⬡   On the outside of the bowl, outside the incised circles between the N and the A of the monogram: almost entirely destroyed.

⬠   Beside the incised circles, opposite the N of the monogram.

✛   Beside the incised circles, above the M of the monogram: flared arms; inscribed [C]I‖[CI‖NN‖HC]?

✛   Beside the A of the monogram.

✛   Inside the bowl: inscribed CI‖CI‖[NN]‖HC.

DATE: Heraclius, A.D. 613–629/30 (see nos. 51, 52).

Principal References: Dalton, *Catalogue,* no. 378.

Source of Illustration: The British Museum, reproduction courtesy of the Trustees.

No. 54 *A* and *B*. PLATE WITH NIELLO CROSS

The Museum of Antiquities, Nicosia, Cyprus; acc. no. J. 456

DESCRIPTION: Large, flat plate with niello cross in center, surrounded by floral wreath (figs. a and b).

Diam. 36.8 cm.; diam. of central roundel 10 cm.; diam. of footring 15.4 cm.

PLACE OF DISCOVERY: Found in Cyprus, in 1902, with nos. 33, 58–66; from the "Second Cyprus Treasure" (see no. 33).

CONTROL STAMPS: Like no. 55, this plate has more than the usual number of stamps, some of which are very worn, others fairly clear, suggesting that the plate was stamped on two occasions (cf. pp. 8, 34). Seven stamps can be identified with certainty (fig. c) – a round, two square, two long, and two cruciform – while the remains of others can also be discerned although their outlines are indistinct. The stamps were worn down when work on the niello decoration was done. They fall readily into two groups, those which are most worn (*A*) and those which are clearer (*B*). Group *A* is related to the stamps on objects nos. 51–53, while group *B* is related to the stamps on objects nos. 55–70. On nos. 55, 56, and 57, the stamps are similar to the corresponding stamps on no. 54*B*. The readings were taken from the object:

54 *A*:

O Near the square stamp of group *B* and below the cross stamps: nimbed bust, type 6a; inscription illegible.

O ? Between the square inscribed ΛΑΜΠ[ΡΟΤΑΤΟC] and the long stamp of group *B*.

□ Damaged monogram of Heraclius; inscribed ΛΑΜΠ[Ρ‖ΟΤΑΤΟC] (see the corresponding stamps on nos. 51, 52).

◠ Beneath the long stamp of group *B*.

✥ Below the long stamp; flared arms.

54 *B*:

□ Double strike; monogram of Heraclius, type a; inscribed ΦΙΛΙ‖ΠΟC, identical with the corresponding stamps on nos. 55–57.

◠ Bust of Heraclius, type 6a; cruciform monogram that reads BACIΛIOV, and is the same as the monogram in the cross stamp; found again in the corresponding stamps of nos. 55–57; inscribed CXOΛAC‖CTIKIC (the C in the middle of the name appears to be duplicated). This name, with minor variations in the spelling, is found again in the long stamps of nos. 55–71. A small X and Θ may be seen below the bust; these letters, also present in the corresponding stamps of nos. 55*A* and 56, remain unexplained (p. 15). This stamp is the same as the corresponding stamp on no. 55*A*, and similar to the long stamp on no. 56, where the inscribed name is abbreviated.

✥ Nearest the long stamp: flared arms; monogram BACIΛIOV as above; inscribed in a circular direction (see the cross stamps on nos. 55–57) CV‖M[Є]‖ωN‖IC.

✥ As above; less clear; inscribed C[V‖MЄ]‖ωN‖IC.

DATE: Both sets of stamps belong to the reign of Heraclius, A.D. 613–629/30. One set is related to the stamps earlier in the Heraclian series, the other to later stamps, thus placing the object near the middle of the series.

Principal References: Dalton, *Arch.* 60, p. 3, no. 2, pl. 1: 2; Rosenberg, pp. 656–657; Matsulevich, "Arg. byz.," pp. 295, 298; *Byz. Art, 1958*, no. 55.

Source of Illustration: The Department of Antiquities, Cyprus.

a. Plate with Niello Cross

b. Detail of Center Medallion

c. The Stamps

a. Plate "B" with Niello Cross from Kalganovka

b. The Stamps

No. 55 *A* and *B*. PLATE "B" WITH NIELLO CROSS FROM KALGANOVKA

THE HERMITAGE, LENINGRAD; acc. no. W. 283

DESCRIPTION: Large, fluted plate, decorated with niello cross in center surrounded by floral wreath (fig. a); almost identical with the design on no. 54. Diam. 27 cm. (Matsulevich).

PLACE OF DISCOVERY: Found in 1878, with nos. 51 and 70, at Kalganovka, district of Solikamsk, Government of Perm (renamed Molotov in 1942). Formerly in the Stroganov Collection.

CONTROL STAMPS: Like no. 54, this plate appears to have been stamped twice at different times for, in addition to the normal complement of five stamps, the round, the hexagon, the square, and the cross are repeated (fig. b). The fact that the duplicate stamps (*B*) are very worn and that three stand alone makes it unlikely that they can be the result of the more common "double strike." Since, however, the repeated stamps seem to be identical with the five that are clearly discernible (*A*), the interval between the times when they were struck cannot have been long. The incision for the niello design on the obverse cuts into the long and cross stamps, indicating that this object was decorated after it was stamped (Matsulevich, "Arg. Byz.," p. 296). The stamps are similar to the corresponding stamps on nos. 54 *B*, 56, and 57. The readings were taken from the photograph and cast:

55 *A*:

○ Imperial bust, type 6c; inscribed [A]NΔ‖P[ЄAC]; identical with the round stamp on no. 56.

⬡ Below the centering point: double strike that has seriously displaced both the inscription and the monogram of Heraclius, type a.

□ To the right of the centering point: monogram of Heraclius; inscribed [ΦI]Λ[I‖ΠO]C; identical with the square stamps on nos. 54 *B*, 55 *B*, 56, 57.

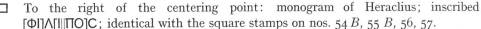
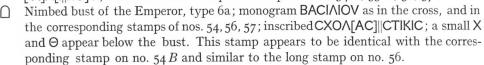

⌂ Nimbed bust of the Emperor, type 6a; monogram BACIΛIOV as in the cross, and in the corresponding stamps of nos. 54, 56, 57; inscribed CXOΛ[AC]‖CTIKIC; a small X and Θ appear below the bust. This stamp appears to be identical with the corresponding stamp on no. 54 *B* and similar to the long stamp on no. 56.

✠ Near the hexagon: monogram as above; inscribed CV‖[MЄ]‖ωN‖IC (see nos. 54 *B*, 55 *B*, 56, 57).

55 *B*:

○ Cutting into the round stamp of 55 *A*.

⬡ Near the centering point.

□ To the left of the hexagon, overlapping the long stamp of 55 *A*: part of the monogram of Heraclius is visible (type a); inscribed [ΦI]Λ[I‖ΠOC].

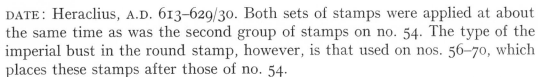

✠ Just above, and partly overlapped by, the square of 55 *A*: inscribed [CV‖MЄ]‖-ωN‖[IC].

DATE: Heraclius, A.D. 613–629/30. Both sets of stamps were applied at about the same time as was the second group of stamps on no. 54. The type of the imperial bust in the round stamp, however, is that used on nos. 56–70, which places these stamps after those of no. 54.

Principal References: Rosenberg, pp. 658–659; Matsulevich, "Arg. byz.," p. 293, no. 2, pl. XLV: 1.
Source of Illustration: The Hermitage.

No. 56. BUCKET WITH MYTHOLOGICAL FIGURES

Kunsthistorisches Museum, Vienna

DESCRIPTION: Bucket decorated with relief depicting six gods (fig. a).

Wt. 2047 gr.; diam. of top 22.7 cm.; diam. of bottom 17.5 cm.; ht. 25.8 cm. (Matsulevich).

PLACE OF DISCOVERY: Found in 1814, in Kuczurmare, Bukovina.

CONTROL STAMPS: Five stamps – a round, a hexagonal, a square, a long, and a cruciform, similar to the corresponding stamps on nos. 54 B, 55, 57 (fig. b). It is difficult to judge whether the stamps were applied before or after the decoration of the bucket. The readings were taken from the photograph:

O   Bust, type 6c; inscribed ANΔ‖PEAC (see no. 55 A).

⬡   Monogram of Heraclius, type a, partly destroyed; small, nimbed bust above the monogram; inscription not clear.

▢   Monogram of Heraclius, type a; inscribed ΦIΛI‖[Π]OC (see nos. 54 B, 55, 57).

⬭   Imperial bust, type 6a; monogram BACIΛIOV (see nos. 54 B, 55 A, 57); a Θ appears below the bust (see nos. 54 B, 55 A); inscribed CXOΛAC‖CTIC; no doubt this is a corrupt spelling of the name CXOΛACTIKIC, found in similar long stamps, nos. 54 B, 55 A, 58–70; it is also abbreviated on no. 58.

✠   Flared arms; monogram as above; inscribed CV‖ME‖ω[N]‖IC]. This stamp is identical with the corresponding stamps on nos. 54 B–57.

DATE: Heraclius, A.D. 613–629/30. These stamps belong to the group 54 B–57, and the name in the long stamp associates this group with nos. 58–70.

Principal References: Rosenberg, pp. 660–661; R. Jaeger, "Ein Beitrag zur Geschichte der altchristlichen Silberarbeiten," *JDAI*, XLIII (1928), *Arch. Anz.*, col. 559; Matsulevich, *Byz. Ant.*, p. 7 f., no. 14, p. 15, pls. 7–11.

Source of Illustration: Kunsthistorisches Museum.

a. Bucket with Mythological Figures

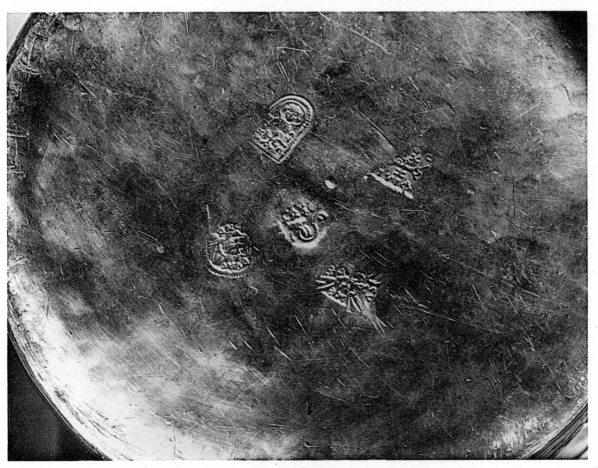

b. The Stamps

a. The Meleager Plate

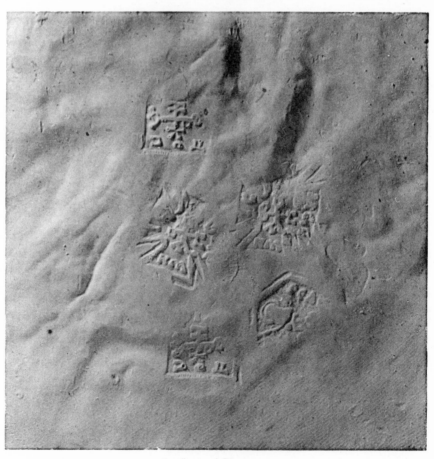

b. Cast of Stamps

No. 57. THE MELEAGER PLATE

THE HERMITAGE, LENINGRAD; acc. no. W. 1

DESCRIPTION: Plate decorated with figures in relief (fig. a). In center, Meleager, at the hunt, leans on his spear; at left (from spectator's point of view) Atalanta leads her horse. On either side stand attendants, the one at left holds a lamb. Below this scene two dogs play near a hunting net.

Wt. 1523 gr.; diam. 28 cm.; diam. of footring 12.5 cm.; ht. of footring 1.2 cm. (Matsulevich).

PLACE OF DISCOVERY: Unknown. Acquired in 1840.

CONTROL STAMPS: Five stamps – a hexagonal, two square, and two cruciform (fig. b). The relief has been worked after the stamps were applied (Matsulevich, pp. 10–12). All the stamps are similar to corresponding stamps on nos. 54 B–56. The readings were taken from the cast and photograph:

○ Monogram of Heraclius, type b, barely visible; small, nimbed bust above the monogram; inscribed [AN]Δ‖PΕAC.

□ Nearest the hexagon: monogram of Heraclius, type a; inscribed ΦIΛ[I]‖ΠOC (see the corresponding stamps on nos. 54 B–56).

□ Above the cross stamps: as above; inscribed [ΦIΛI]‖ΠOC.

⊕ Between the square stamps: flared arms; monogram BACIΛIOV; inscribed in a circular direction CV‖ME‖ωN‖IC. This stamp is identical with the corresponding stamps on nos. 54 B–56.

⊕ Same as above; inscribed CV‖ME‖ωN‖IC.

DATE: Heraclius, A.D. 613–629/30. These stamps belong to the same period as the stamps on nos. 54 B–56.

Principal References: Rosenberg, pp. 662–663; Matsulevich, *Byz. Ant.*, p. 2 f., no. 1, pp. 9–17, figs. 1, 2, pl. 1.

Source of Illustration: The Hermitage.

No. 58. THE DAVID PLATES: DAVID AND GOLIATH

THE METROPOLITAN MUSEUM OF ART, NEW YORK, Gift of J. Pierpont Morgan; acc. no. 17.190.396

DESCRIPTION: Large plate with three scenes in relief (fig. a): at top, Meeting of David and Goliath; in central band, Slaying of Goliath; at bottom, David Beheading Goliath (I Sam. 17).

Diam. 49.4 cm.; diam. of footring 20.7 cm.

PLACE OF DISCOVERY: Found in Cyprus, in 1902, with nos. 33, 54, 59–66; from the "Second Cyprus Treasure" (see no. 33).

CONTROL STAMPS: Five stamps – a round, a hexagonal, a square, a long, and a cruciform (fig. b). They appear to have been damaged, especially the long stamp, during the hammering of the relief. The fact that they are almost identical with the corresponding stamps on nos. 59–66 clarifies the reading of a number of individual names and monograms. Yet the combination of the stamps varies among the plates of the set: no. 60, like no. 58 and probably no. 59, has one stamp of each shape; on no. 61 only four stamps can be positively discerned; on nos. 62 and 63 the hexagon has been replaced by an extra cruciform stamp; nos. 64 and 65 have an additional cruciform stamp, as well as the remains of a hexagonal one, making six in all; on no. 66 are a hexagon, two long, and two cruciform stamps. On no. 58 (the largest plate in the set) the name CXOΛACTIKIC in the long stamp appears in an abbreviated form (see no. 56). The readings were taken from the object in each case:

O   Bust of Heraclius, type, 6c; inscribed [Θ]ЄOXA‖PI[CTOC].

O   Overlapped by the square; barely discernible.

□   Monogram of Heraclius, type a; the instrument slipped and disfigured the monogram (see the corresponding stamp on no. 43); inscribed ✝ KOM‖ITAC.

∩   Imperial bust, type 6c; monogram in enlarged characters (see no. 48), ΘЄOΔѠPOV (see no. 20); inscribed CXOΛ[A]‖CTIC.

✠   Flared arms; monogram as above, in small letters; inscribed in a circular direction ✝ K‖OC‖M‖AC.

DATE: Heraclius, A.D. 613–629/30. The relationship between the inscription in the long stamp and the corresponding inscriptions on nos. 54 B–56 places this group of stamps and those on nos. 59–66 close to the previous group. The more developed form of the imperial bust in the long stamp—on nos. 54 B–56 the bust is nimbed—suggests that this series follows upon the series nos. 54 B–56 (see p. 10).

Principal References: Smith, p. 46 f., pl. LXVI; Rosenberg, pp. 640–641.

Source of Illustration: The Metropolitan Museum of Art.

a. David Plate: David and Goliath

b. The Stamps

a. David Plate: Marriage of David and Michal

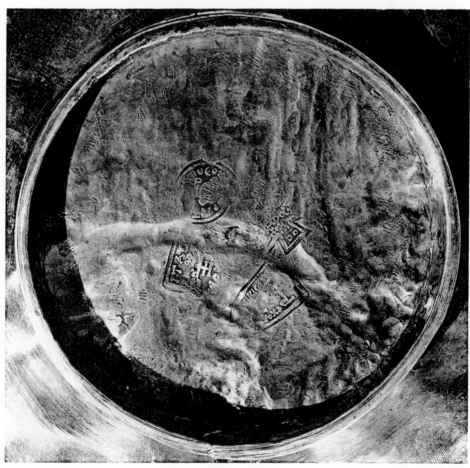

b. The Stamps

No. 59. THE DAVID PLATES: MARRIAGE OF DAVID AND MICHAL

THE MUSEUM OF ANTIQUITIES, NICOSIA, CYPRUS; acc. no. 452

DESCRIPTION: Plate with relief depicting Marriage of David and Michal (I Sam. 18:27) (fig. a).

Diam. 26.8 cm.; diam. of footring 11.8 cm.

PLACE OF DISCOVERY: Found in Cyprus, in 1902, with nos. 33, 54, 58, 60–66; from the "Second Cyprus Treasure" (see no. 33).

CONTROL STAMPS: Four stamps are distinctly visible – a round, a square, a long, and a cruciform (fig. b). There is, in addition, the suggestion of a hexagonal outline on the top arm of the cross. The stamps were damaged during the hammering of the relief, as is apparent from the impressions in the deep hollow formed by the joined arms on the obverse. They are almost identical with the corresponding stamps on nos. 58, 60–66 (see no. 58).

O   Bust of Heraclius, type 6c; inscribed ΘЄΟΧ[Α]‖PICTO[C].

⬭   ?

☐   Monogram of Heraclius, type a; inscribed [+]ΚΟΜ‖ΙΤΑC.

⬭   Bust not clear; monogram ΘЄΟΔШΡΟV; inscribed CΧΟΛ[Α‖C]ΤΙΚΙC.

✛   Flared arms; monogram as above; inscribed [+ Κ]‖OC‖[Μ‖ΑC].

DATE: Heraclius, A.D. 613–629/30 (see no. 58).

Principal References: Dalton, *Arch.* 60, p. 3, no. 3, pl. II; Rosenberg, pp. 648–649; P. Dikaios, *A Guide to the Cyprus Museum* (Nicosia, 1947), p. 115, pl. XXIII, fig. 2; *Byz. Art, 1958,* no. 34.

Source of Illustration: Victoria and Albert Museum, reproduction courtesy of The Department of Antiquities, Cyprus.

No. 60. THE DAVID PLATES: INTRODUCTION OF DAVID TO SAUL

THE METROPOLITAN MUSEUM OF ART, NEW YORK, Gift of J. Pierpont Morgan;
acc. no. 17.190. 397

DESCRIPTION: Plate with relief of Meeting of David and Saul (I Sam. 16:21) (fig. a).

Diam. 26.5 cm.; diam. of footring 12 cm.

PLACE OF DISCOVERY: Found in Cyprus, in 1902, with nos. 33, 54, 58, 59, 61–66; from the "Second Cyprus Treasure" (see no. 33).

CONTROL STAMPS: Three stamps are distinctly visible – a square, a long, and a cruciform (fig. b); under the centering point and close to the long stamp, part of a hexagonal outline can be seen; under the long stamp are the remains of the inscription in a round stamp. It is difficult to determine whether the stamps were applied before or after the plate was decorated, but, since it belongs to a set, it was probably decorated at the same time as its companion pieces, that is, after the stamps had been applied (see nos. 58, 59, 61, etc.). The stamps are almost identical with the corresponding stamps on nos. 58, 59, 61–66 (see no. 58).

O   Badly worn; only a portion of the rim is visible to the right and below the bust in the long stamp: inscribed [ΘЄOXA]‖PIC[TOC].

O   Not clear.

□   Monogram of Heraclius; inscribed + KO[M‖IT]AC.

∩   Bust of Heraclius, type 6c; monogram ΘЄOΔШPOV; inscribed [CX]OΛ[A]‖C[TIKIC].

✠   Flared arms; inscribed + K‖O[C‖M‖AC].

DATE: Heraclius, A.D. 613–629/30 (see no. 58).

Principal References: Dalton, *BM*, p. 357, fig. 2; *idem, Arch.* 60, p. 2; Sambon, p. 124, no. 3, pl. XIX, right; Smith, p. 45, pl. LXIV; Rosenberg, pp. 646–647.

Source of Illustration: The Metropolitan Museum of Art.

a. David Plate: Introduction of David to Saul

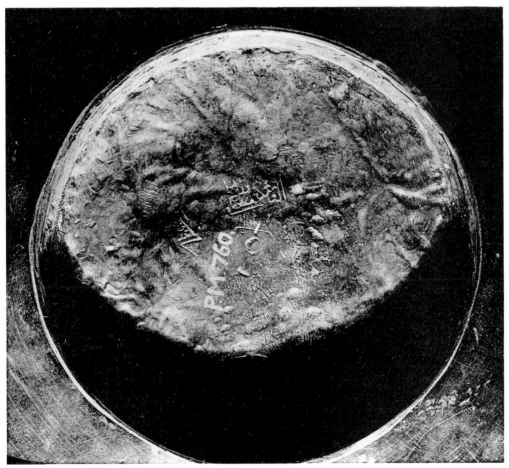

b. The Stamps

a. David Plate: David Trying on Saul's Armor

b. The Stamps

No. 61. THE DAVID PLATES: DAVID TRYING ON SAUL'S ARMOR

THE METROPOLITAN MUSEUM OF ART, NEW YORK, Gift of J. Pierpont Morgan; acc. no. 17.190.399

DESCRIPTION: Plate with relief of David Trying on Saul's Armor (I Sam. 17:38) (fig. a). This plate shows particularly well the technique of joining together two sheets of silver after the relief has been moulded. Inside the footring, the relief is revealed in repoussé, but on the outside the plate is perfectly smooth. Breaks in the silver are visible on the rim and on the footring where the second sheet has been joined to the first. This technique was used for all the David plates (p. 1).

Diam. 26 cm.; diam. of footring 12 cm.

PLACE OF DISCOVERY: Found in Cyprus, in 1902, with nos. 33, 54, 58–60, 62–66; from the "Second Cyprus Treasure" (see no. 33).

CONTROL STAMPS: Four stamps are distinctly visible – a round, a square, a long, and a cruciform (fig. b). These stamps appear to have been applied before the decoration of the plate, since the cross stamp is clearest where the relief has been hollowed out to form David's head. They are almost identical with the corresponding stamps on nos. 58–60, 62–66 (see no. 58).

O   Bust of Heraclius, type 6c; inscribed ΘЄOXA‖PI[C]TOC.

□   Monogram of Heraclius, type a; inscribed + KOM‖[ITA]C.

∩   Bust of Heraclius, type 6c; monogram ΘЄOΔѠPOV, mostly destroyed; inscribed CXOΛA‖CTI[KIC].

✠   Flared arms; monogram as above; inscribed + K‖O[C]‖M‖[A]C.

DATE: Heraclius, A.D. 613–629/30 (see no. 58).

Principal References: Dalton, *BM*, p. 361, pl. II, fig. 5; Sambon, p. 124, no. 4, pl. XIX, left; Smith, p. 45 f., pl. LXV; Rosenberg, pp. 644–645; E. Rosenbaum, "The Andrews Diptych and Some Related Ivories," *Art Bulletin*, XXXVI (1954), p. 256, note 31, fig. 16.

Source of Illustration: The Metropolitan Museum of Art.

No. 62. THE DAVID PLATES: ANOINTING OF DAVID

THE METROPOLITAN MUSEUM OF ART, NEW YORK, Gift of J. Pierpont Morgan; acc. no. 17.190.398

DESCRIPTION: Plate with relief of Anointing of David (I Sam. 16:13) (fig. a).

Diam. 26 cm.; diam. of footring 12 cm.

PLACE OF DISCOVERY: Found in Cyprus, in 1902, with nos. 33, 54, 58–61, 63–66; from the "Second Cyprus Treasure" (see no. 33).

CONTROL STAMPS: Five stamps – a round, a square, a long, and two cruciform (fig. b). The centering point cuts into the cross stamp, and, since this plate belongs to a set, it was probably decorated at the same time as its companion pieces, that is, after the stamps were applied (see nos. 58, 59, 61, etc.). The stamps are almost identical with the corresponding stamps on nos. 58–61, 63–66 (see no. 58).

O   Bust of Heraclius, type 6c; inscribed ΘЄOXA‖PICTOC.

□   Flattened out; monogram of Heraclius can be discerned; inscribed [+ K]OM‖[ITA]C.

⌂   Bust of Heraclius, type 6c; monogram ΘЄOΔѠPOV; inscribed [CXOΛA]‖CTI[KI]C.

✙   In the center of the plate, broken by the centering point: monogram ΘЄOΔѠPOV as above; inscribed + K‖O[C]‖M‖[AC].

✙   As above; inscribed [+ K]‖OC‖M‖[AC].

DATE: Heraclius, A.D. 613–629/30 (see no. 58).

Principal References: Dalton, *BM*, p. 361, pl. II, fig. 4; Sambon, p. 123, no 2, pl. XX, center; Smith, p. 44, pl. LXIII; Rosenberg, pp. 642–643.

Source of Illustration: The Metropolitan Museum of Art.

a. David Plate: Anointing of David

b. The Stamps

a. David Plate: David Slaying Lion

b. The Stamps

No. 63. THE DAVID PLATES: DAVID SLAYING LION

THE METROPOLITAN MUSEUM OF ART, NEW YORK, Gift of J. Pierpont Morgan; acc. no. 17.190.394

DESCRIPTION: Plate with relief of David Slaying the Lion (I Sam. 17:34–36) (fig. a).

Diam. 14 cm.; diam. of footring 6.5 cm.

PLACE OF DISCOVERY: Found in Cyprus, in 1902, with nos. 33, 54, 58–62, 64–66; from the "Second Cyprus Treasure" (see no. 33).

CONTROL STAMPS: Five stamps (fig. b) – a round, a square, a long, and two cruciform, almost identical with the corresponding stamps on nos. 58–62, 64–66 (see no. 58). The centering point cuts into the cross stamp, and, since this plate belongs to a set, it was probably decorated at the same time as its companion pieces, that is, after the stamps were applied (see nos. 58, 59, 61, etc.).

○   Nimbed bust, type 6c; inscribed [Θ]ЄΟΧΑ‖PIC[TOC].

□   Monogram of Heraclius, type a; inscribed + KOM‖[ITA]C.

⌂   Bust of Heraclius, type 6c; monogram ΘЄΟΔШPOV; inscribed [C]XOΛΑ‖[C]TIKIC.

✚   In the center of the plate, broken by the centering point: flared arms; monogram as above; inscribed + K‖OC‖[M]‖.C.

✚   Beside the central cross stamp: same as the above; inscribed + [K]‖OC‖[M]‖AC.

DATE: Heraclius, A.D. 613–629/30 (see no. 58).

Principal References: Dalton, *BM*, p. 361, pl. I, fig. 1; Sambon, p. 122 f., no. 1, pl. XX, lower left; Smith, p. 44; Rosenberg, pp. 636–637.

Source of Illustration: The Metropolitan Museum of Art.

No. 64. THE DAVID PLATES: DAVID AND SOLDIER

THE METROPOLITAN MUSEUM OF ART, NEW YORK, Gift of J. Pierpont Morgan; acc. no. 17.190.395

DESCRIPTION: Plate with relief of David and Soldier (I Sam. 30:11 ff. ?) (fig. a).

Diam. 14 cm.; diam. of footring 6.5 cm.

PLACE OF DISCOVERY: Found in Cyprus, in 1902, with nos. 33, 54, 58–63, 65, 66; from the "Second Cyprus Treasure" (see no. 33).

CONTROL STAMPS: Five stamps are distinctly visible (fig. b) – a round, a square, a long, and two cruciform, all nearly identical with the corresponding stamps on the other plates in the David set, nos. 58–63, 65, 66 (see no. 58). In addition, a sixth stamp, hexagonal, can be discerned beneath the round stamp in the center (p. 8). Like the other pieces of the set, this plate was probably decorated after it was stamped (see nos. 58, 59, 61, etc.).

O   Imperial bust, type 6c; inscribed [Θ]ЄOXA‖[PICT]OC.

O   Illegible.

□   Monogram of Heraclius, type a; inscribed + KOM‖[IT]AC.

◻   Bust of Heraclius, type 6c; monogram ΘЄOΔШPOV; inscribed [CXOΛA]‖CTIKIC.

✠   On a line with the round and the square: monogram as above; inscribed + K‖[OC‖M‖ AC].

✠   On a line with the round and the long: monogram as above; inscription not clear.

DATE: Heraclius, A.D. 613–629/30 (see no. 58).

Principal References: Dalton, *BM*, p. 361, pl. 1, fig. 3; Sambon, p. 124, no. 5, pl. xx, lower right; Smith, p. 47; Rosenberg, pp. 638–639.

Source of Illustration: The Metropolitan Museum of Art.

a. David Plate: David and Soldier

b. The Stamps

a. David Plate: David Summoned to Samuel (?)

b. The Stamps

No. 65. THE DAVID PLATES: DAVID SUMMONED TO SAMUEL(?)

THE MUSEUM OF ANTIQUITIES, NICOSIA, CYPRUS; acc. no. 454

DESCRIPTION: Plate with relief of David as Shepherd, and Messenger Approaching Him (? I Sam. 16:11f.) (fig. a).

Diam. 14 cm.; diam. of footring 6.5 cm.

PLACE OF DISCOVERY: Found in Cyprus, in 1902, with nos. 33, 54, 58–64, 66; from the "Second Cyprus Treasure" (see no. 33).

CONTROL STAMPS: Five stamps are distinctly visible (fig. b) – a round, a square, a long, and two cruciform, all nearly identical with the stamps on the rest of the David set, nos. 58–64, 66 (see no. 58). The remains of a sixth stamp, a hexagon, can be seen near the center cross stamp (see p. 8; no. 64). Like the other plates in the David set, this piece was probably decorated after it was stamped (see nos. 58, 59, 61, etc.).

O   Only part of the outline is distinct.

◖   Illegible.

□   Monogram of Heraclius, type a; inscribed   +KOM‖[ITAC].

◖   Barely visible, near the central cross stamp: part of the monogram ΘЄΟΔѠΡΟV and the inscription CXOΛ[A‖CTIKIC] can be determined.

✠   Next to the central cross stamp: illegible.

✠   Near the center: part of the monogram ΘЄΟΔѠΡΟV; inscribed [+ K‖ΟC]‖M‖[AC].

DATE: Heraclius, A.D. 613–629/30 (see no. 58).

Principal References: Dalton, *Arch.* 60, p. 8, no. 5, fig. 4a; Rosenberg, pp. 650–651; Dikaios, *A Guide to the Cyprus Museum*, p. 116f.; *Byz. Art, 1958*, no. 36.

Source of Illustration: Victoria and Albert Museum, reproduction courtesy of Mr. John Beckwith and the Department of Antiquities, Cyprus.

No. 66. THE DAVID PLATES: DAVID SLAYING BEAR

The Museum of Antiquities, Nicosia, Cyprus; acc. no. 453

DESCRIPTION: Plate with relief of David Slaying the Bear (I Sam. 17:34, 35) (fig. a).

Diam. 14 cm.; diam. of footring 6.5 cm.

PLACE OF DISCOVERY: Found in Cyprus, in 1902, with nos. 33, 54, 58–65; from the "Second Cyprus Treasure" (see no. 33).

CONTROL STAMPS: Five stamps (fig. b) – a hexagonal, two long, and two cruciform, almost identical with the corresponding stamps on the other plates in the David set, nos. 58–65 (see no. 58). Like other plates in the set, this piece was probably decorated after it was stamped (see nos. 58, 59, 61, etc.).

○ Part of the monogram of Heraclius can be discerned; inscription not entirely legible, ...OV.

◠ Near the top of the hexagon: part of a bust can be seen; monogram ΘΕΟΔѠΡΟV; inscribed CX[ΟΛΑ‖CTΙΚ]ΙC.

◠ Near the visible part of the inscription in the hexagon: part of a bust; monogram ΘΕΟΔѠΡΟV as above; inscribed CX[ΟΛΑ‖CTΙΚΙC].

✚ Nearest the first long stamp: monogram ΘΕΟΔѠΡΟV as above; inscribed [✚]Κ‖[Ο]C‖ Μ‖[ΑC].

✚ Nearest the second long stamp: double strike; monogram as above; inscribed [✚Κ‖ΟC]‖Μ‖[ΑC].

DATE: Heraclius, A.D. 613–629/30 (see no. 58).

Principal References: Dalton, *Arch.* 60, p. 7f., no. 4, fig. 4b; Rosenberg, pp. 652–653; Dikaios, *A Guide to the Cyprus Museum*, p. 116, pl. XXIII, fig. 1; *Byz. Art, 1958*, no. 35.

Source of Illustration: Victoria and Albert Museum, reproduction courtesy of Mr. John Beckwith and the Department of Antiquities, Cyprus.

a. David Plate: David Slaying Bear

b. The Stamps

a. Plate with Niello Cross from Piatigor'e

b. The Stamps

No. 67. PLATE WITH NIELLO CROSS FROM PIATIGOR'E

THE HERMITAGE, LENINGRAD; acc. no. W. 217

DESCRIPTION: Small, fluted plate, decorated in center with niello cross surrounded by ivy wreath (fig. a).

Wt. 295 gr.; diam. 14.2 cm. (Matsulevich).

PLACE OF DISCOVERY: Piatigor'e, district of Çerdyn, Government of Perm (renamed Molotov in 1942).

CONTROL STAMPS: Remains of five stamps – two square, one long, and two cruciform (fig. b). Since the circle inscribed within the footring cuts off part of the stamps, they must have been applied before the decoration had been completed (Matsulevich, "Arg. byz.," p. 297). They are identical with the corresponding stamps on plates in the David set, nos. 58–66. The readings were taken from the photograph and cast:

▢   Overlapping a cross stamp: inscribed [+]KOM‖[ITAC].

▢   On the opposite side of the circle from the cross stamps: monogram of Heraclius, type a; inscribed [+KOM]‖ITAC.

⌂   Only the outline is dimly seen between the two cross stamps. It would appear to have been struck twice.

✠   On a line with the first square stamp and the long stamp: monogram ΘΕΟΔѠΡΟV, partly destroyed; inscribed [+K‖OC‖M‖A]C.

✠   Near the first square: monogram as above; inscribed + K‖[OC‖M‖A]C.

DATE: Heraclius, A.D. 613–629/30 (see no. 58).

Principal References: Rosenberg, pp. 654–655; Matsulevich, "Arg. byz.," p. 294, no. 7.

Source of Illustration: The Hermitage.

No. 68. STROGANOV PLATE WITH NIELLO CROSS

THE HERMITAGE, LENINGRAD; acc. no. W. 281

DESCRIPTION: Plate with cross in center surrounded by ivy wreath. Curved lines of fluting radiate from center (fig. a).

Wt. 939 gr.; diam. 26 cm. (Matsulevich).

PLACE OF DISCOVERY: Found in 1780(?), near the village of Sludka on the Kama River, Government of Perm (renamed Molotov in 1942). Formerly in the Stroganov Collection in Rome.

CONTROL STAMPS: Five stamps – a hexagonal, a square, two long, and a cruciform (fig. b). They were damaged during the working of the niello design on the obverse. The readings were taken from the cast and photograph:

○ Outline barely visible between the cross and the clearest long stamp.

▢ Monogram of Heraclius, type a; inscription not clear.

◌ Farthest from the square stamp, on a line with the square and the centering point: bust of Heraclius, type 6c; cruciform monogram ΔAMIANOV? (Jaeger, as published by Rosenberg); inscribed CXOΛA‖CTIKIC (see the corresponding stamps on nos. 54B–70).

◌ Between the first long stamp and the square: same as above, less clear.

⳨ Flared arms; monogram as above; inscribed in a circular direction [A]N‖ΔP‖[E‖AC]. See no. 69.

DATE: Heraclius, A.D. 613–629/30. The position of the stamps in the sequence is determined by their relationship to those of the David set, on the one hand, and to those of the following numbers, on the other. They come before the stamps of Constans II, nos. 75–78.

Principal References: Rosenberg, pp. 668–669; Matsulevich, *Byz. Ant.*, p. 81, fig. 12; *idem,* "Arg. byz.," p. 293, no. 1, p. 294, pl. XLIV:1.

Source of Illustration: The Hermitage.

a. Stroganov Plate with Niello Cross

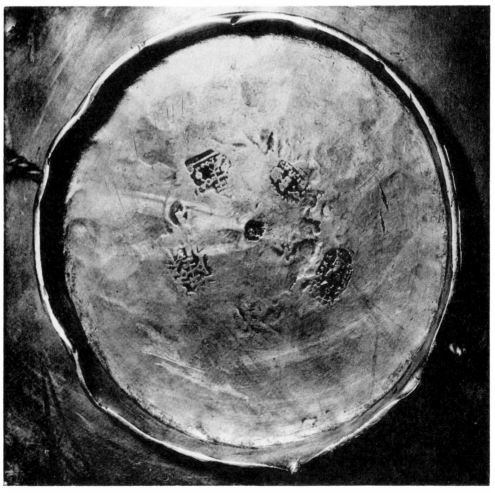

b. The Stamps

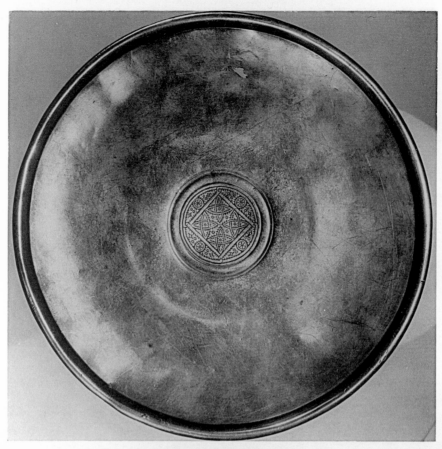

a. Plate with Center Niello Pattern from Viatka

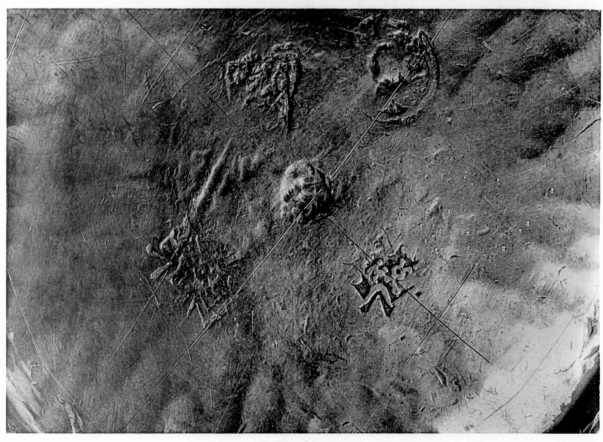

b. The Stamps

No. 69. PLATE WITH CENTER NIELLO PATTERN FROM VIATKA

THE HERMITAGE, LENINGRAD; acc. no. W. 110

DESCRIPTION: Simple plate with geometric niello design in center (fig. a).

Diam. *ca.* 28 cm. (Rosenberg).

PLACE OF DISCOVERY: Found in the River Tomyz, district of Glazov, Government of Viatka (renamed Kirov in 1934).

CONTROL STAMPS: Four indistinct stamps within footring – a round, a square, and two cruciform (fig. b). It is difficult to say whether they were applied before or after the decoration was finished. The readings were taken from the photograph:

○   Imperial bust, type 6c(?); inscribed ....IKIC.

□   Monogram of Heraclius, indistinct.

✥   On a line with the square and the centering point: monogram ΔAMIANOV(?); inscribed AN‖[Δ]P‖Є‖[AC]. See no. 68.

✥   On a line with the round and the centering point: same as the above; inscribed AN‖[ΔP]‖Є‖[AC].

DATE: Heraclius, A.D. 613–629/30. The relationship between these stamps and those of no. 68 places them in the same period.

Principal References: Rosenberg, pp. 666–667.

Source of Illustration: The Hermitage.

No. 70. THE MAENAD PLATE

THE HERMITAGE, LENINGRAD

DESCRIPTION: Plate with relief of dancing Maenad and Silenus with wine-skin on his shoulder (fig. a).

Wt. 1181 gr.; diam. 25.8 cm.; diam. of footring 11.7 cm. (Matsulevich).

PLACE OF DISCOVERY: Found in 1878, with nos. 51 and 55, at Kalganovka, district of Solikamsk, Government of Perm (renamed Molotov in 1942). Formerly in the Stroganov Collection.

CONTROL STAMPS: Five stamps within footring – two round, a square, a long, and a cruciform (fig. b). They were applied before the decoration of the plate was finished since they are clearest (especially the square, the long, and the cross) where there are hollows on the bottom of the plate (Matsulevich, pp. 20–21). Beside the stamps the name ΑΝΔΡΕΟΥ has been scratched in. The readings were taken from the object:

O   Bust of Heraclius, type 6c; inscribed ΜΑΡΤ‖ΥΡ[Ε?].

O   The same, but worn.

☐   Monogram of Heraclius, "type c" (i.e., partially destroyed or incomplete since it lacks the Ρ); inscribed ΠΑΤΡ‖ΙΚ[ΙϹ].

◠   Bust of Heraclius, type 6c; cruciform monogram; inscribed ϹΧΟΛΑ‖ϹΤΙΚΙϹ (see the corresponding inscriptions on nos. 54 B–69).

✠   Flared arms; the cruciform monogram appears to repeat the monogram in the square (p. 15, Table III, and no. 71); inscribed ΑΝ‖ΔΡ‖Ε‖[ΑϹ] (see nos. 68, 69).

DATE: Heraclius, A.D. 613–629/30. The relationship between these stamps and the stamps on nos. 54 B–69 dates them in the same period.

Principal References: Rosenberg, pp. 664–665; Matsulevich, *Byz. Ant.*, p. 3, no. 2, pp. 18–22, fig. 3, pl. 2; *Byz. Art, 1958*, no. 47.

Source of Illustration: Victoria and Albert Museum, reproduction courtesy of the Hermitage and Mr. John Beckwith.

a. The Maenad Plate

b. The Stamps

a. Bowl with Angels

b. The Stamp

No. 71. BOWL WITH ANGELS

THE HERMITAGE, LENINGRAD

DESCRIPTION: Deep bowl with relief, on outside, of angels standing under arches (fig. a). The arches rest on palm leaves springing from a central roundel containing a cross, a motif also found in the relief of the British Museum Censer, no. 35.

PLACE OF DISCOVERY: Unknown.

CONTROL STAMPS: One stamp – cruciform, on base of bowl (fig. b). It is difficult to judge whether it was applied before or after the bowl was decorated. The reading was taken from cast and photograph:

☩ Flared arms; cruciform monogram resembling the monogram in the cross stamp of no. 70; it may belong to Heraclius, type c (see no. 70); inscribed in a circular direction [+C]‖E‖ΡΓ‖[IC]; this inscription is similar to the corresponding inscription on no. 75, but the letters have different positions in the arms of the cross.

DATE: Heraclius, A.D. 613–629/30 (see nos. 70 and 75).

Principal References: Rosenberg, pp. 724–725.

Source of Illustration: The Hermitage.

No. 72. PLATE WITH CENTER ROSETTE FROM TURUSHEVA

THE HERMITAGE, LENINGRAD; acc. no. W. 389

DESCRIPTION: Plate with formal rosette design in center and radiating lines to rim (fig. a).

Diam. 27.5 cm.; diam. of footring 11.8 cm.; ht. of footring 1.6 cm. (Matsule-vich).

PLACE OF DISCOVERY: Found in 1927, with no. 76, in Turusheva, district of Omutninsk, Government of Viatka (renamed Kirov in 1934).

CONTROL STAMPS: Five stamps – a round, a hexagonal, a square, a long, and a cruciform (fig. b). Since they are badly worn around the centering point and since the hexagon is broken by the incised rings on the base, the plate must have been decorated after the stamps were applied. They are identical with the stamps on no. 73. The readings were taken from the photograph and cast:

○ Bust of Heraclius, type 7; inscribed [X]PICTO‖[ΦΟΡΟV] (see the long stamp on no. 75).

◑ This stamp has been struck twice; the position of the inscription in relation to the sides of the hexagon is unusual in the Imperial series (see also nos. 2, 5, 9, 73, and the description for no. 2); monogram of Heraclius, type a; the small bust above the monogram is not only nimbed but appears to be winged (see no. 73); inscribed [ΠΑΤΡ]‖IK[IC].

□ Monogram of Heraclius, type a; inscription illegible.

◘ Only the bottom half is visible; monogram MHNA(?); inscribed CEP‖ΓIC.

✛ Monogram as above; inscribed [CXO]‖ΛΑ‖[CTI]‖KIC (see nos. 73, 74).

DATE: Heraclius, A.D. 629/30–641. The bust of the Emperor in the round stamp dates these stamps and those on no. 73 in the last years of the Emperor's reign. The inscription in the round stamp relates them to later Imperial stamps (no. 75).

Principal References: Matsulevich, "Prikam'e," p. 140 ff., fig. 3, pl. 1.

Source of Illustration: The Hermitage.

a. Plate with Center Rosette from Turusheva

b. The Stamps

a. Plate with Niello Cross from Malaia Pereshchepina

b. The Stamps

No. 73. PLATE WITH NIELLO CROSS FROM MALAIA PERESHCHEPINA

THE HERMITAGE, LENINGRAD; acc. no. 824

DESCRIPTION: Plate with niello cross in center surrounded by wreath (fig. a). Fluting radiates from center to rim.

Wt. 1472 gr.; diam. 30.9 cm. (Matsulevich).

PLACE OF DISCOVERY: Found in 1912, in Malaia Pereshchepina, Government of Poltava, South Russia, with nos. 2, 30, 31, 79.

CONTROL STAMPS: Five stamps – a round, a hexagonal, a square, a long, and a cruciform (fig. b). The niello pattern on the obverse cuts into the round stamp, indicating that the plate was stamped before it was decorated (Matsulevich, "Arg. byz.," p. 296). All the stamps are identical with those on no. 72. The readings were taken from the photograph and cast:

○ Bust of Heraclius, type 7; inscribed XPICTO||Φ[OPOV].

◓ Monogram of Heraclius; inscribed [ΠA]TP||IK[IC]; above the monogram a small, nimbed bust which appears to be winged (p. 11). The letters are inscribed differently than those of the usual hexagonal Imperial stamp (see nos. 2, 5, 9, 72).

□ Monogram of Heraclius, type a; inscribed [CEP]||Γ[I]C?

◠ Bust of Heraclius, type 7; monogram MHNA; inscribed [CE]P||ΓIC.

✠ Monogram as above; inscribed C[XO||Λ]A||[CTI||KIC] (see nos. 72 and 74).

DATE: Heraclius, A.D. 629/30–641 (see no. 72).

Principal References: Rosenberg, pp. 696–697; Matsulevich, "Arg. byz.," p. 294, no. 6, pl. XLV:3.

Source of Illustration: The Hermitage.

209

No. 74. PLAIN, SMALL DISH

THE STATE HISTORICAL MUSEUM, MOSCOW; acc. no. 84846

DESCRIPTION: Small dish without ornament, on high footring (fig. a).

PLACE OF DISCOVERY: Found near the Alkino station of the Ufa railway in 1953.

CONTROL STAMPS: One cruciform stamp, struck twice, on inside of footring (fig. b). It appears to have been struck before the plate was finished, since it is damaged by the centering point. The reading was taken from the photograph:

✠ The double strike has displaced part of a monogram which has not been deciphered; flared arms; inscribed in a circular direction CXO‖[ΛΑ‖CT]I‖[KI]C (see the corresponding stamps on nos. 72–73).

DATE: Heraclius, A.D. 629/30–641. The relationship between the inscription on this stamp and the corresponding inscriptions on nos. 72 and 73 dates it in the same period.

Principal References: Unpublished.

Source of Illustration: The State Historical Museum.

a. Plain, Small Dish

b. The Stamp

OBJECTS WITH IMPERIAL STAMPS FROM THE REIGN OF CONSTANS II, A.D. 641–668

a. The Nereid Jug

b. The Stamps

No. 75. THE NEREID JUG

THE HERMITAGE, LENINGRAD; acc. no. W. 256

DESCRIPTION: Jug with flat sides (fig. a). On either side a Nereid riding a sea monster, surrounded by sea-gulls, fish, and shells. Handle missing.

Wt. 1132 gr.; ht. 25.2 cm.; diam. of roundels of flat sides 13.5 cm.; width of narrow sides 4.8 cm.; base 9.2 cm. × 6.8 cm. (Matsulevich).

PLACE OF DISCOVERY: Uncertain; probably in the Government of Perm (renamed Molotov in 1942) (Matsulevich).

CONTROL STAMPS: Four stamps on base of jug – a round, a square, a long, and a cruciform (fig. b). They appear to have been applied before the vessel was finished, since they are worn near the raised rim of the base and around the centering point (Matsulevich, p. 89); yet they must have been applied when the jug was at least partly fashioned for they were applied very close together within the rim (p. 2). The readings were taken from photograph and cast:

O   Imperial bust of Constans II with globus crucifer, type 8; inscribed [IⲰA]N‖N[H]C (see the corresponding stamp on no. 76 and the related ones on nos. 77, 78).

☐   Close to the round stamp: cruciform monogram that does not spell the name of an emperor (Table II and p. 12); inscribed [MA]KE‖ΔⲰNNO[V].

◖   Imperial bust as above, type 8; cruciform monogram like that in the cross stamp, reads KⲰNCTANTINOV (see p. 14); inscribed [X]PICTO‖ΦOPO[V] (see round stamps on nos. 72, 73).

✠   Flared arms; monogram as above; inscribed +‖CE‖[PΓ]‖IC (see the corresponding stamp, no. 71).

DATE: Constans II, A.D. 641–51 (bust in round stamp; cf. p. 10f.). The position of this group of stamps in the series is determined, on the one hand, by the relationships to nos. 76 and 77 (round stamp, secondary monogram, name in cruciform stamp) and, on the other, by the relationship to no. 71 (name in cruciform stamp) and nos. 72 and 73 (which have in the round stamp the name inscribed in the long stamp of no. 75). Though nos. 71, 75, 76, and 77 all have the name CEPΓIC in the cruciform stamp, the placing of the letters differs in each instance.

Principal References: Rosenberg, pp. 722–723; Matsulevich, *Byz. Ant.,* p. 5 f., no. 8, pp. 89–91, fig. 19, pls. 19–21.

Source of Illustration: The Hermitage.

No. 76. PLATE WITH NIELLO CROSS FROM TURUSHEVA

THE HERMITAGE, LENINGRAD; acc. no. W. 390

DESCRIPTION: Flat plate with cross in center surrounded by ivy wreath (fig. a).

Wt. 241.5 gr.; diam. 14.2 cm.; diam. of footring 6.6 cm.; ht. of footring 1 cm. (Matsulevich).

PLACE OF DISCOVERY: Found in 1927, with no. 72, near Turusheva, district of Omutninsk, Government of Viatka (renamed Kirov in 1934).

CONTROL STAMPS: Five stamps – a round, a hexagonal, a square, and two cruciform (fig. b). They were damaged while the niello pattern was being worked, since the wreath cuts into the stamps (into one of the cross stamps and the square especially). The plate was thus stamped before it was decorated. Numerous graffiti may be seen on the back of the plate; on the outside of the footring is scratched the name ΘΕΟΔΟΡΟV. The readings were taken from the photograph and cast:

○ Imperial bust with globus crucifer, type 8; inscribed IѠ[AN‖NHC] (identical with the corresponding stamp on no. 75).

⟨⟩ Monogram of Heraclius, type a; inscription not clear.

□ Cruciform monogram ΠΑVΛΟV(?), found also in the square stamps of nos. 77 and 78; inscribed ΘΕΟΦ‖ANIC (identical with the corresponding stamp on no. 77); for the irregularity in the monogram, see Table II and p. 12.

✠ Near the square stamp: monogram KѠNCTANTINOV as in the corresponding stamps of nos. 75 and 77; inscribed [+]‖C‖ΕΡΓ‖IC· This stamp is similar to the stamps on nos. 75 and 77, but the letters in the arms are differently placed.

✠ As above, less clear.

DATE: Constans II, A.D. 641–651. The relationships between these stamps and those on nos. 75 and 77 place this object between these two objects in the series.

Principal References: Matsulevich, "Prikam'e," p. 143 f., pl. II: 1, 3; *idem, B–A,* p. 124 f., fig. 1.

Source of Illustration: The Hermitage.

a. Plate with Niello Cross from Turusheva

b. The Stamps

a. The Obolenskiĭ *Trulla*

b. The Stamps

No. 77. THE OBOLENSKII *TRULLA*

THE HERMITAGE, LENINGRAD; acc. no. W. 292

DESCRIPTION: *Trulla* with design of fishermen and sea creatures in relief on outside of bowl. On handle, Poseidon holding trident and standing on back of dolphin (fig. a).

Wt. 875 gr.; diam. 13.5 cm.; ht. 6.8 cm.; length, with handle, 26.7 cm. (Matsulevich).

PLACE OF DISCOVERY: Uncertain. Matsulevich (*Byz. Ant.*, p. 6) suggests that this *trulla* may have been part of a treasure found in 1853 in the village of Peshnigort, Solikamsk District, Government of Perm (renamed Molotov in 1942). Formerly in the Obolenskii Collection.

CONTROL STAMPS: Five stamps – a round, a hexagonal, a square, and two cruciform (fig. b). It is difficult to determine whether they were applied before or after the decoration had been completed. The readings were taken from the photograph and cast:

O   Imperial bust, type 8; inscribed [IⲰ]AN‖NOV. This stamp is the same as the corresponding stamp on no. 78, and similar to the round stamps on nos. 75 and 76.

⬡   Unique in the Imperial series; the hexagon contains the nimbed bust of a military saint (pp. 11, 12); inscribed IⲰA‖NNOV.

□   Monogram ΠΑVΛOV; inscribed ΘEOΦ‖AN[IC] (see the corresponding stamps on nos. 76 and 78).

✚   Nearest the square: monogram KⲰNCTANTINOV as on nos. 75 and 76; inscribed +C‖[Є]P‖ΓI‖[C]. This stamp is similar to the stamps on nos. 75 and 76, but the letters inscribed in the arms of the cross are arranged differently in each case.

✚   Same as the above; inscribed [+C]‖ЄP‖ΓI‖[C].

DATE: Constans II, A.D. 641–651. The relationship between these stamps and those on nos. 75, 76, and 78 places them after no. 76 and before no. 78.

Principal References: Rosenberg, pp. 720–721 (drawings of stamps only); Matsulevich, *Byz. Ant.*, p. 6, no. 10, pp. 65–71, 75, pls. 12–15; *idem*, "Arg. byz.," p. 300, pl. XLIV: 2.

Source of Illustration: The Hermitage.

No. 78. PLATE WITH BUST OF SAINT

The British Museum, London

DESCRIPTION: Plate with central medallion, surrounded by band of niello ornament, containing relief of nimbed saint, full face (fig. a). No traces of gilding.

Wt. 926 gr.; diam. 24.5 cm.; depth 6–7.8 cm.; diam. of footring 9.9 cm.

PLACE OF DISCOVERY: Found near the monastery of Acheiropoietos, six miles west of Kyrenia, Cyprus, with nos. 28 and 35; from the "First Cyprus Treasure." Acquired in 1899.

CONTROL STAMPS: Five stamps – two round, a hexagonal (?), a square, and a long (fig. b). The outline of the hexagon is not clear; it might easily be a round stamp. The bottom of the plate has greatly deteriorated which makes it difficult to read the stamps and even more difficult to judge whether they were applied before or after the decoration of the plate was finished. The readings were taken from the object:

O   Imperial bust, type 8; inscribed IⳜ[A]‖NNOV (see the corresponding stamp on no.77).

O   Between the hexagon and the square: a single cruciform monogram IⳜANNOV? (pp. 8, note 32; 12, 21).

O   Misshapen, on the left of the round stamp above: monogram like that of Heraclius, type a; inscribed ITA‖ΛOV?

□   Opposite the round stamp and aligned with it and the centering point: monogram ΠAVΛOV, as in the square stamps of nos. 76 and 77; inscription illegible.

∩   Between the square and the first round stamp: imperial bust, type 8; monogram not visible; inscribed TAPO.‖TAP. .

DATE: Constans II, A.D. 641–651. The relationships between the regular round stamp and the corresponding stamp on no. 77, and between the monogram in the square and the corresponding monograms on nos. 76 and 77 place this object at the end of the series of Imperial stamps (see p. 21).

Principal References: Dalton, *Arch.* 57, pp. 159–165; *idem, Catalogue*, no. 398, pl. XXIV; E. Kitzinger, *Early Medieval Art in the British Museum* (London, 1940), p. 25, pl. 11.

Source of Illustration: Victoria and Albert Museum, reproduction courtesy of Mr. John Beckwith and the Trustees of the British Museum.

a. Plate with Bust of Saint

b. The Stamps

UNDATED OBJECTS WITH IMPERIAL (?) STAMPS

a. Amphora from Malaia Pereshchepina

b. The Stamps

No. 79. AMPHORA FROM MALAIA PERESHCHEPINA

The Hermitage, Leningrad; acc. no. W.828

DESCRIPTION: Silver gilded amphora with narrow bands of ornament around the neck, the body, and the foot (fig. a). Handles in shape of two fish.

Wt. 7800 gr.; ht. 48 cm.; diam. of base 12.5 cm.; thickness of neck 2.2 cm.; width of central band of ornament 4.8 cm. (Matsulevich).

PLACE OF DISCOVERY: Found in 1912, in Malaia Pereshchepina, Government of Poltava, with nos. 2, 30, 31, 73.

CONTROL STAMPS: "Unter der Vergoldung auf dem Boden ein byzantinischer Kreuzstempel" (Matsulevich, p. 7) (fig. b, center). The object was evidently stamped before it was gilded, and it is perhaps this gilding that has erased the stamps. Only the cross stamp is clear, but there may be the blurred remains of a hexagon above and to the left of the cross and the faint suggestion of a box monogram of the Justinianic type. The shape of the cross stamp with arms slightly flared indicates a relatively early position in the Imperial series of stamps (p. 15). The object was examined from the photograph.

DATE: Sixth century.

Principal References: Rosenberg, pp. 694–695 (no stamps given); Matsulevich, *Byz. Ant.*, p. 7, no. 13, pp. 107–109, figs. 23, 24, pl. 28.

Source of Illustration: The Hermitage.

No. 80. CHALICE FROM ANTIOCH

THE METROPOLITAN MUSEUM OF ART, NEW YORK, Fletcher Fund; acc. no. 47.100.34

DESCRIPTION: Chalice, in several fragments, recently lined with another metal (see fig.). Gilded inscription around rim: +VΠЄΡ ΑΝΑΠΑVCЄωC ΧΑΡΟVΦΑ Κ(αι) CωTHPIAC ΘЄΚΛHC; around foot: [Κ(αι) TωN] TЄΚΝωΝ ΑV[TωN].

Diam. at top 17.5 cm.; ht. 17.1 cm.

PLACE OF DISCOVERY: Antioch, 1910? or with the "Hama treasure," nos. 13, 34, 89, 98, and possibly no. 18 (see p. 20).

CONTROL STAMPS: Before this chalice was lined, stamps were reported to have been visible inside the base (Downey, p. 349f.). These can perhaps be seen faintly, in reverse, on the outside of the base, but they are illegible. The object was examined in the original.

DATE: On the basis of the inscription, Downey dates the chalice in the sixth century (p. 349).

Principal References: Diehl, p. 105, note 2; *WAG,* no. 392; G. Downey, *AJA,* LV (1951), p. 349ff.

Source of Illustration: The Metropolitan Museum of Art.

Chalice from Antioch

OBJECTS STAMPED IN THE FOURTH AND FIFTH CENTURIES

a. Deep bowl with Beaded Brim

b. The Stamp

No. 81. DEEP BOWL WITH BEADED BRIM

EHEM. STAATLICHE MUSEEN, BERLIN-CHARLOTTENBURG (formerly in the Antiquarium)

DESCRIPTION: Deep bowl on low foot with flat, broad brim edged with beads (fig. a). Concentric circles engraved on rim. Very similar to nos. 82 and 85.

Wt. 489 gr.; diam. at rim 16.5 cm.; ht. 7–7.3 cm. (Zahn).

PLACE OF DISCOVERY: "Aus Syrien" (Schlunk).

CONTROL STAMPS: One square stamp containing a Tyche seated *en face*, wearing a helmet and a long tunic, and holding a sphere in one hand and a scepter in the other (fig. b); underneath the figure the inscription: ΑΒΑΛΑΤΟC CΦΡΑΓΙCΕΝ. The photograph does not indicate whether the stamp was applied before or after the plate was finished.

DATE: Comparing the stamp with contemporary coins, Zahn (col. 273) dates the bowl in the last third or last quarter of the fourth century (p. 4f.).

Principal References: R. Zahn, "Spätantike Silbergefässe," *Amtl.Ber.*, XXXVIII (1917), col. 270ff.; Rosenberg, pp. 618–619; R. Jaeger, "Ein Beitrag zur Geschichte der altchristlichen Silberarbeiten," *JDAI*, XLIII (1928), *Arch. Anz.*, col. 559; Peirce and Tyler, *L'art byz.*, I, pl. 59 a, c; H. Schlunk, *Kunst der Spätantike im Mittelmeerraum* (Berlin, 1939), no. 105.

Source of Illustration: Staatliche Museen, Berlin.

No. 82. DEEP BOWL WITH BEADED BRIM

The State Historical Museum, Moscow; acc. no. 54791

DESCRIPTION: Deep bowl on low foot with flat, broad brim edged with beads (fig. a). This bowl is very similar to nos. 81 and 85.

PLACE OF DISCOVERY: Found at Sulin, Don River district. Formerly in the P. S. Ivanova Collection.

CONTROL STAMPS: A single square stamp containing a Tyche seated *en face* and holding a scepter and a sphere (fig. b). Above the sphere is a small cross. Beneath the figure the letters TIM; to the right of the figure another letter (Φ or Θ ?). It is difficult to say whether the stamp was applied before or after the decoration of the bowl. The stamp was examined from the photograph.

DATE: The stamp is similar to that on no. 81, and may provisionally be dated in the same period, that is, in the last third or last quarter of the fourth century.

Principal References: Protasov, p. 68f. and pl. IX: 2; Matsulevich, *Byz. Ant.*, p. 76, note 3.

Source of Illustration: The State Historical Museum.

a. Deep Bowl with Beaded Brim

b. The Stamp

a. Small Fluted Bowl

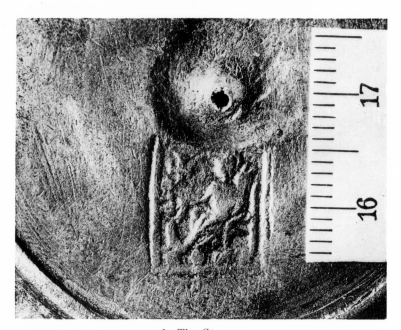

b. The Stamp

No. 83. SMALL, FLUTED BOWL

THE STATE HISTORICAL MUSEUM, MOSCOW; acc. no. 42421

DESCRIPTION: Deep, round, fluted bowl (fig. a).

Diam. *ca.* 11 cm. (Rosenberg).

PLACE OF DISCOVERY: District of Botosani, Rumania.

CONTROL STAMPS: One square stamp containing a Tyche seated in profile to left (fig. b). She wears a helmet and holds an unidentified object in her right hand and a scepter (?) in her left. Her foot rests upon a ship's prow. In the left-hand corner a cross is engraved and, along the left side, the letters ΔIO. Beneath the figure: CONS. The stamp was damaged when work was done around the centering point and the bowl must, therefore, have been stamped before it was finished. The stamp was examined from the photograph.

DATE: Zahn (col. 293) dates this stamp in the fourth or fifth century. The bowl was found with some coins of Emperor Theodosius II (d. 450) and Valentinian III (d. 455). Cf. p. 5.

Principal References: Zahn, "Spätantike Silbergefässe," *Amtl.Ber.*, XXXVIII (1917), cols. 292–293, fig. 99; Protasov, pp. 64–68 and pl. IX: 1; Rosenberg, pp. 620–621.

Source of Illustration: The State Historical Museum.

No. 84. VASE WITH NINE MUSES

Oruzheinaia Palata Museum, Moscow

DESCRIPTION: Tall vase with nine muses depicted in central band, and ornamental bands above and below (figs. a and b).

Wt. 2250 gr.; diam. of base 11.3 cm.; ht. 39 cm.; width of central frieze 15 cm. (Matsulevich).

PLACE OF DISCOVERY: Found in 1918–1919, in a barbarian grave at the village of Bol'shoi Kamenets on the Sudzha River, a tributary of the Psel River in the Dniepr River basin.

CONTROL STAMPS: Single, rectangular stamp cut off by the ring of the base and applied, therefore, before the vessel was finished (fig. c). The stamp shows a seated figure, holding a sphere. Little more is distinguishable from the photograph. The stamp has been struck twice.

DATE: The stamp is similar to those on nos. 81–83 and may be dated in the late fourth or fifth century.

Principal References: L. A. Matzoulevitch (Matsulevich), *Une sépulture d'un roi barbare en Europe Orientale, trouvailles nouvelles aux sources de la Soudza* (Moscow-Leningrad, 1934) (in Russian, with French summary on pp. 119–125).

Source of Illustration: The Hermitage (figs. a, b), and Prof. Leonid Matsulevich, courtesy of Mme. Jeannette Matsulevich (fig. c).

a   b

Vase with Nine Muses

c. The Stamp

a. Deep Bowl with Beaded Brim

b. The Stamp

No. 85. DEEP BOWL WITH BEADED BRIM

DESCRIPTION: Deep bowl on low foot, with broad brim edged with beads (fig. a). Concentric circles engraved on inside of bowl. This bowl is almost identical with no. 81, and very similar to no. 82.

Diam. 14.5 cm.; diam. of bowl without brim 9 cm.; ht. 6 cm.; diam. of footring 5.3 cm.

PLACE OF DISCOVERY: "From Constantinople" (*WAG*).

CONTROL STAMPS: Single, oblong stamp, struck twice, on the base (fig. b). It is broken by the centering point in a way that suggests the plate was worked on after it had been stamped. The details of the stamp are too damaged to be distinguishable. The object was examined in the original.

DATE: The stamp resembles those of nos. 81–84, and should belong to the fourth or fifth century A.D.

Principal References: WAG, no. 379, pl. LII.

Source of Illustration: The Metropolitan Museum of Art.

OBJECTS WITH IRREGULAR STAMPS

a. Plate from Cesena

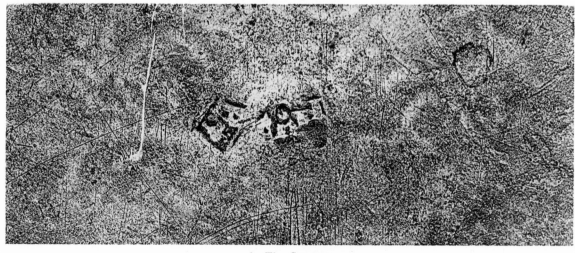

b. The Stamps

No. 86. PLATE FROM CESENA

BIBLIOTECA MALATESTIANA, CESENA

DESCRIPTION: Large platter with raised brim (fig. a) and central tondo containing two scenes, one above the other: top – banquet scene; bottom – horse and hunter in front of palace (?). Pastoral subjects, interspersed with medallions, incised on brim. Silver gilded against niello background.

Wt. 600 gr.; diam. 63 cm.; diam. of tondo 25 cm. (Arias).

PLACE OF DISCOVERY: Found in Cesena, with another plate "che verrà illustrato altrove" (Arias, p. 309) and a Gothic coin minted probably in Rome in the time of Theodoric or Athalaric (cf. W. Wroth, *Catalogue of the Coins of the Vandals, Ostrogoths, and Lombards...in the British Museum* [London, 1911], p. 105, no. 31, pl. XIV, 5).

CONTROL STAMPS: There are two stamps for which no analogies have yet been found (fig. b). One seems to contain the letter A; the other the letter P and an ivy leaf. The shapes of the stamps are not clear. It is impossible to determine whether they were applied before or after the plate was decorated. The stamps were examined frcm the photographs.

DATE: Arias dates the plate, on stylistic grounds, in the late fourth century.

Principal References: P. E. Arias, "Il piatto argenteo di Cesena," *Annuario della Scuola Archeologica di Atene*, XXIV–XXVI (N.S. VIII–X, 1946–1948), pp. 309–344.

Source of Illustration: Soprintendenza alle Antichità, Bologna.

No. 87. DEEP, FLUTED DISH

PRESENT LOCATION UNKNOWN (formerly Spink and Son, Ltd., London [1956])

DESCRIPTION: Deep dish with fluted edges, made of single, thin sheet of silver (fig. a). Two concentric circles around centering point on inside of dish.

Wt. approx. 19 oz.; diam. of dish 31.3 cm.; depth approx. 4.3 cm.; diam. of base 20.1 cm.; length of sides approx. 8.5 cm.

PLACE OF DISCOVERY: Unknown.

CONTROL STAMPS: Single stamp in center of bottom of dish, on reverse of centering point, which, in this instance, is on inside of dish (fig. b). The stamp must have been applied before the plate was finished since it has been worn evenly at the edges, in a circular fashion, by the lathe. In the center of the plate, on the bottom, there is a slight bump, which was formed when the centering point was used, possibly at the time the stamp was applied. The stamp is roughly square, and contains the monogram of Christ. The object was examined in the original.

DATE: ?

Unpublished.

Source of Illustration: Dumbarton Oaks Photographic Collection.

a. Deep Fluted Dish

b. The Stamp

a. Albanian Bowl

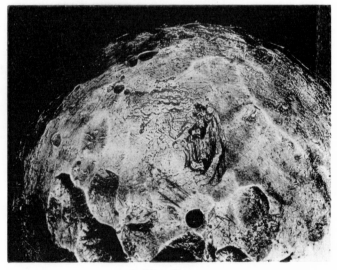

b. The Stamp

No. 88. ALBANIAN BOWL

The Metropolitan Museum of Art, New York, Gift of J. Pierpont Morgan;
acc. no. 17. 190. 1707

DESCRIPTION: Deep bowl (censer?) with geometric diamond pattern around the exterior (fig. a); set within the diamonds are birds, flowers, and various other objects.

Wt. 481.5 gr.; diam. of top 13.2–13.7 cm.; diam. of footring 7.3 cm.; ht. of bowl 10.4 cm. (Strzygowski).

PLACE OF DISCOVERY: Found, with no. 103, in 1902–1907, in the vicinity of the village of Vrap, Albania.

CONTROL STAMPS: One stamp visible – hexagonal (?), possibly containing a monogram similar to, but not identical with, the Anastasius-Justinian type (fig. b) (see p. 22). No inscription can be traced. It is difficult to say whether the stamp was applied before or after the vessel was decorated. The object was examined in the original:

DATE: Strzygowski dates the bowl, on stylistic grounds, in the fifth or sixth century (p. 16).

Principal References: J. Strzygowski, *Altai-Iran und Völkerwanderung* (Leipzig, 1917), pp. 14–17, pl. IV, figs. 13–15; Rosenberg, pp. 628–629.

Source of Illustration: The Metropolitan Museum of Art.

No. 89. HANGING LAMP FROM HAMA

THE WALTERS ART GALLERY, BALTIMORE; acc. no. 57.640

DESCRIPTION: Lamp of double-curved shape and without ornament (fig. a); chain missing.

Ht. 14.3 cm.; diam. 16.6 cm. (*WAG*).

PLACE OF DISCOVERY: Found in Hama, Syria, in 1910, with nos. 13, 34, 98 and possibly nos. 18 and 80 (p. 20, note 75).

CONTROL STAMPS: Five stamps – a round, a hexagonal, a square, a long, and a cruciform (fig. b). There is no sign that any work was done on the object after it was stamped, and the stamps make their deepest impression around the centering point, where the silver is slightly raised, indicating that most of the work was done before they were applied. Although they are similar in shape and general design to stamps from the Imperial series, there are certain differences in all the stamps that set them apart from Imperial stamps. The readings were taken from the object:

O   A group of figures in a composition resembling the lower part of an Ascension; no inscription.

◌   The worn outline can be traced between the cross and the long stamp: a cruciform monogram is visible, with letters that do not spell the name of an emperor; the inscription is not entirely legible: .....TVP; the letters of the inscription are placed all around the monogram, as in some exceptional cases in the Imperial series (nos. 2, 5, 9, 72, 73). By contrast to these other exceptions, the monogram itself is here in its normal position within the hexagon.

□   Monogram of the Emperor Phocas: the **K** and the **A** have been interchanged (see nos. 32–36). The inscription is not entirely legible: ...Λ||.TOV. The genitive ending thus appears in the upper left-hand corner, which suggests that this inscription also has been reversed.

◠   Nimbed, imperial bust with crown having trefoil ornament (?) and pendants (cf. Table I:1?); illegible cruciform monogram; inscribed ΘЄOV|| [Π]OΛЄO[C] (see the corresponding stamp on no. 90).

⊹   Struck twice; flared arms; no sign of a monogram. The letters inscribed in the arms of the cross read neither in a vertical nor a circular direction, but toward the center of the cross: NI||K||AC||OV.

DATE: Phocas, A.D. 602–610. The name in the long stamp refers to the city of Antioch (p. 20).

Principal References: Diehl, p. 109, no. 11, pl. XXVII: 2; Rosenberg, pp. 730–731; *WAG*, no. 403.

Source of Illustration: The Walters Art Gallery.

248

a. Hanging Lamp from Hama

b. The Stamps

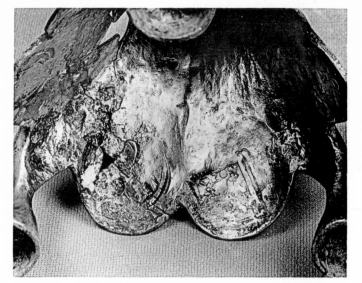

b. Round and Square

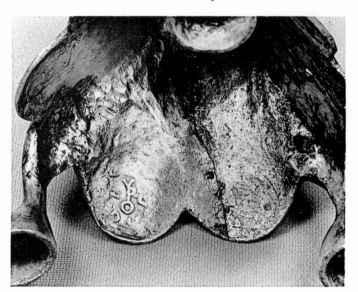

c. Hexagonal

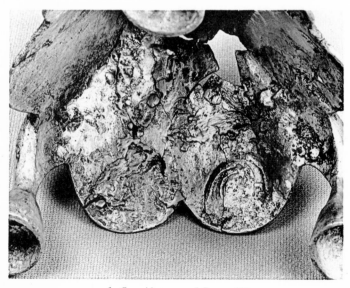

d. Cruciform and Long (?)

The Stamps

a. Candlestick

No. 90. CANDLESTICK

DESCRIPTION: Slender candlestick or lampstand, without ornament (fig. a). It has been broken into several fragments.

Wt. 333.2 gr.; ht. 21.3 cm.

PLACE OF DISCOVERY: Antioch. Found by Lassus in 1938, in excavations below the level of a pavement "of a late period" (Ross).

CONTROL STAMPS: Remains of five stamps – a round, a hexagonal, a square, a long, and a cruciform. Since they are applied inside the base, on the lobes between the legs, and since one of the lobes cuts off the long stamp, it is likely that they were struck before the object was given its definitive shape (see no. 19). The readings were taken from the object:

○ (fig. b) Only part of the outline is clear; inside there is some indication of a design that does not appear to belong to an imperial bust (see no. 89). There is no sign of an inscription.

⬡ (fig. c) Cruciform monogram that does not spell the name of an emperor; inscription around the monogram with letters placed all around the edge of the hexagon; this rarely occurs in stamps of the Imperial series, where the letters are normally placed on either side of the monogram on two of the sides of the hexagon. The inscription is illegible. The stamp is similar to, but not identical with, the hexagon on no. 89.

□ (fig. b) Adjacent to the round stamp: part of monogram of Phocas, like that in the corresponding stamp of no. 89. The inscription is placed backwards and reads ...OTOV. The stamp, in so far as it is preserved, is identical with the corresponding stamp on no. 89, even to the irregularity in the arms of the V.

⬚ (fig. d) On the other side of the round stamp: only the upper part of a nimbed bust is clearly visible; inscribed [ΘЄOV]‖Π[OΛЄOC] (see the corresponding inscription on no. 89; this inscription supplies the missing letter in the inscription of no. 89).

✚ (fig. d) Only a corner is visible in the lobe of the base, adjacent to the long stamp.

DATE: Phocas, A.D. 602–610. The relationship between these stamps and the stamps on no. 89 dates them in the same period and assigns these stamps also to Antioch (p. 20).

Principal References: M. C. Ross, "A Small Byzantine Treasure Found at Antioch-on-the-Orontes," *Archaeology,* V (1952), pp. 30–32; *DOC,* no. 15.

Source of Illustration: Dumbarton Oaks.

No. 91. VALDONNE PLATE "A"

THE LOUVRE, PARIS

DESCRIPTION: Simple, decorated plate with concentric circles, and with crossed lines in center (fig. a). This plate is thinner than the Valdonne Plate "B," no. 92, and was probably made to fit inside it (Villefosse).

Wt. 296 gr.; diam. 17 cm. (Prou).

PLACE OF DISCOVERY: Found, with no. 92, in 1900, in Valdonne, Commune of Peypin, Bouches-du-Rhône.

CONTROL STAMPS: Five stamps – a square, two long, and two cruciform. They must have been applied before the plate was finished as they were damaged by subsequent hammering (fig. b). The stamps are crude and similar in workmanship to the stamps on no. 92. The readings were taken from the object:

☐   Inscribed in Latin characters, backwards: +AR‖BAL‖DO+.

⌂   Profile bust, with palm branch in front.

⌂   Same as above.

✠   Simple cross design.

✠   Same as above.

DATE: *ca.* 650 A.D. (p. 20f.).

Principal References: A. Héron de Villefosse, discussion in *Bulletin de la Société des Antiquaires de France* (25 mai, 1910), pp. 246–256; M. Prou, "Les contre-marques mérovingiennes de la coupe de Valdonne (Bouches-du-Rhône)," *Revue Charlemagne*, I (1911), pp. 182–185; Rosenberg, pp. 738–739.

Source of Illustration: Archives Photographiques, Paris.

a. Valdonne Plate "A"

b. The Stamps

a. Valdonne Plate "B"

b. The Stamps

No. 92. VALDONNE PLATE "B"

THE LOUVRE, PARIS

DESCRIPTION: Plate decorated with concentric circles, and with lobed cross in center (fig. a). This plate is thicker than the Valdonne Plate "A," no. 91, and was probably made to contain it (Villefosse).

Wt. 409 gr.; diam. 17.5 cm. (Prou).

PLACE OF DISCOVERY: Found, with no. 91, in 1900, in Valdonne, Commune of Peypin, Bouches-du-Rhône.

CONTROL STAMPS: Five stamps – three round and two cruciform. They must have been applied before the plate was finished, for they appear to have been damaged when the base was subsequently beaten (fig. b). They are similar in workmanship to the stamps on no. 91 and belong to the same stamping system. The readings were taken from the object:

O   Cruciform monogram: ΘΕΟΔΩΡΟΥ?

O   Same as above.

O   Cruciform monogram tentatively read as ΚΥΡΙΕ ΒΟΗΘΕΙ, though not all of the letters are present.

⊕   Cruciform monogram not deciphered.

⊕   Cruciform monogram, not clear.

DATE: This plate is a companion piece to the Valdonne Plate "A," no. 91, and can also be dated about the middle of the seventh century.

Principal References: Same as for no. 91; Rosenberg, pp. 736–737.

Source of Illustration: Archives Photographiques, Paris.

No. 93. THE NEREID PLATE IN TURIN

GALLERIA SABAUDA, TURIN; formerly in the Gualino Collection

DESCRIPTION: Large platter with central roundel depicting small putto, fish, dolphins, and Nereid riding sea lion (fig. a). Inscribed around roundel: + SPES MEA DEVS MEVS EXAVDI ORATIONEM MEAM ET ADIMPLE DESIDERIVM MEVM.

Diam. 48.5 cm.; diam. of roundel 18.7 cm. (Monneret de Villard).

PLACE OF DISCOVERY: Ugo Monneret de Villard saw this plate in the hands of an antique dealer in Cairo before it became a part of the Gualino Collection.

CONTROL STAMPS: Two stamps – a rectangular stamp containing five lines of Latin inscription (figs. c, d) and a square (fig. b). It is difficult to judge from the reproduction whether the stamps were applied before or after the plate was decorated. The readings were taken from cast and photographs:

☐   An A and ω in ligature.

☐   .XVDN
        . STINIAN
        NDICTIOV   The inscription refers to the fifteenth year of the reign of Justinian,
        DECEMBR   to the fifth indiction, to December, and to Carthage.
        . . KART

DATE: December, 541 (p. 19).

Principal References: U. Monneret de Villard, *La scultura ad Ahnas* (Milan, 1923), p. 38f., fig. 25; Rosenberg, p. 740 (with commentary by L. Venturi); Peirce and Tyler, *L'art byz.*, II, pl. 154a.

Source of Illustration: Soprintendenza alle Gallerie del Piemonte.

a. The Nereid Plate in Turin

d. Cast of Second Stamp

b. First Stamp

c. Second Stamp

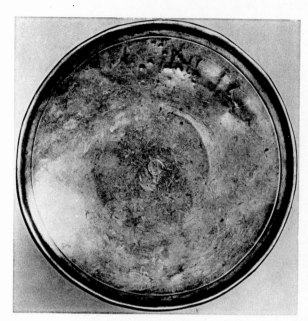

a. Plain Plate

b. The Stamps

c. Cast of Stamps

No. 94. PLAIN PLATE

The Hermitage, Leningrad; acc. no. W. 90

DESCRIPTION: Plain flat plate with footring (fig. a).

Diam. *ca.* 24.5 cm. (Rosenberg).

PLACE OF DISCOVERY: Uncertain.

CONTROL STAMPS: Two stamps – one in the shape of a rosette with eight leaves; the other rectangular with three lines of inscription (figs. b and c). They are similar to the stamps on nos. 95–97. The rosette seems to have been damaged in the course of subsequent work on the base. The readings were taken from the photographs and cast:

Rosette: Inscribed with one Greek character in each leaf: [+Θ]ЄOΔ[ω]POV?

Rectangle: Inscribed in Latin characters:

[ddN]NhЄRAC
[LIЧS] ЄThЄR
ACON [STPPAV]*

DATE: The form of inscription in the rectangle appears frequently on the coinage of Heraclius from A.D. 613–641 (Wroth, I, pp. 186–254, *passim*, and Grierson, *Num. Chron.* X, pp. 59, 69).

Principal References: Rosenberg, pp. 626–627; Matsulevich, *Viz.vrem.*, p. 189, fig. 4.

Source of Illustration: The Hermitage.

---

* I am grateful to Prof. Andrew Alföldi, who supplied this reading.

No. 95. EAGLE SIGNUM

DESCRIPTION: Large eagle with snake entwined around legs; from head of standard (fig. a).

Wt. 1035 gr.; length 21 cm.; ht. 13.2 cm. (Grinchenko).

PLACE OF DISCOVERY: Found in 1930 in Voznesenka (Neskrebovka), on the Dniepr River.

CONTROL MARKS: Two stamps – one a rosette with eight leaves, on the wing of the bird (fig. c), the other a rectangle, on the tail (fig. b). They are similar to the stamps on nos. 94, 96, 97. They seem to have been applied before the bird was decorated, since the decoration cuts into the rectangular stamp on the tail. Engraved on the breast of the bird is the monogram: ΠЄΤΡΟV. The stamps were examined from the photographs:

Rosette: According to Matsulevich, the Greek characters inscribed in the leaves of the rosette can be read as the name Theodore, but he also points out that the stamp is not identical with the rosette of no. 94.

Rectangular: Three lines of inscription which have not been read.

DATE: The find is dated on the basis of other associated objects in the seventh century. This date corresponds to the dates of similar stamps on nos. 94, 96, and 97.

Principal References: V. A. Grinchenko, "Pam'iatka VIII st. kolo s. Voznesenki na Zaporizhzhi," *Arkheologiia*, III (1950), pp. 37–63, fig. 5; Matsulevich, *Viz.vrem.*

Source of Illustration: Courtesy of Prof. Matsulevich.

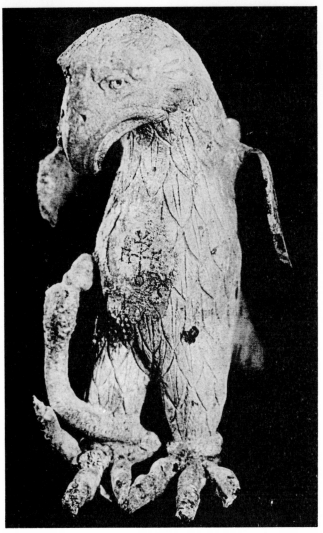

a. Eagle Signum

b. Back View

c. Side View

a. Spoon "A" from Novobaiazet

b. Rectangle

c. Rosette

The Stamps

No. 96. SPOON "A" FROM NOVOBAIAZET

The State Historical Museum, Moscow; acc. no. 47748

DESCRIPTION: Spoon with plain handle (fig. a).

PLACE OF DISCOVERY: District of Novobaiazet, former Government of Erivan, Russian Armenia (see nos. 6, 97).

CONTROL STAMPS: Two stamps – a rosette with eight leaves (fig. c) and a rectangle (fig. b). They were applied before the spoon was finished since they have been damaged in the shaping of the handle. They resemble in shape the stamps on nos. 94, 95, 97. The stamps were examined from the photographs:

Rosette: Greek characters not deciphered.

Rectangle: +dNCONST
          ANTIN[ᕝS]
          ..PPAVG

DATE: These stamps are similar to the stamps on nos. 94 and 95 and probably also belong to the seventh century. The inscription may then refer either to Constans II, 641–668, or to Constantine IV, 668–685. The former seems the more probable since these stamps closely resemble those on no. 94 from the reign of Heraclius.

Principal References: (Ia. I. Smirnov), *Vostochnoe Serebro, Atlas drevnei serebrianoĭ i zolotoĭ posudy vostochnago proiskhozhdeniia* (St. Petersburg, 1909), pl. CXXIII, figs. 51, 52, 53; Rosenberg, pp. 624–625.

Source of Illustration: The State Historical Museum.

No. 97. SPOON "B" FROM NOVOBAIAZET

THE STATE HISTORICAL MUSEUM, MOSCOW; acc. no. 47749

DESCRIPTION: Spoon with twisted handle (fig. a).

PLACE OF DISCOVERY: District of Novobaiazet, former Government of Erivan, Russian Armenia (see nos. 6, 96).

CONTROL STAMPS: Two stamps – a rosette (fig. c) and a rectangle (fig. b), similar to the stamps on nos. 94–96. They appear to have been damaged during the shaping of the handle. The stamps were examined from the photographs:

Rosette: Greek characters in the leaves not deciphered.

Rectangle: Three lines of Latin inscription:

[dN]CON[ST]

[AN]TINЧ[S]

. . . PPAV[G]

DATE: The stamps resemble those on no. 96 and can be dated in the same period, most probably in the reign of Constans II, A.D. 641–668.

Principal References: (Ia. I. Smirnov), *Vostochnoe Serebro, Atlas drevneĭ serebrianoĭ i zolotoĭ posudy vostochnago proiskhozhdeniia* (St. Petersburg, 1909), pl. CXXIII, figs. 48, 49, 50; Rosenberg, pp. 622–623.

Source of Illustration: The State Historical Museum.

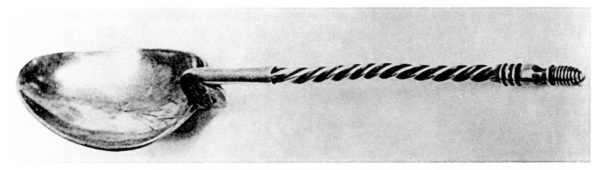

a. Spoon "B" from Novobaiazet

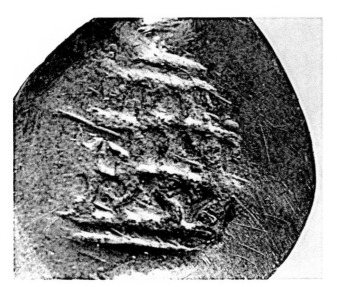

b. Rectangle

c. Rosette

The Stamps

a. Inscribed Plate with Cross

b. Rectangular Stamp

c. Back of Plate showing Stamps

No. 98. INSCRIBED PLATE WITH CROSS

THE WALTERS ART GALLERY, BALTIMORE; acc. no. 57.637

DESCRIPTION: Simple plate with cross inscribed in center and inscription around cross (fig. a): ✚ VΠЄP ЄVXHC ΠЄΛΑΓΙΟV ΚΑΙ CⲰCΑΝΝΑC ΚΑΙ TⲰΝ TЄΚΝⲰΝ ΑVTⲰΝ ΑΜΗΝ.

Diam. 37.8 cm. (*WAG*).

PLACE OF DISCOVERY: Found in Hama, Syria, in 1910, with nos. 13, 34, 89, and possibly with nos. 18 and 80 (p. 20, note 75).

CONTROL STAMPS: Two stamps (fig. c) – one is circular, without inscription, but with an eight-pointed star; the other is rectangular and contains three lines of inscription which have not been read (fig. b). It is not clear whether the stamps were applied before or after the plate was decorated. The object was examined in the original.

DATE: The closest analogies for these stamps are those found on nos. 94–96, from the seventh century.

Principal References: Diehl, p. 107, no. 4, pl. XXVII: 1; *WAG*, no. 401.

Source of Illustration: The Walters Art Gallery.

No. 99. SASSANIAN PHALERA

THE DUMBARTON OAKS COLLECTION, WASHINGTON, D. C.; acc. no. 52.9

DESCRIPTION: Phalera in the shape of a human face with strongly Sassanian features (fig. a).

Wt. 173 gr.; ht. 13.2 cm.; width 12 cm.

PLACE OF DISCOVERY: Said to have been found in Constantinople. Acquired in 1952.

CONTROL STAMPS: Three stamps – two round and one hexagonal – on the front of the mask, on the chin. They were certainly applied after the relief had been fashioned for they are placed carefully on the blank areas of the face itself, and indentations on the reverse show where they were struck on the rounded surface. The stamps were not applied on the back of the object as was customary. The readings were taken from the object:

O (fig. b) On the left of the chin: standing orans figure of a female saint; inscribed H‖ΑΓΙ[Α]‖Δ.Θ. . . .

O (fig. c) On the center of the chin: same as above, but inscription less clear.

О (fig. d) On the right side of the chin: bust of Christ with crossed nimbus; inscribed ΑΓ[ΙΟC], ΑΓΙΟ[C], ΑΓΙΟ[C]?

DATE: On the basis of comparisons with other stamps (see p. 21), as well as on the evidence of the style of the object itself, the phalera has been assigned to the seventh or early eighth century by A. Alföldi and E. Cruikshank.

Principal References: A. Alföldi and E. Cruikshank, "A Sassanian Silver Phalera at Dumbarton Oaks," *Dumbarton Oaks Papers*, II (1957), pp. 237–245; DOC, no. 18.

Source of Illustration: Dumbarton Oaks.

a. Sassanian Phalera

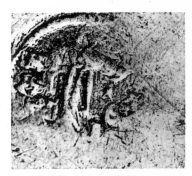

b. First Round Stamp

c. Second Round Stamp

d. Hexagonal Stamp

a. Plate "B" with Niello Cross from Klimova

b. The Stamps

No. 100. PLATE "B" WITH NIELLO CROSS FROM KLIMOVA

The Hermitage, Leningrad; acc. no. W. 193

DESCRIPTION: Large plate with crudely worked cross in center surrounded by wreath (fig. a).

Wt. 4817 gr.; diam. 53 cm. (Matsulevich).

PLACE OF DISCOVERY: Klimova, district of Solikamsk, Government of Perm (renamed Molotov in 1942). Found, with nos. 9 and 36, in 1907.

CONTROL STAMPS: Five round stamps applied at regular intervals on the bottom of the dish, one in the exact center and four near the footring equidistant from each other and from the center (fig. b). The centering point has damaged the central stamp, suggesting that the plate was worked on after it was stamped (Matsulevich, "Arg. byz.," p. 296). Two round stamps contain the figure of Christ with crossed nimbus; the other three contain identical cruciform monograms which have not been deciphered. If it were not for the absence of a P they would read CЄPΓIOV. The stamps were examined from the photograph:

DATE: Seventh century (p. 21).

Principal References: Rosenberg, pp. 734–735; Matsulevich, "Arg. byz.," p. 293, no. 4.

Source of Illustration: The Hermitage.

No. 101. THE ZALESIE BOWL

KUNSTHISTORISCHES MUSEUM, VIENNA

DESCRIPTION: Round, shallow bowl without footring, decorated with barbaric pattern of leaves and punched dots around central roundel, which is framed with large beads and contains a bird (figs. a and b). The bird and the roundel of beads may be by different hands than the rest of the design (Fettich).

Diam. 16.6 cm.; ht. 3.5–3.8 cm. (Fettich).

PLACE OF DISCOVERY: Found in Zalesie, in the Ukraine (former Galicia) in 1838; in the Kunsthistorische Museum since 1846.

CONTROL STAMPS: Five illegible, round (?) stamps (figs. c, d, e). All appear to be identical. Since they are placed in the blank areas of the design on the back of the plate, they must have been applied after the design had been executed. The stamps were examined from the photographs.

DATE: The relationship between these stamps and those on no. 100 places them in the seventh or early eighth century (p. 21).

Principal References: N. Fettich, *Archäologische Studien zur Geschichte der späthunnischen Metallkunst = Archaeologia Hungarica*, XXXI (1951), pp. 109–110, pls. I, II: 4–6.

Source of Illustration: Kunsthistorisches Museum.

a. The Zalesie Bowl

c. A Stamp

b. Side View

d. Two Stamps

e. Two Stamps

Stamps on Ewer from Pokrovskoie

No. 102. EWER FROM POKROVSKOIE

ARCHAEOLOGICAL MUSEUM, ALMA ATA

DESCRIPTION: Not available.

PLACE OF DISCOVERY: Found in a mound near the village of Pokrovskoie, Central Asia.

CONTROL STAMPS: Five cross-shaped stamps (see fig.), showing designs which resemble cruciform monograms but do not include actual letters. Like the stamps of the Valdonne plates (nos. 91, 92), they are of crude design, but in this instance it is uncertain whether they were applied before or after the plate was finished. The stamps were examined from the photograph.

DATE: Like those of the Valdonne plates, these stamps probably represent late provincial copies of Imperial stamps. The five-fold repetition of a single shape recalls irregular stamps late in the sequence (nos. 100, 101; see p. 21f.). These stamps can reasonably be dated in the late seventh or in the eighth century.

Principal References: Matsulevich, *Byz. Ant.*, p. 62, where he refers to a publication by W. Gorodeckii (*Izvestija sredne-aziatskogo komiteta po delam muzeev*, I [Tashkent, 1926], p. 79f., figs. 4–7), which was not available to this author.

Source of Illustration: The Hermitage.

No. 103. ALBANIAN EWER

The Metropolitan Museum of Art, New York, Gift of J. Pierpont Morgan;
acc. no. 17.190.1704

DESCRIPTION: Ewer with narrow band of incised ornament around the body and gilded inscription around the neck (fig. a): + ΦΟΝΗ ΚΥΡΕΙΟΥ ΕΠΕΙ ΤΟΝ VΔΑΤΟΝ (Psalm 29:3).

Wt. 654.5 gr.; ht. with handle 23.5 cm.; diam. of top 6.7 cm.; diam. of footring 8.2 cm. (Strzygowski).

PLACE OF DISCOVERY: Found, with no. 88, in 1902–1907, in the vicinity of the village of Vrap, Albania.

CONTROL STAMPS: Five monograms within circles *incised* on the bottom of the ewer (fig. b). Each one is different and together they form an inscription which Strzygowski reads ΚΥΡΙΕ ΒΩΗΘΗ ΤΟΥ ΔΟΥΛΟΥ COY ΖΗΝΟΒΙΟΥ ΑΜΗΝ. They were incised after the vessel was finished, since there is little sign of wear and they cut into the solder of the footring. The object was examined in the original.

DATE: Strzygowski dates this ewer, on stylistic grounds, between the sixth and the ninth century (p. 21). The cross monograms set within circles may be associated with the stamps on nos. 78, 100, 101, and dated accordingly in the seventh century —or, at least, at the end of the Imperial series (p. 22).

Principal References: J. Strzygowski, *Altai-Iran und Völkerwanderung* (Leipzig, 1917), pp. 19–22, figs. 19, 20; *WAG*, no. 415.

Source of Illustration: The Metropolitan Museum of Art.

a. Albanian Ewer

b. Incised Monograms

REFERENCES CITED IN ABBREVIATION

PRIMARY SOURCES:

Amm. Marc.: Ammianus Marcellinus, *Rerum gestarum libri qui supersunt* (Loeb ed., 1950–1952).

Cassiodorus: Cassiodorus, *Variae* (ed. Mommsen, *Monumenta Germaniae Historica, Auctores antiquissimi*, XII, Berlin, 1894).

CIL: *Corpus Inscriptionum Latinarum*, III (1873–1902).

Cod. Just.: *Corpus Iuris Civilis*, II, *Codex Iustinianus* (ed. P. Krueger, Berlin, 1929).

Cod. Theod.: *Theodosiani libri XVI* (ed. Mommsen and Meyer, Berlin, 1905).

Corippus: Corippus, *De laudibus Iustini Augusti minoris* (Bonn ed., 1836).

CP: *Chronicon Paschale* (Bonn ed., 1832).

Dessau: H. Dessau, *Inscriptiones latinae selectae*, I (Berlin, 1892).

Ed. Just.: *Corpus Iuris Civilis*, III, *Iustiniani XIII Edicta* (ed. Schoell and Kroll, Berlin, 1928).

Evagrius: Evagrius, *Ecclesiastical History* (ed. Bidez and Parmentier, London, 1898).

FHG: Karl Müller, *Fragmenta Historicorum Graecorum*, IV (Paris, 1851).

Mal.: Ioannes Malalas, *Chronographia* (Bonn ed., 1831).

Mansi: J. D. Mansi, *Sacrorum conciliorum nova et amplissima collectio*, VIII (Florence, 1762).

Nov. Just.: *Corpus Iuris Civilis*, III, *Iustiniani Novellae* (ed. Schoell and Kroll, Berlin, 1928).

Nov. Theod.: *Leges Novellae ad Theodosianum pertinentes* (ed. Mommsen and Meyer, Berlin, 1905).

PG: *Patrologia Graeca* (ed. J.-P. Migne, Paris).

PL: *Patrologia Latina* (ed. J.-P. Migne, Paris).

P. Oxy.: *The Oxyrhynchus Papyri*, XVI (ed. Grenfell, Hunt, and Bell, London, 1924).

Proc., *Anec.*: Procopius, *Anecdota* (Loeb ed., 1935).

Proc., *BP*: Procopius, *De bello persico* (Loeb ed., 1954).

Proc., *BV*: Procopius, *De bello vandalico* (Loeb ed., 1953).

Theoph.: Theophanes, *Chronographia*, I (ed. C. de Boor, Leipzig, 1883).

SECONDARY SOURCES:

Bréhier: L. Bréhier, "Les trésors d'argenterie syrienne et l'école artistique d'Antioche," *Gazette des Beaux-Arts*, LXII (1920), pp. 173–196. There is also an English translation of the same article: *The Treasures of Syrian Silverware and the Art School of Antioch* (Paris, 1921).

Bury: J. B. Bury, *The Imperial Administrative System in the Ninth Century* (London, 1911).

Bury, *History*: J. B. Bury, *A History of the Later Roman Empire* (London, 1923).

Byz. Art, 1958: *Byzantine Art*, Catalogue of the Exhibition Sponsored by the Edinburgh Festival Society in Association with the Royal Scottish Museum and the Victoria and Albert Museum (London, 1958).

Dalton, *Arch.* 57: O. M. Dalton, "A Byzantine Silver Treasure from the District of Kyrenia, Cyprus, Now Preserved in the British Museum," *Archaeologia*, LVII (1900), pp. 159–174.

Dalton, *Catalogue*: O. M. Dalton, *Catalogue of Early Christian Antiquities and Objects from the Christian East in the British Museum* (London, 1901).

Dalton, *Arch.* 60: O. M. Dalton, "A Second Silver Treasure from Cyprus," *Archaeologia*, LX (1906), pp. 1–24.

Dalton, *BZ*: O. M. Dalton, "Byzantine Silversmith's Work from Cyprus," *Byzantinische Zeitschrift*, XV (1906), pp. 615–617.

Dalton, *BM*: O. M. Dalton, "Byzantine Plate and Jewellery from Cyprus in Mr. Morgan's Collection," *Burlington Magazine*, X (1906–1907), pp. 355–362.

Delbrueck: R. Delbrueck, *Die Consulardiptychen und verwandte Denkmäler* (Berlin-Leipzig, 1929).

Diehl: Ch. Diehl, "Un nouveau trésor d'argenterie syrienne," *Syria*, VII (1926), pp. 105–122.

DOC: *Catalogue of the Byzantine and Early Mediaeval Antiquities in the Dumbarton Oaks Collection*, I: *Metalwork, Ceramics, Glass, Glyptics, Paintings*, by Marvin C. Ross (Washington, D. C., in the press).

REFERENCES IN ABBREVIATION

DOH: *Handbook of the Dumbarton Oaks Collection* (Washington, D. C., 1955).

Grierson, *Num. Chron.* X: Philip Grierson, "Dated Solidi of Maurice, Phocas and Heraclius," *Numismatic Chronicle*, 6th Series, X (1950), pp. 49–70.

Grünhagen: W. Grünhagen, *Der Schatzfund von Gross Bodungen* (*Römisch-Germanische Forschungen*, 21, Berlin, 1954).

Kitzinger (1958): E. Kitzinger, "Byzantine Art in the Period Between Justinian and Iconoclasm," *Berichte zum XI. Internationalen Byzantinisten-Kongress, München, 1958* (Munich, 1958), IV, 1.

Lethaby and Swainson: W. R. Lethaby and Harold Swainson, *The Church of Sancta Sophia in Constantinople* (London-New York, 1894).

Matsulevich, *Byz. Ant.*: L. Matzulewitsch, *Byzantinische Antike* (Berlin-Leipzig, 1929).

Matsulevich, "Arg. byz.": L. Maculevič, "Argenterie byzantine en Russie," *L'art byzantin chez les Slaves. Deuxième recueil dédié à la mémoire de Théodore Uspenskii*, II (Paris, 1932), pp. 292–301.

Matsulevich, "Prikam'e": L. Matsulevich, "Vizantiiskii Antik i Prikam'e," *Materialy i issledovaniia po arkheologii SSSR* (*Akad. Nauk*), I (Moscow-Leningrad, 1940), pp. 139–158.

Matsulevich, *B-A*: L. Matzoulevitch, "Byzantine Art and the Kama Region," a summary in English of the preceeding article of 1940 by Matsulevich, trans. by Mrs. David Huxley, ed. Dr. Henry Field, *Gazette des Beaux-Arts*, 6th Series, XXXI–XXXII (1947), pp. 123–126.

Matsulevich, *Viz.vrem.*: L. Matsulevich, "Voiskovoi znak V v.," *Vizantiiskii vremennik*, XVI (1959), pp. 183–205.

Peirce and Tyler, *L'art byz.*: H. Peirce and R. Tyler, *L'art byzantin* (Paris, 1934), vols. I, II.

Pink: K. Pink, *Römische und byzantinische Gewichte in Oesterreichischen Sammlungen* (Baden bei Wien, 1938).

Protasov: N. D. Protasov, "K izucheniiu kleim na vizantiiskoi serebrianoi posude," *Institut Arkheologii i Iskusstvoznanii* (Moscow University), *Trudy Otdeleniia Arkheologii*, I (1926), pp. 64–75.

Ratto: R. Ratto, *Monnaies byzantines et d'autres pays contemporaines à l'époque byzantine* (Sales Catalogue, Lugano, 1930).

Rosenberg: M. Rosenberg, *Der Goldschmiede Merkzeichen*, IV (Berlin-Leipzig, 1928), pp. 613–740.

Sabatier: J. Sabatier, *Déscription générale des monnaies byzantines* (Paris, 1862).

Sambon: A. Sambon, "Trésor d'orfèvrerie et d'argenterie trouvé à Chypre et faisant partie de la collection de M. J. Pierpont Morgan," *Le Musée*, III (1906), pp. 121–129.

Smirnov: Ia. I. Smirnov, "O niekotorykh khristianskikh zolotykh i serebrianykh predmetakh kiprskago proiskhozhdeniia," *Zapiski imperatorskago russkago arkheologicheskago obshchestva*, N.S., XII (1901), pp. 505–510.

Smith: C. H. Smith, *Collection of J. Pierpont Morgan. Bronzes: Antique Greek, Roman, etc., Including Some Antique Objects in Gold and Silver* (Paris, 1913).

Stein, *Studien*: E. Stein, *Studien zur Geschichte des byzantinischen Reiches vornehmlich unter den Kaisern Justinus II u. Tiberius Constantinus* (Stuttgart, 1919).

Stein, *BE*: E. Stein, *Histoire du Bas-Empire*, II (Paris, 1949).

WAG: *Early Christian and Byzantine Art, Catalogue of the Exhibition held at the Baltimore Museum of Art, Organized by the Walters Art Gallery* (Baltimore, 1947).

Walters: H. B. Walters, *Catalogue of Silver Plate* (*Greek, Etruscan, and Roman*) *in the British Museum* (London, 1921).

Wroth: W. Wroth, *Catalogue of the Imperial Byzantine Coins in the British Museum* (London, 1908), vols. I, II.

PERIODICALS:

AJA: *American Journal of Archaeology*.

Amtl.Ber.: *Amtliche Berichte aus den Königlichen Kunstsammlungen* (*Berliner Museen*).

BCH: *Bulletin de correspondance hellénique*.

JDAI: *Jahrbuch des Deutschen Archäologischen Instituts*.

Prakt.: *Praktika tes en Athenais Archaiologikes Hetaireias*.

INDEX I

LIST OF STAMPED OBJECTS ACCORDING TO PRESENT LOCATION

INDEX II

LIST OF STAMPED OBJECTS ACCORDING TO PLACE OF DISCOVERY